3 3V-8-1,

American Indian Culture

American Indian Culture

Volume 1

Acorns—Headdresses

Edited by

Carole A. Barrett
University of Mary

Harvey J. Markowitz
Washington and Lee University

SALEM PRESS, INC.
Pasadena, California   Hackensack, New Jersey

Most of the essays appearing within are drawn from *Ready Reference: American Indians* (1995), *Great Events from History: Revised North American Series* (1997), and *Racial and Ethnic Relations in America* (1999); essays have been updated and new essays have been added.

Library of Congress Cataloging-in-Publication Data
American Indian culture / edited by Carole A. Barrett, Harvey J. Markowitz.
    p. cm. — (Magill's choice)
Includes bibliographical references and index.
    ISBN 1-58765-192-0 (set : alk. paper) — ISBN 1-58765-193-9 (vol. 1 : alk. paper) — ISBN 1-58765-194-7 (vol. 2 : alk. paper) — ISBN 1-58765-247-1 (vol. 3 : alk. paper)
    1. Indians of North America—Social life and customs. I. Barrett, Carole A. II. Markowitz, Harvey. III. Series.
    E98.S7A44 2004
    970.004'97—dc22

                                                            2004001362

First Printing

Contents

Contents

Contents

Contents

Publisher's Note

American Indian Culture joins three other publications in the Magill's Choice series of core teaching tools for public, school, and college libraries: *American Indian Biographies* (1 volume, 1999, to be reissued in an expanded edition in 2005), covering 329 Native North Americans from the sixteenth century to the present day; *American Indian Tribes* (2 volumes, 2000), with surveys of the ten major culture areas of North America and nearly 300 tribes and nations; and *American Indian History* (2 volumes, 2003), with 224 essays covering the major events and developments in the history of Native Americans of North America, from the earliest prehistoric traditions through the activism of the present day.

The current three volumes add 275 entries to the more than 800 covered in the companion publications. These essays are a mixture of both new and old: 259 are drawn from three previous Salem Press publications: *Ready Reference: American Indians* (3 volumes, 1995), winner of the American Library Association's Outstanding Reference Source Award; *Great Events from History: Revised North American Series* (4 volumes, 1997); and *Racial and Ethnic Relations in America* (3 volumes, 1999). Updating of the bibliographies of previously published essays was accompanied by the addition of more than 180 new bibliographies as well as new citations to nearly all existing bibliographies. Care was taken to review datedness among the previously published essays, and several of the more time-sensitive topics—"Demography," "Elderly," "Gambling," "Land Claims," and "Pan-Indianism"—were significantly revised and updated. In addition, 16 essays were newly commissioned for this publication.

Arranged alphabetically by topic, each of the essays addresses a cultural phenomenon characteristic of the indigenous peoples of North America. Essays range in length from 250 to 3,000 words and cover the range of culture from lifeways, religious rituals, and material culture to art forms and modern social phenomena. Twenty separate essays cover both "Architecture" and "Arts and

Crafts" in ten North American culture areas: the Arctic, California, the Great Basin, the Northeast, the Northwest Coast, the Plains, the Plateau, the Southeast, the Southwest, and the Subarctic. In other entries, students will find everything from brief discussions of the importance of acorns or wild rice to a survey of agriculture; from a history of the atlatl to an essay on weapons in general; from entries on particular dance forms, such as the Ghost Dance, the Sun Dance, and the Buffalo Dance, to an overview of dances and dancing. Although the emphasis is on the traditional cultural heritage of North American indigenous peoples, modern social trends are surveyed and analyzed as well: such essays cover alcoholism, the impact of disease (both pre-contact and post-contact), education, family life, gaming, tourism, and urban Indians.

It is perhaps as important to mention what will not be found here as what we have included: Key historic events, movements, laws, acts, treaties, organizations, reports, wars, battles, court cases, and other historical overviews are covered in the companion two-volume publication *American Indian History*; coverage of tribes and nations is addressed in *American Indian Tribes*; and more than three hundred biographies of historic Native American personages appear in *American Indian Biographies*.

Each essay is arranged in a ready-reference format that calls out the following elements at the top: *name of topic* by key word; *tribe or tribes* affected or involved (topics are often, but not always, pantribal); and finally a brief synopsis of the topic's *significance*. These reference features are followed by a description and discussion of the topic's importance in American Indian culture. All essays end with a list of "Sources for Further Study," which, as stated above, have been expanded and updated to offer the most recent and accessible print resources pertinent to the topic; Web sites are listed in the appendix "Web Resources." All essays are fully cross-referenced to one another in the "See also" section at the essay's end, where the name of the contributor also appears.

The three volumes are illustrated with more than 135 photographs, drawings, maps, and tables, and several appendixes at the end of volume 3 serve as research tools:

- Educational Institutions and Programs *(expanded)*
- Festivals and Pow-wows *(expanded)*
- Glossary
- Mediagraphy
- Museums, Archives, and Libraries
- Organizations, Agencies, and Societies
- Tribes by Culture Area
- Bibliography *(expanded)*
- Web Resources *(expanded)*

Subtopics addressed in the text are accessible through three indexes:

- Category Index: essays by subject, from "Agriculture and Foodstuffs" through "Weapons and Warfare"

- Culture Area Index: essays organized by the ten major North American culture areas as well as "Pantribal" for those of general application

- Subject Index: a general and comprehensive index including concepts, forms of material culture, tribes, people, and organizations

Finally, the front matter to all three volumes contains the full alphabetized list of contents for ready reference.

A few comments must be made on certain editorial decisions. Terms ranging from "American Indian" to "Native American" to "tribe" are accepted by some and disapproved of by others. We have used "American Indian" in the title of this set, as it is today a widely accepted collective name for the first inhabitants of North America and their descendants. We have allowed authors to use either "American Indian" or "Native American" in their articles rather than impose a term editorially, recognizing that individual writers have their own preferences.

The inclusion of line drawings, maps, and 90 photographs illustrates the social concepts and material culture presented in the text. Where available historical or rare images were not of the best quality, the editors erred on the side of inclusion.

The editors wish to acknowledge the invaluable guidance and assistance of Professors Carole A. Barrett of the University of Mary and Harvey J. Markowitz of Washington and Lee University, both of whom specialize in American Indian studies. They surveyed the table of contents, recommended new entries, and generously wrote many of them. In addition, we wish to thank the contributing writers, whose names appear on the following pages.

Contributors

Thomas L. Altherr
*Metropolitan State College
of Denver*

T. J. Arant
Appalachian State University

Mary Pat Balkus
Radford University

Carl L. Bankston III
Tulane University

Russell J. Barber
*California State University,
San Bernardino*

Carole A. Barrett
University of Mary

Bette Blaisdell
Independent Scholar

Kendall W. Brown
Brigham Young University

Gregory R. Campbell
University of Montana

Byron D. Cannon
University of Utah

Thomas P. Carroll
John A. Logan College

Cheryl Claassen
Appalachian State University

Richmond Clow
University of Montana

Richard G. Condon
University of Arkansas

Michael Coronel
University of Northern Colorado

Patricia Coronel
Colorado State University

LouAnn Faris Culley
Kansas State University

Michael G. Davis
Northeast Missouri State University

Jennifer Davis
University of Dayton

Ronald J. Duncan
Oklahoma Baptist University

Dorothy Engan-Barker
Mankato State University

James D. Farmer
Virginia Commonwealth University

Michael Findlay
California State University, Chico

Roberta Fiske-Rusciano
Rutgers University

William B. Folkestad
Central Washington University

Contributors

Raymond Frey
Centenary College

Lucy Ganje
University of North Dakota

Lynne Getz
Appalachian State University

Marc Goldstein
Independent Scholar

Nancy M. Gordon
Independent Scholar

William H. Green
University of Missouri, Columbia

Eric Henderson
University of Northern Iowa

Donna Hess
South Dakota State University

C. L. Higham
Winona State University

Carl W. Hoagstrom
Ohio Northern University

John Hoopes
University of Kansas

Andrew C. Isenberg
University of Puget Sound

M. A. Jaimes
University of Colorado at Boulder

Jennifer Raye James
Independent Scholar

Helen Jaskoski
*California State University,
Fullerton*

Joseph C. Jastrzembski
University of Texas at El Paso

Bruce E. Johansen
University of Nebraska at Omaha

Marcella T. Joy
Independent Scholar

Charles Louis Kammer III
The College of Wooster

Nathan R. Kollar
St. John Fisher College

Philip E. Lampe
Incarnate Word College

Elden Lawrence
South Dakota State University

Denise Low
Haskell Indian Nations University

William C. Lowe
Mount St. Clare College

Kenneth S. McAllister
University of Illinois at Chicago

Heather McKillop
Louisiana State University

Kimberly Manning
*California State University,
Santa Barbara*

Harvey Markowitz
Washington and Lee University

Lynn M. Mason
Lubbock Christian University

Patricia Masserman
Independent Scholar

Howard Meredith
*University of Science and Arts
of Oklahoma*

Linda J. Meyers
Pasadena City College

David N. Mielke
Appalachian State University

Laurence Miller
*Western Washington State
University*

David J. Minderhout
Bloomsburg University

Molly H. Mullin
Duke University

Bert M. Mutersbaugh
Eastern Kentucky University

Gary A. Olson
San Bernardino Valley College

Nancy H. Omaha Boy
Rutgers University

Max Orezzoli
Florida International University

William T. Osborne
Florida International University

Martha I. Pallante
Youngstown State University

Zena Pearlstone
*California State University,
Long Beach*

Victoria Price
Lamar University

Jon Reyhner
*Montana State University,
Billings*

Jennifer Rivers
Brigham Young University

Moises Roizen
West Valley College

John Alan Ross
Eastern Washington University

Richard Sax
Madonna University

Glenn J. Schiffman
Independent Scholar

Michael W. Simpson
Eastern Washington University

Sanford S. Singer
University of Dayton

Roger Smith
Linfield College

Contributors

Daniel L. Smith-Christopher
Loyola Marymount University

Pamela R. Stern
University of Arkansas

Ruffin Stirling
Independent Scholar

Leslie Stricker
Independent Scholar

Harold D. Tallant
Georgetown College

Nicholas C. Thomas
*Auburn University at
Montgomery*

Gale M. Thompson
Saginaw Valley State University

Leslie V. Tischauser
Prairie State College

Diane C. Van Noord
Western Michigan University

Mary E. Virginia
Independent Scholar

Susan J. Wurtzburg
University of Canterbury

Clifton K. Yearley
*State University of New York at
Buffalo*

Alphabetical List of Contents

Volume 1

Volume 2

Alphabetical List of Contents

Volume 3

American Indian Culture

Acorns

Tribes affected: Tribes in California and the prehistoric Northeast
Significance: *Acorns provided a starchy food staple for various Indian groups.*

Acorns, the nuts of oak trees, average 40-50 percent carbohydrates, 3-4 percent protein, and 5-10 percent fat, making them a nutritious foodstuff providing about 168 calories per ounce. This abundant and easily collected nut became the dietary mainstay for various Indian groups, particularly in the Northeast and California.

The earliest unequivocal evidence of the dietary use of acorns comes from the Lamoka culture of New York, probably around 3500 B.C.E. Archaeological sites in Massachusetts dating from a millennium later also have produced clear evidence of the eating of large quantities of acorns. By the historic period, however, Northeastern Indians were using acorns only sparingly as food.

Seven Oak Trees Used by California Indians		
Common Name	*Species*	*Desirability Rating*
Tan oak	*Lithocarpus densiflora*	1.0
Black oak	*Quercus kelloggii*	1.5
Blue oak	*Quercus douglasii*	1.5
Valley oak	*Quercus lobata*	1.9
Coast live oak	*Quercus agrifolia*	2.0
Oregon oak	*Quercus garryana*	2.0
Engelmann oak	*Quercus engelmannii*	2.2

Source: Heizer, Robert F., ed., *California.* Vol. 8 in *Handbook of North American Indians,* edited by William C. Sturtevant. Washington, D.C.: Smithsonian Institution, 1978.

Note: Acorns were of great importance to California Indians even in areas in which not many were available. "Desirability rating" scale created by Martin A. Baumhoff (1963); the lower the number, the more preferable the acorns.

In California, major use of acorns began later, around 1000 B.C.E., but it ultimately was more important, often forming the bulk of the diet. Six species of acorn were gathered, and families commonly obtained enough in one season to last them two years. The acorns typically were stored in baskets or wooden granaries, some as much as 5 feet in diameter and 8 feet high. To reduce infestation by vermin, the base of a granary might be painted with pitch, or fragrant laurel leaves might be included. The acorns were ground as needed, and bitter tannin was leached out by washing the acorn meal repeatedly with hot water. The acorn meal was boiled into gruel or baked into pancake-biscuits on heated rocks. This staple supported many California Indians into the late nineteenth century.

Russell J. Barber

See also: Hunting and Gathering; Subsistence.

Adobe

Tribes affected: Pueblo peoples
Significance: *Adobe, an energy-efficient building material, made possible the typical buildings of the Puebloans of the Southwest.*

"Adobe" comes from the identical Spanish word, which in turn is taken from the Arabic word *attoba*, meaning "the brick." Adobe bricks are made of clay and straw mixed with water and dried in the sun. The word can be used to describe the bricks themselves or the clay or soil from which they are made, as well as the mortar sometimes made from them and the structures built with them.

Adobe is used as a building material primarily in the southwestern United States by the Pueblo peoples, which include such well-known tribes as the Hopi and Zuñi. They build large community dwellings of masonry and adobe that endure, in some cases, for centuries.

Some of the oldest standing structures in the United States are

A single-family Zuñi adobe dwelling in 1879. *(National Archives)*

made of this material. Adobe is energy-efficient, as it insulates well against both heat and cold. Buildings made of adobe can rise up to five stories in height. It is a building material well suited to the desert environments in which it is most commonly used.

Michael W. Simpson

See also: Architecture: Southwest; Pit House; Pueblo.

Adoption

Tribes affected: Pantribal
Significance: *Native Americans had very different ideas about family from those now accepted in America; many more people were considered family to begin with, and adoption was a widespread practice.*

In most American Indian cultures, a family was not only the nuclear family but also parents, parents-in-law, aunts, uncles, cousins, and other related individuals who might need the "sponsorship" of a family. An example of one to be adopted would be a great aunt whose children had died or moved to another camp or tribe. Individuals who had been adopted became part of the family.

Adoption could be temporary or permanent. For example, the Ute allowed their children to live with Spanish-speaking residents of trading partners so that the children would learn a second language and culture. These children then belonged to both families, although they continued to identify themselves as Ute. Among most nations, related children, such as a cousin's child, might be reared by the parents until a certain age and then allowed to live with relatives who might have special skills or children of similar age. While these were not considered adoptions by Indians, they are frequently cited in the non-Indian literature about Indians as adoptions. A Cheyenne girl who showed particular interest in quillwork at nine years of age might go to live with an aunt who was skilled in this work. Her parents, brothers, sisters, and cousins often continued to interact with her on a daily basis.

Adoptions, as defined by American society, also took place with orphans or captives. When a person of any age was claimed as a relative, full family status was accorded to him or her by all members of the family, and the person was treated as though he or she had been born into the family. That may be the reason that some children who had been captured and reared by Indians preferred to stay with them, even when "rescued." Indian families were very loving and supportive; children were cherished, and adults gave freely to all children. Among the Lakota, children without parents were taken in by relatives, but other adults continued to give them horses and beaded clothing and to treat them kindly throughout their lives.

In another form of adoption, a bereaved parent mourning the death of a beloved child might be offered another child by a friend or relative. The Winnebagos were known to have done this. Again, these children were not considered as "belonging" to the receiving family. The giving family was extending to the receiving family the right to love, educate, adore, make gifts for, share stories with, and train the child. The child did not give up his or her birth family so much as he or she added another family. The child might reside in one home or the other at different times. The benefits of both families were stronger relationships, resulting in a stronger support system.

Nancy H. Omaha Boy

Sources for Further Study

Bensen, Robert, ed. *Children of the Dragonfly: Native American Voices on Child Custody and Education*. Tucson: University of Arizona Press, 2001.

Holt, Marilyn Irvin. *Indian Orphanages*. Lawrence: University Press of Kansas, 2001.

See also: Captivity and Captivity Narratives; Children; Slavery.

Agriculture

Tribes affected: Pantribal
Significance: *Although the North American Indians have a long tradition of agriculture, it has not been successfully integrated with white agriculture; Indian agriculture has steadily declined.*

The beginnings of agriculture among the Indians of North America stretch far back into prehistory, perhaps as far back as seven thousand years. Exactly when it began—when the native peoples of North America began relying on deliberately cultivated crops for a portion of their caloric requirements—is a matter of debate. What is not in debate is where it began: Mexico is clearly the location of the earliest efforts to produce cultivated crops. From there, knowledge and seeds appear to have radiated outward, notably northward.

The progress of agriculture was very slow. It began with the domestication of one or two wild plants, the gathering of their seeds, and deliberate planting and raising of them at a prepared site in order to be able to harvest the resulting crop. Most likely the first efforts were more like gardens than agricultural fields, for the Indians were constrained by two factors that did not affect residents of the Old World: The Indians lacked metal tools and they lacked domesticated animals. All agriculture was hand labor, with tools that lacked the precise usefulness of modern, metal tools.

In time, however, the Indians were able to produce larger and larger portions of their caloric requirements from agriculture. That reduced their dependence on fruits and nuts they could gather and on game they could kill. By the time of European contact, some Indian tribes were supplying as much as 50 to 60 percent of their nutritional requirements from crops they planted, cultivated, and harvested.

The story of Indian agriculture falls naturally into three phases. The first phase, covering perhaps five thousand years, is all the time that transpired before Christopher Columbus initiated the flood of Europeans into the Western Hemisphere. The second phase (at least in North America) is that covering the period from Columbus' discovery to the close of the American Revolution, roughly from 1500 to 1783. The third phase, in the United States, is the period after 1783, when the Indians were wards of the federal government.

Pre-contact Agriculture. The pre-contact agriculture of the North American Indians began in the highlands of Mexico. There, the earliest cultivated plants were the gourds, the cucurbits. In the earliest adaptations from wild plants, gourds were used as containers; the pulp was too bitter to eat. The seeds, however, did become a regular foodstuff, constituting the "peanuts" of Indian agriculture. As new varieties of cucurbit emerged (from careful seed selection by the Indians), squashlike vegetables were produced and eaten regularly.

During much of the millennium prior to European contact, most Indians lived in relatively permanent villages. They came to specialize in the production of food for the group. The women were responsible for the planting, cultivation, and much of the harvesting work; the men remained the hunters, going off on hunting expeditions, sometimes for weeks at a time.

The Indians settled in places where the soil could be easily worked with simple tools, often only a digging stick. The favored locations were stream bottoms, alluvial plains, and, to a lesser extent, ridge tops. These places generally had light, sandy soil that could be easily worked with tools made from forked sticks, clam shells, and stone.

If the land chosen for cultivation had shrubs and trees growing on it, the Indians generally girdled the trees and uprooted the shrubs. The latter, together with the herbaceous cover, were burned; the crops were planted around the stumps of any remaining trees. In most cases, the Indians burned over a field assigned to be cultivated each year; in this way they provided some lime and potash for the new crop.

Once the land was cleared for cultivation, a process carried out by the men of the tribe, the women took over. Planting was done with the aid of a dibble stick, thrust into the ground and worked around to provide a hole into which the seed could be dropped. Once the planted vegetables had come up, the Indian women weeded the crop at least once, sometimes twice. In the rare cases where irrigation was practiced, in the Southwest, the men were responsible for the construction and the maintenance of the irrigation ditches; otherwise agriculture was women's work.

The harvesting was also largely women's work, though the men sometimes helped with it. Depending on the crop, the harvested material needed to be prepared so that it would keep; this was usually accomplished by drying. The material was hung up in the sun until all the moisture was gone. It was then packed, often in baskets made from plant material (corn stalks, willow withes, and other flexible plant materials), and stored, frequently in pits.

By the end of the prehistoric period, the Indians were cultivating a wide variety of crops. The most important of these, squashes, beans, and corn, had all come from central Mexico. The squashes came first; beans came later, probably around 1000 C.E., but in time came to constitute an important part of the Indian diet. Their usefulness depended on the possession of pottery vessels in which they could be cooked.

Without a doubt, the most important Indian crop was maize, a cultivated version of the wild plant teosinte, a native of the central Mexican highlands. How early a cultivated maize had developed in North America is under dispute among archaeologists. There is, however, evidence that maize as a cultivated crop was widespread among Native Americans by 1000 C.E.

Prior to the development of maize, there is archaeological evidence of the cultivation of some native grasses that produced seeds rich in oil. Sumpweed (*Iva annua*), goosefoot (*Chenopodium bushianum* or *berlandieri*), and sunflower (*Helianthus annus*) were the most important of these native plants that were domesticated by the Indians. Cultivation of these native species declined after the arrival of maize, as the latter fulfilled far more easily the carbohydrate nutritional needs of the Indians.

One important food plant that was never fully domesticated (although there is some evidence of domestication by the Chippewas) but was harvested for many centuries by the Indians of the northern tier of the United States was wild rice. The Indians of Minnesota to this day have exclusive rights to the wild rice growing in those northern swamps.

Two important crops that were not food crops were tobacco and cotton. Tobacco was grown (mostly by men, not women) for its ceremonial use. Tobacco was being grown all over what is now the United States by the resident Indians at the time of European contact. Cotton was grown only in the Southwest, generally in irrigated plots; it was developed as a crop sometime after 500 C.E. The southwestern Indians also developed the necessary skills to convert the fiber to cloth.

1500-1783. The arrival of the European colonists profoundly altered Indian agriculture in two principal ways: The Europeans, by trading manufactured items with the Indians for agricultural products, turned a portion of Indian agriculture into commercial agriculture. Additionally, the Europeans brought many new crops, some of which were eagerly adopted by the Indians.

The story of how the first Europeans to arrive as colonists survived only because they acquired food from the Indians is familiar to every American schoolchild. The Europeans brought with them manufactured products, notably axes, whose use the Indians could readily appreciate, and they were eager to acquire them. The Indians themselves had two things to offer: crops they had grown and skins from wild animals. The latter were in demand in Europe and financed much of the early development of the European colonies; the former were needed by the colonists for survival until they could develop their own fields.

One of the most important crops brought by the Europeans was wheat. The Spaniards introduced wheat to the Indians of the Southwest, and it became a major crop for the Indians of that area. The Indians of the Mississippi Valley also began growing wheat, as did the Plains Indians. The Spaniards also introduced the plow, and although some Indians (notably the Cherokee) were initially reluctant to use plows, many other tribes readily adopted plow agriculture. In some areas Indians actually traded plow services from the colonists for skins and agricultural products.

The Europeans added crops other than wheat to the traditional Indian produce. Both potatoes and tomatoes became part of the Indian diet as a result of European introduction. Watermelons and cantaloupes were also introduced by the Europeans. The Europeans introduced the idea of orchards, particularly peach orchards, and some tribes took to the idea. Peach orchards were particularly popular with the Indians of the Southwest. Apricots and apples were also grown in orchards after being introduced.

A major agricultural change introduced by the Europeans was the raising of livestock. The Indians had obtained all their meat from game prior to European contact. The Europeans brought horses, mules, cattle, sheep, and goats. Sheep and goats became particularly popular with the Indians of the Southwest, where grazing is the only possible agricultural use of much of the dry land of that area. It is widely known that the Plains Indians acquired horses from the Spaniards and that the acquisition profoundly altered their lifestyle. Some of the midwestern and eastern Indians recognized the value of oxen and began to use them for plowing.

1783-1887. The victory of the colonists in the American Revolution had a profound impact on Indian agriculture. The federal government, as soon as it was well organized, developed a definitive policy with respect to the Indians still living in the territory ceded by the British in 1783. That policy essentially involved separating the two groups—pushing the Indians into areas not inhabited by white Americans so as to open up more of the land for settlement by the colonists. With the Louisiana Purchase, this policy of separating the Indians from the white Americans became more explicit. By acquiring vast lands in the trans-Mississippi region, the federal government obtained western areas where it could establish new reservations to which the Indians could be "removed," thus effectively separating them from the European Americans.

At the same time, considerable effort was devoted to inculcating white agricultural practices. In the 1790's, Congress passed what were known as the Trade and Intercourse Acts, defining the relationship between Indians and white Americans. These acts stressed the development of white farming practices among the Indians and provided funds for tools (mostly plows and hoes) and even livestock to enable the Indians to become typical small farmers like the vast majority of white citizens of that time. The Indian agents appointed by the federal government for each tribe were instructed to promote such agricultural practices among the Indians.

1887-1934. In 1887, however, an abrupt change occurred in the Indian policy of the federal government. Although agriculture had been slowly gaining among the Indians, Congress became convinced that it could significantly lessen the costs of Indian support (needed to supplement the produce of Indian agriculture) if it created the incentive of private property. It therefore passed what was widely known, from its author, Senator Henry Dawes, as the Dawes Severalty Act, otherwise called the General Allotment Act. This act authorized the president to divide reservation land into individual allotments: Each head of household was to receive 160 acres, a single man 80 acres, and a child 40 acres. The title to the land was held in trust by the federal government for twenty-five years, at the end of which time full title to the land would be transferred to the Indian owner. If that owner should die before the twenty-five years had elapsed, the land was to be divided among all his heirs. If the reservation contained more land than was needed to allot each member of the tribe his prescribed share, then the remainder of the land was opened to white settlement. The funds derived from selling these "surplus" lands to whites were to be set aside in a trust fund for the benefit of the tribe.

Although the underlying concept of the General Allotment Act and the allotment policy was that it would hasten the time when all Indians would become at least subsistence farmers, it in fact had the opposite effect. There were a number of reasons for this failure. Most critics of the policy stress the fact that it attempted to impose, by legislation, a private-property culture on peoples whose own culture largely lacked such a concept. To Indians, the land was made available by the Great Spirit for the use of his children; that it should be used to amass individual wealth was wholly outside their sense of the appropriate.

Also crucially important was the fact that the land assigned to the Indians under the allotment system was incapable of providing subsistence for a family in the amount allotted. An allotment of 160 acres was simply too little land in an area of light rainfall, where tillage agriculture, if it could be carried on at all, depended on heavy capital investment in plows and harvesting equipment. Raising livestock was a practical option, but it required many more acres than the 160 allotted. The allotment policy discouraged the development of tribal herds run on a cooperative basis, actually the most hopeful revenue for Indian agriculture in the plains states. The result was, instead, that the Indians gave up attempts at agriculture and instead began leasing their land to whites who had the capital and the expertise to farm it.

By the 1920's, it was clear that the allotment policy was a failure. The secretary of the interior commissioned a report to be produced by a group of specialists headed by Lewis Meriam. Their report, known as the Meriam Report (1928), had three principal recommendations regarding agriculture. First, any notion of remaking the Indians into commercial farmers should be abandoned—the most that could be hoped for would be subsistence agriculture. Second, more government programs should be directed toward women to encourage subsistence gardening, poultry raising, and modern methods of food preservation. Third, the focus of Indian agriculture should shift from tillage to livestock raising, for which Indian men showed greater aptitude. The report recognized that most Indian land was only suitable for grazing anyway.

These recommendations laid the basis for a reversal of Indian agricultural policy under the New Deal of President Franklin Roosevelt. The Roosevelt Administration appointed a new commissioner of Indian affairs, John Collier, who had new ideas about how to conduct Indian policy. Collier pushed tribal initiatives, particularly cooperative agricultural efforts. These efforts had some success among Plains Indians. The Indian Reorganization Act of 1934 ended allotments for any tribes that agreed with the new policy. Any former reservation land that had been opened to white homesteading but not taken would be returned to the tribe, and some funds were provided for the purchase of additional land.

Since 1934. The steady decline in Indian land under the allotment policy was reversed, but only a modest portion of the more than 50 million acres once assigned to Indians but lost under allotment was recovered. Prior to allotment, Indians had had more than 100 million acres under their control; by the 1970's that figure had dropped to around 50 million.

The period since World War II has seen vacillating Indian policy on the part of the government. Agriculture has continued to decline among Indians, so that now no more than 10 percent are agriculturally active. In most recent years, the federal government, although recognizing its continuing responsibility to the Indians, has largely given up attempting to encourage agriculture among them.

Nancy M. Gordon

Sources for Further Study

Carlson, Leonard A. *Indians, Bureaucrats, and Land: The Dawes Act and the Decline of Indian Farming*. Westport, Conn.: Greenwood Press, 1981. An intensive study of the effect of the allotment system on the participation of Indians in agriculture. Carlson includes an economic model of the behavioral response that might be expected to allotment-type inducements. Selected bibliography.

Ford, Richard I., ed. *Prehistoric Food Production in North America*. Ann Arbor: University of Michigan Press, 1985. A collection of papers by archaeologists involved in seeking data on prehistoric agriculture. The detail is fairly exhaustive, but the general picture is clear. Notes and bibliography.

Hurt, R. Douglas. *Indian Agriculture in America: Prehistory to the Present*. Lawrence: University Press of Kansas, 1987. A good general survey. The bulk of the book is devoted to discussing the Indian policy of the federal government as it relates to agriculture. The author is critical of the policy pursued as lacking in consideration for the special constraints imposed by Indian culture. Bibliographic note, extensive notes to text.

Lewis, David Rich. *Neither Wolf nor Dog: American Indians, Environment, and Agrarian Change*. New York: Oxford University Press, 1994. An examination of the effects of the federal agrarian system on three Native American groups—Hupas, Northern Utes, and Tohono O'odhams.

Russell, Howard S. *Indian New England Before the Mayflower*. Hanover, N.H.: University Press of New England, 1980. The author of the preeminent history of New England agriculture looks at the culture that preceded it. Part 4, "The Bountiful Earth," describes the agriculture of the New England Indians. Notes, extensive bibliography, and index.

Smith, Bruce D., with contributions by C. Wesley Cowan and Michael P. Hoffman. *Rivers of Change: Essays on Early Agriculture in Eastern North America*. Washington: Smithsonian Institution Press, 1992. An alternate view of how prehistoric North American cultures evolved from hunting and gathering societies to agricultural-based societies.

Thomas, Peter A. "Contrastive Subsistence Strategies and Land Use as Factors for Understanding Indian-White Relations in New England." *Ethnohistory* 23 (1976): 1-18. A thoughtful consideration of the thorny question of whether the Indians or the European settlers were more efficient and effective users of the land. References.

See also: Anasazi Civilization; Beans; Corn; Food Preparation and Cooking; Irrigation; Squash; Subsistence; Technology.

Alcoholism

Tribes affected: Pantribal
Significance: *American Indians, whether living on or off reservations, have extremely high rates of alcoholism; many Indian problems with crime, health, and poverty are related to heavy drinking.*

The most severe health problem among contemporary American Indians is alcoholism. The reasons for the problem are complex, but central among them are poverty, a pervasive sense of despair (particularly among young reservation Indians), and the stresses involved in adjusting to non-Indian life. Both Indian and non-Indian sources, contemporary and historical, also point to drinking as one reaction to the profound disruption of Indian societies that began soon after Europeans landed in the Americas and which intensified through the years.

Early Contact Years. With the exception of parts of the Southwest, alcoholic beverages did not exist in North America before the Europeans came, though they were widely used by Central and South American natives. Early French and English explorers, trappers, and merchants often gave Indians liquor as a gift or exchanged it for food or furs. By the early 1600's, for example, French Canadian traders were encouraging the use of alcohol among the Huron, even though the Catholic church deplored such practices and the French government outlawed the sale or use of liquor in trade. As early as 1603, French priests in Canada reported that many natives were drinking alcohol heavily during their ceremonies and dances. Whiskey and rum quickly became prime items of trade—and killers of Indians. European traders cultivated the desire for liquor among Indians, creating a market; they realized that trading liquor was a cheap way to obtain valuable furs. John Stuart stated in 1776 that English traders obtained five times as many animal skins from the Choctaws of the Southeast through trading alcohol than through the trade of English manufactured goods of any real value. This situation, he said, was making the Choctaws "poor, wretched, . . . and discontented."

The white stereotype of the dangerous firewater-drinking Indian became established early. Regardless of what some whites believed, the truth is simply that some Indians drank and others did not. Drinking patterns varied by individual and by tribe; a number of cultures, among them the Pawnee, were known for not drinking at all. Eighteenth century accounts suggest that, among the Iroquois, there were occasional drunken revels that would essentially engulf a whole village or town and end when the liquor was gone; life would then return to normal. Indian drinking behavior was no more dangerous or violent than that of the Europeans who lived along the frontier. A difference, however, was that Indian cultures, having no previous experience with alcohol intoxication, did not have a set of social norms or expectations governing drinking, as European cultures did. There were no religious strictures or stigma attached to being under the influence of alcohol, and being drunk may have developed religious overtones in some Indian cultures. The Lakota Sioux called alcohol "the magic water," for example, and some scholars have noted a link between drinking liquor until drunk and the traditional Indian practice of going on a vision quest seeking wisdom and strength through fasting, meditation, and prayer until a state of altered consciousness is achieved. Alcohol intoxication may also have been considered akin to being influenced or possessed by a supernatural being.

Many tribal political and religious leaders soon recognized the danger that alcohol posed to traditional culture. Many tribal leaders tried to ban alcohol from their villages, but such efforts rarely succeeded. A number of post-contact religious movements, or revitalization movements, among American Indians included abstinence from liquor as a central tenet: One was the Longhouse religion established by Handsome Lake; another was the Pan-Indian movement led by Tenskwatawa.

In the Indian Trade and Intercourse Acts of 1834, the United States government prohibited the sale of alcohol to Native Americans, but enforcing the law proved impossible. Smugglers made huge profits, and bootlegging became one way of becoming very rich on the frontier. Alcohol remained illegal on Indian reservations until 1953, when Congress permitted its sale if local tribal governments voted to allow it. Easier access to alcoholic beverages led to a steady increase in cases of alcoholism among Native Americans.

Impact on the Indian Population. A report issued by the American Indian Policy Review Commission, established by Congress in 1975 to survey major reservation problems, concluded that alcohol abuse was the most severe health care problem faced by Native Americans. It found that almost one-half of Indian adults had some sort of chemical dependency, with alcohol being the chemical most often abused. Statistics at the time of the commission's report emphasized the prevalence of the problem: Seventy-one percent of all arrests on reservations involved alcohol, and the death rate from drunk driving on reservations was three times the rate for the general population. Death from cirrhosis of the liver, almost always caused by alcoholism, was more than four times greater for Indians (27.3 per 100,000) than for other Americans (6.1 per 100,000). The suicide rate among Native Americans—which drinking undoubtedly influences—was more than double the national rate. Another alcohol-related health problem, one which has been recognized relatively recently, is fetal alcohol syndrome (FAS), a disease that stunts growth and interferes with brain development in the babies of alcoholic mothers. Native American women have been found to have babies born with fetal alcohol syndrome at a rate greater than ten times that of the rest of the U.S. population.

A 1985 study reported that one-third of all Indian deaths were related to alcohol—three times as many as the U.S. average. In 1986, recognizing the severity of the problem, Congress enacted the Indian Alcohol and Substance Abuse Prevention and Treatment Act.

Those who have studied Indian drinking generally believe that alcohol abuse among Native Americans results from the same factors that lead to high levels of alcoholism among other populations: It is a means of coping with unemployment, poverty, and alienation. The economic situation of American Indians, particularly those on isolated reservations, is grim compared with that of most Americans. In the late twentieth century, following the awakening (and suppression) of Indian activism in the 1960's and 1970's, younger Indians became increasingly aware of past injustices toward Indians and increasingly desperate regarding what seemed to be the lack of future opportunities.

Other aspects of Indian alcoholism are the social factors thought, by some, to encourage drinking actively. It has been suggested that drinking may amount to a form of social protest: By not obeying the rules of white society, a Native American displays contempt for those who destroyed his or her culture and who now do not offer opportunities in theirs. Drinking is tolerated by many adults on reservations, and there is little pressure put on alcoholics to seek help or change their ways. One study of a reservation in North Dakota found that most residents faced almost daily pressure from friends and family members to drink. Many adults supported the idea that individuals have the right to become publicly intoxicated. In addition, drunkenness was seen as a way of acknowledging that one is no better than one's neighbor and that one knows how to have a good time; viewed in this way, drinking may be seen as representing a sense of community.

There is hope that the situation will begin to improve. Groups such as Alcoholics Anonymous have opened chapters in Indian communities. In addition, the search for an Indian answer to alcoholism has involved the reawakening of interest in Indian spiritual and cultural traditions. Because Indian alcoholism so often involves group activity, approaches involving groups and entire communities have proved more beneficial than have private counseling and treatment. As Indian cultural pride and solidarity increase, as more Indians themselves work for the Indian Health Service (which serves reservation communities), and as sufficient funding becomes available, new possibilities exist for stemming the tide of alcoholism.

Leslie V. Tischauser

Sources for Further Study

Dorris, Michael. *The Broken Cord*. New York: Harper & Row, 1989.

Fixico, Donald Lee. *The Urban Experience in America*. Albuquerque: University of New Mexico Press, 2000.

French, Laurence Armand. *Addictions and Native Americans*. Westport, Conn.: Praeger, 2000.

_____. *Counseling American Indians*. Lanham, Md.: University Press of America, 1997.

Indian Health Service, Task Force on Indian Alcoholism. *Alcoholism: A High Priority Health Problem*. Washington, D.C.: U.S. Government Printing Office, 1977.

Kunitz, Stephen J., and Jerrold E. Levy. *Drinking, Conduct Disorder and Social Change: Navajo Experiences*. New York: Oxford University Press, 2000.

Mancall, Peter C. *Deadly Medicine: Indians and Alcohol in Early America*. Ithaca, N.Y.: Cornell University Press, 1995.

Mihesuah, Devon A. *American Indians: Stereotypes and Realities*. Atlanta, Ga.: Clarity, 1996.

See also: Employment and Unemployment; Medicine and Modes of Curing: Post-contact; Relocation; Stereotypes; Urban Indians.

American Indian Studies

Tribes affected: Pantribal
Significance: *American Indian studies programs, which began in the late 1960's, seek to preserve and understand American Indian history and culture.*

Since the late 1960's, American Indian studies (or Native American studies) programs have served as the most important scholarly approach to knowing and understanding American Indian culture. Traditional teachings of tribal and village elders remain the solid foundation of American Indian and Native American studies. These culture bearers provide the understanding essential to legitimate study of the native peoples of the Americas.

Establishment of Programs. Dependence upon European American (notably Anglo-American) source materials has made for distortion in scholarly studies. As professor Henrietta Whiteman has stated, "Cheyenne history, and by extension Indian history, in all probability will never be incorporated into American history, because it is holistic, human, personal, and sacred. Though it is equally as valid as Anglo-American history it is destined to remain complementary to white secular American history." This specific difficulty led in large part to the creation of American Indian studies programs in existing institutions of higher learning. Despite limited funds, Native American programs began to emerge as interdisciplinary curricula. Most American Indian studies programs focus on long-term goals involved with cultural preservation, unlike Western, objective academic disciplines such as history and ethnology. American Indian studies use teaching, research, and service to cross cultural boundaries and create an atmosphere for understanding. In many instances, the American Indian studies degree programs are the only non-Western courses of study on campus.

American Indian or Native American studies programs vary considerably in method and subject matter. These also represent different degrees of institutional support, budget size, and quality of program leadership. In the late 1960's and early 1970's, various programs began to emerge at the University of California, Berkeley, and the University of California, Los Angeles. Other programs developed in the California State University system on campuses at Long Beach, Fullerton, and Northridge. At that time, California had the largest Native American population in the United States. Oklahoma had the second-largest native population. Two degree programs were created in Oklahoma in the early 1970's, one at Northeastern State University at Tahlequah, the capital of the Cherokee Nation, and one at the University of Science and Arts of Oklahoma in Chickasha. The Native American studies degree program at the University of Oklahoma was accepted by the higher regents in 1993. Other American Indian studies degree programs were created at the University of Minnesota, the University of Washington, Evergreen College, Washington State University, the University of Arizona, the University of Illinois (Chicago), Dartmouth College, the University of North Dakota, Montana State University, the University of New Mexico, and Cornell University, among others. By the mid-1980's, eighteen programs offered a major leading to a bachelor's degree. Of these, six programs also offered a master's degree.

Tribally Controlled Colleges. Tribally controlled colleges added new energy to American Indian studies. In 1968, the Navajo Nation created the first tribally controlled institution of higher learning. Navajo Community College was a success and led to the passage of the Tribally Controlled Community College Assistance Act of 1978. This act provides for some federal support for tribally controlled colleges initiated by tribes in the western United States. Initially, this helped support thirteen tribally controlled colleges. Since the act's passage, at least nine additional colleges have been initiated. Colleges that followed the creation of Navajo Community College include Sinte Glista College, Standing Rock College, Blackfeet Community College, Dull Knife Memorial College, Salish Kootenai College, Little Bighorn College, and Stone Child

College, among others. Lummi College of Aquaculture in Washington has expanded to become the Northwest Indian College. Sinte Glista College on the Rosebud Sioux Reservation has grown to become the first fully accredited tribally controlled four-year institution of higher learning.

In all these examples, the tribally based community colleges have not only aided the education of individual Indian young people but also improved the development of the tribal communities that they serve. Of primary importance is that Indian people are now controlling institutions that directly affect them. The tribally controlled colleges are far outstripping the state-supported and private colleges and universities in retention of American Indian students. The tribally controlled colleges have become important centers of research. These colleges are proving to be better suited to the needs of American Indian students and communities than their state-supported and private counterparts. The tribally controlled colleges offer hope to tribes that have, all too often, survived in a climate of despair.

Issues and Concerns. In the early 1990's, American Indian studies emerged in a period of questioning current methods and practices concerning spirit, philosophy, structures, roles, contexts, and intent. The quest for meaning appeared in many guises. The interest in the emotional component of community life, the expansion of traditional approaches to knowledge and wisdom, the acceptance of grammar and logic stemming from native languages, and the hope of differentiating Western-based interpretation from traditional knowledge all reflected the aim of uncovering purpose, meaning, and perspectives on truth in presentation. There was pervasive anxiety that the individual is being submerged in community. There was additional attention being given to the way people feel as well as the way they behave. There was also a movement in American Indian studies toward narrative storytelling in the literature. American Indian studies places human beings and the comprehensible societies in which they live into the story. These are real stories, however, not dry and forbidding pieces of analysis.

The quest for meaning only multiplies the pluralism of current research and teaching. The very process of recovering deeper motivations and attitudes, dragging the latent out of the manifest, requires such personal feats of imagination and use of language that questions about plausibility and proof are bound to arise. Senior faculty at one state-supported university in Oklahoma challenged the continuation of a bachelor's degree in American Indian studies, stating, "While the program is inessential to a liberal arts education, it is not inconsistent with one." This type of Euro-American bias makes it difficult to pursue knowledge and wisdom in an atmosphere with freedom of thought and feeling.

The obverse of the quest for meaning is an uneasiness with the material conditions of life that until recently seemed so compelling. A clear, single idea emerges from the doubts that have been expressed about the power of economic development. As American Indian studies turns to more emotional content, the demand is for a more elusive process of comprehension. Analytical and technical research is increasingly limited, as mental patterns, attitudes, and symbolic acts become more prominent.

Questions of the use of quantification arise because of the almost exclusive use of United States and Western social science data. What is at stake is a profound epistemological question, not just a disagreement over collection of data. American Indian studies many times are very personal and intuitive. The insights are justified within a specific tribal context with powerful rhetorical and imaginative methods. They appeal to an interest in behavior that is very different from Anglo-American intellectual concerns, but never claim to be definitive.

The establishment of an agenda for American Indian studies, of a set of methods or purposes indigenous to the Americas, or of a special task for its practitioners, hardly seems plausible. American Indian studies is united in its respect of tribal traditions. There is observation of certain fundamental rules for using evidence so as to be intelligible across cultural boundaries. None of these skills is difficult to learn; neither is the telling of a sustained story, which is a special mark of scholars and teachers in American Indian studies. The one form of synthesis used most often by those in American Indian studies blends the disparate methods of current research in examinations of tribally specific localities. This synthesis convincingly links physical conditions, economic and demographic developments, social arrangements, intellectual and cultural assumptions, and political behavior, with mythic patterns and images.

Archives and Tribal Records. The most important repository of American Indian knowledge remains with the tribal elders. There is no substitute for this significant information. This knowledge and wisdom can be gained only with real commitment over a significant period of time. Tribal elders have become wary of "instant experts," whether Indian or non-Indian. All scholarship must access this wisdom and knowledge to reflect tribal tradition and history.

Once removed from this vital core of information are the tribal archives and records. These are held in a variety of ways. For example, the Wichita and Affiliated Tribes maintain their tribal archives as a part of the Wichita Memory Exhibit Museum at the tribal complex on reserve land north of Anadarko, Oklahoma. A second example is that of the Navajo Nation, which collects and preserves its records as a part of the Navajo Tribal Council Reference Library in Window Rock. A third example is that of the Cherokee Nation, which maintains a portion of its records in the Archives of the Cherokee National Historical Society in Tahlequah, while the records of the Cherokee Nation from 1839 through 1906 are held in the Indian Archives of the Oklahoma Historical Society, which functions as a trustee for the United States government. These records were placed in trust in 1906, just before Oklahoma statehood, before the National Archives of the United States was created. Each tribe maintains its records in an individual way. Contact with the tribes is the best means to understand their respective record-keeping systems.

U.S. National Archives. Large numbers of records about American Indian peoples are held by the National Archives of the United States. These are housed in the Washington National Records Center, Suitland, Maryland, and in eleven regional Federal Archives and Records Centers throughout the United States. Additional records holdings concerning American Indian peoples are contained at the presidential libraries administered by the National Archives and Records Service. The papers of the presidents and many of those of other high officials, including the files of individual members of Congress, are regarded as their personal property. These personal papers are collected in large part by state-supported university manuscripts collections.

The basic organizational unit in the National Archives collections is the record group. This refers to the records of a single agency, such as the Bureau of Indian Affairs and its predecessors. The National Archives endeavors to keep records in the order in which they were maintained by the respective agency. The agency filing system was designed for administrative purposes, not for the benefit of researchers. There are important guides to assist in research efforts, however. The two most important of these are *Guide to the National Archives of the United States* (1974) and *Guide to Records in the National Archives of the United States Relating to American Indians* (1981). Another useful volume is *Indian-White Relations: A Persistent Paradox* (1976), which includes papers and proceedings of the National Archives Conference on Research in the history of Indian-white relations.

Additional materials concerning Indian-white relations are contained in the United States Supreme Court decisions, the research that was used in the Indian Land Claims Act of 1946, and in the manuscript collections of major universities throughout the western United States.

American Indian studies has long been limited in perspective because of the heavy dependence upon documents generated by Euro-American policymakers, businesspersons, and military personnel. Scholarly works accepted many of the assumptions of those who produced these sources. American Indian people were perceived either negatively as an enemy or romantically as part of the environment. In the last decade, scholarship in American Indian studies has changed significantly from this approach. More balanced efforts are being made by American Indian scholars utilizing native languages and tribal sources. All American culture and society is being shown in a new light as a result of the creative images and ideas of American Indian studies.

Howard Meredith

Sources for Further Study

Carnegie Foundation for the Advancement of Teaching. *Tribal Colleges: Shaping the Future of Native America*. Princeton, N.J.: Author, 1989. Reviews the colleges that have been established for Native Americans.

Grounds, Richard A., George E. Tinker, and David E. Wilkins, eds. *Native Voices: American Indian Identity and Resistance*. Lawrence: University Press of Kansas, 2003. A scholarly examination of law, politics, and religion as related to Native American studies programs.

Heth, Charlotte, and Susan Guyette. *Issues for the Future of American Indian Studies*. Los Angeles: American Indian Studies Center, University of California, Los Angeles, 1985. Examines the field of American Indian studies.

Hill, Edward E., comp. *Guide to the Records in the National Archives of the United States Relating to American Indians*. Washington, D.C.: National Archives and Records Service, G.S.A., 1981. Helps researchers find information contained in the archives.

See also: Education: Post-contact; Ethnophilosophy and Worldview; Language Families; Oral Literatures; Tribal Colleges.

Anasazi Civilization

Significance: *This Basket Maker civilization of the Southwest emerged, advanced architecture and agriculture, and then vanished.*

The Anasazi, believed to be descendants of ancient Desert Archaic people, are the best known of the Southwest prehistoric cultures, flourishing about 200-1250 C.E. in what is now the Four Corners area (the junction of New Mexico, Arizona, Utah, and Colorado). Different groups of Anasazi spoke at least six languages, which were not mutually understood. The term "Anasazi" derives from an English-language corruption of a Navajo term, Anaasa'zi, which describes the many stone ruins of the Four Corners region and may mean "ancient ones," "enemies of the ancient ones," or "ancient enemy."

The earliest Anasazi are known as the Basket Makers because of their extraordinary skill in basketry. These early people were indistinctive initially, with a few cave sites and rock shelters along the San Juan River and open sites in the Rio Grande Valley. Inhabitants of these early villages planted maize and squash, a skill learned from their ancestors, but also hunted and foraged.

The villages, perhaps occupied seasonally, comprised a few pit houses: low, circular houses dug into the ground, approximately seven feet across. Stone slabs were used for some houses. Upper walls and roofs of many dwellings were made of wood and adobe or wattle and daub. The houses had fire pits and were entered by ladders placed in the smokehole of the roof. Tunnellike side entries faced the east. Larger pit houses were for ceremonial use. Smaller slab-lined structures were used for storing food. Baskets (some woven tightly enough for cooking), sandals, and other articles were of high caliber, highly stylized with geometric motifs. These designs gave rise to later Anasazi pottery painting traditions. Anasazi rock art of the period illustrates humans with broad shoulders, trapezoid-shaped bodies, and very large hands and feet. Elaborate headdresses, hair ornaments, necklaces, earrings, and sashes adorn the figures. Found near the villages, the art appears to have been part of community life.

As the Basket Maker Anasazi population grew and their territory expanded, their villages became larger. Almost all had ritual rooms, which the later Hopi called "kivas." Pit houses became deeper, more complex, and spacious. Earth-covered wooden roofs were supported by four posts with crossbeams. Some houses were dome-shaped. Storage bins, benches, a central fire pit, and a draft deflector between the fire and the ventilator shaft were found in many dwellings. Roof or side entrances were retained.

Within the village were many outdoor work and cooking areas. Slab-lined storage buildings and ramadas—roofed, open-walled structures shading work and living areas—were built on the surface. Some kivas were modified houses, but many were larger, some thirty-five feet across. Excavated holes called *sipapu* were

Area of Anasazi Culture

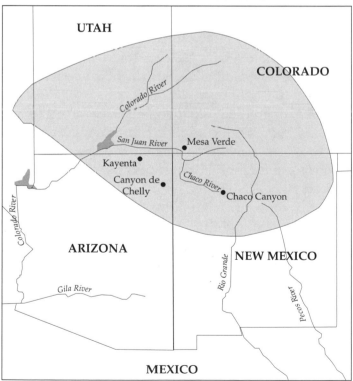

dug near the center of the floor in many homes and in most kivas. Turquoise or other offerings were placed in the *sipapu*, the opening to the underworld from which people emerged.

Farming became increasingly important to the Anasazi. To ensure successful crops, check dams and devices were used in fields near villages. By 600 C.E., beans, introduced from Mexico, were cultivated. By 700 C.E., cotton, the bow and arrow, and stone tools were used generally. Maize was ground on large stone mortars using two-handed grinding stones.

Basketry, sandalmaking, and weaving also became increasingly elaborate. Feathers and rabbit fur were woven into robes. Pottery making developed as both an occupation and a basis for trade. Pots were used for rituals, storing food and water, and cooking and serving food.

The quantity and variety of rock art increased. Rock art was near or in villages, on mesa boulders, near hunting trails, or in other open locations. Subjects included birds, animals, hunting scenes, and figures playing the flute. Human handprints covered some cliff walls in massed profusion. Home, village, and the kiva were the focus of community life, which endeavored to encourage and ensure agricultural prosperity.

The Pueblo period of the Anasazi began about 700 C.E. Villages varied in size from small complexes to those with more than a hundred dwellings. Architecture gradually developed into rectangular surface buildings of dry masonry or stone and adobe that followed a linear arrangement with multiroom units. Buildings usually faced a plaza located to the south or southeast. One or more kivas were built in the plaza. Kiva architecture included an encircling bench attached to the wall, roof support poles, a central fire pit, a ventilator shaft, and a *sipapu*. The kiva was entered by ladder through a roof opening that also allowed smoke to escape. Jars, bowls, and ladles were frequent forms for pottery. Turkeys and dogs were domesticated. Infants were bound to cradle boards so that the child could be near the mother. By 900 C.E., trade activities and movement of the people had engendered a certain amount of cultural uniformity, although some local differences occurred in agriculture, architecture, and pottery.

The Anasazi realized their cultural apogee between 1000 and 1300. The building of Chaco Canyon, the cliff houses of Mesa Verde, and the ruins of Kayenta date from this time. Many communities of this period and virtually all of the Chaco-style "great houses" were planned or renovated into single, self-enclosed structures. New rooms were attached to older ones. Linear units grew into L-shapes when a room was added at the end of a row to enclose space. L-shapes became U's and U's turned into rectangles. If a village grew or became old enough, the public space of the plaza was enclosed. "Great kivas" were usually built in the Chaco plazas in addition to smaller ones. Rooms were organized into units of two or three, with a doorway facing the plaza. Ladders led to upper-level units.

The Chaco Canyon district included nine great houses and eighteen great kivas within an eight-mile area. Families occupied suites of rooms in the great houses. Other rooms were for storage, turkey pens, trash, or sometimes burial chambers. Anasazi ate stews of meat, corn mush, squash, and wild vegetables and corn-meal cakes.

Beginning about 1050, the Chaco Anasazi built a complex of twelve elaborate towns that became their religious, political, and commercial center. Grandest of all the great houses was Pueblo Bonito, a five-story D-shaped structure with eight hundred rooms and thirty-seven kivas, covering three acres. It took 150 years before the planned village of Pueblo Bonito realized the conceptions of the original designers.

Skilled as astronomers, the Anasazi built celestial observatories on clifftops. Of these, Fajada Butte is the most famous. Three stone slabs lean against a vertical cliff face on which two spiral petroglyphs are carved. Each day before noon, sun daggers fall through the slabs onto the spirals in different places and, depending on the time of year, mark the solstices and equinoxes.

The Chaco Anasazi built an elaborate road system of about fifteen hundred miles. The thirty-foot-wide roads were paved and curbed. Straight paths cut through or were built over gullies, hills, or cliffs. Roadside shrines were constructed in widened parts of the road. These roads may have served some ceremonial purpose.

By 1150, the Chacoan culture began to decline. The peace-loving people of Pueblo Bonito walled up the doors and windows facing the outside of the great houses. Stones closed the entrance to the pueblos, leaving access by ladder only. Slowly the people left the basin, never to return.

About 1100, the Mesa Verde Anasazi began to abandon many small settlements in the mesa. Large pueblos developed, which initially followed the traditional Mesa Verde pattern with the kiva in front of the main dwelling. Soon, the kivas were enclosed within the circle of houses and walls. Stone towers were built, perhaps as watchtowers. Walls were made of large rectangular sandstone blocks with little mortar. Mud plaster was applied inside and out. One hundred years later, the Mesa Verde Anasazi moved into the caves below the mesa, although they continued to farm the mesa. Some of the cliff dwellings became quite large. Cliff Palace numbered two hundred rooms with twenty-three kivas. The Mesa Verde Anasazi prospered for some time in their cliff dwellings, but decline fell upon these Anasazi, too. A savage, twenty-three-year drought occurred in the Southwest. The Mesa Verdeans left as the crisis intensified.

By 1300, few Anasazi remained in their once-large domain. As their legacy they left descendants who became the Hopi, Zuñi, and other Pueblo peoples, as well as some of their religious and social traditions. Today the adobe pueblos of the Southwest serve as reminders of the great stone houses of their Anasazi forebears.

Mary Pat Balkus

Sources for Further Study

Brody, J. J. *The Anasazi*. New York: Rizzoli International Press, 1990. Presents a definitive view of the Anasazi, from prehistoric tribes to modern Pueblo people. Color photographs and illustrations.

Frazier, Kendrick. *People of Chaco: A Canyon and Its Culture*. Rev. and updated ed. New York: W. W. Norton, 1999. Concentrates on the Anasazi of Chaco Canyon, with details of each archaeological site. Photographs and illustrations.

Gabriel, Kathryn. *Roads to Center Place*. Boulder, Colo.: Johnson Books, 1991. Provides insight into the development of the Chaco roads. Photographs and illustrations.

Lister, Robert H., and Florence C. Lister. *Those Who Came Before*. Tucson: University of Arizona Press, 1983. Focuses on historical events that led to exploration, excavation, and interpretation of artifacts. Photographs and illustrations.

Pike, Donald. *Anasazi: Ancient People of the Rock*. Palo Alto, Calif.: American West, 1974. Illustrated with color photographs by David Muench.

Stuart, David E. *Anasazi America*. Albuquerque: University of New Mexico Press, 2000. An examination of the Anasazi people.

See also: Agriculture; Architecture: Southwest; Baskets and Basketry; Cliff Dwellings; Hohokam Culture; Kivas; Mogollon Civilization; Pottery; Pueblo.

Appliqué and Ribbonwork

Tribes affected: Northwest Coast, Eastern Woodlands, Southeast tribes

Significance: *The personalized designs for these traditional garment decorations both express individual style and maintain group identity.*

Clothing is a silent communication of personal or cultural values and beliefs. Observers may not understand the meanings being expressed, but they are usually aware that a certain style is not accidental. Decorations such as appliqué and ribbonwork may lend similarity (if not uniformity) to the clothing of a people. Styles of clothing and decoration may be maintained over time as part of a people's culture; some garments themselves are literally passed down through many generations. Since such garments are usually handmade, they are a visible history of a family, clan, or a people and are thought to carry the essence of the original wearer.

Appliqué. Appliqués are cutout decorations of contrasting color or fabric stitched to a garment. They are often embellished with stitching, beads, or shells. The Kwakiutl people of the Northwest Coast are famous for their appliquéd button blankets. Worn as ceremonial shawls, the red blankets carry large blue or black appliquéd crests of Raven, Wolf, or Eagle Clans. Outlines of gleaming mother-of-pearl and abalone buttons (as many as three thousand) emphasize the crests and trim the edges of these magnificent blankets. In addition to expressing wealth, the wearing of these blankets imparts the qualities of clan animals.

The Kwakiutl people are well known for the ceremonial potlatch, an extravagant giveaway once banned by the Canadian government. On the eve of the potlatch, women wear button blankets as they dance in the smoke-filled great house. While the women sing mourning songs, the iridescent buttons sparkle in the firelight, helping to drive away sadness so the celebration can proceed. The next day, the men in their crested button blankets perform the Chiefs' Dance to begin the potlatch.

After contact with Europeans provided new fabrics, Eastern Woodlands women put aside their deerskin outfits and decorated their cotton shawls and skirts with wide borders of silk appliqué. These formal outfits are worn in ceremony and at social gatherings. In the mid-twentieth century, younger Woodlands women adapted this style to create the cape dancer's outfit now often seen at pow-wows. The young dancers whirl in their one-of-a-kind satin shawls decorated with bright, bold appliqués and yards of fringe. For ceremonies and pow-wows, Woodlands men wear aprons and leggings of black velvet decorated in stylized nature designs. These are typically rendered in colorful combinations of appliqué, embroidery, and beads.

Ribbonwork. Seminole and Miccosukee women of Florida have raised the use of decorative ribbons to an art form. One of the most recognizable styles in North America, some of these attractive designs have been used for many decades. The practice may have begun after contact with Spanish officials who wore striped brocade on dress uniforms. In the trading days of the late 1800's, the hand-cranked sewing machine was readily adopted by Southeast women to adorn calico skirts and shirts. The early patterns of wide bands of single contrasting colors soon evolved into elaborate multicolored patchwork strips. The strips are combined with bands of ribbon in a manner similar to that used in quilting and sewn together.

Both men and women wear garments of this distinctive type. The early tradition was knee-length shirts for elderly men and longer shirts for younger men. Women and girls wore full-length ribbon skirts topped with a lightweight cape edged in ribbons. Later a popular waist-length jacket was rendered in a Seminole ribbon style for men.

Traditional Seminole patterns are still used and are often altered as the tailor expresses her own ideas. Complex designs have names, such as *checkers* or *rattlesnake*, suggested by something they resemble. Designs are treasured but are not claimed as personal property. They are shared with friends and handed down within families. Copying of designs by those who admire them is considered an honor to the originator.

The use of ribbons in ceremonial dress was carried to Oklahoma by the Creek, formerly of the Southeast. In the Ribbon Dance, women wear rainbow-colored headdresses of cascading ribbons as they parade through the public square. The annual ceremony reaffirms and honors the role of women within the community.

Gale M. Thompson

Sources for Further Study

Billard, Jules B., et al. *The World of the American Indian*. Washington, D.C.: National Geographic Society, 1974. More than 440 color illustrations, maps of culture areas, poems and chants, and tribal location supplement. Back-pocket map, index, and acknowledgments.

Garbarino, Merwyn. *The Seminole*. New York: Chelsea House, 1989. Culture, history, and effect of European contact on the Seminole people; Seminole resistance under leader Osceola; color and black-and-white photographs; and designs of Seminole ribbonwork clothing.

MacCauley, Clay. *The Seminole Indians of Florida*. Foreword by Jerald T. Milanich, introduction by William C. Sturtevant. Gainesville: University Press of Florida, 2000. A definitive report on the Seminole people which provides an examination of their clothing and ornaments, crafts, housing, and other features of their daily existence.

Maxwell, James A., et al. *America's Fascinating Indian Heritage*. Pleasantville: Reader's Digest, 1978. Comprehensive account of culture areas, prehistory (including Mesoamerican), cultural, political, and social issues of early twentieth century. Includes more than seven hundred color illustrations as well as descriptions of ceremonies. List of museums, historic villages, and archaeological sites.

Owen, Roger G., et al. *The North American Indians: A Sourcebook*. Macmillan: New York, 1967. Collection of original (edited) articles dating from 1888 to 1963 and arranged by culture areas; history, evolution, and demography; and social perspectives of the mid-twentieth century. Includes references, additional reading list, and a directory of 250 educational films.

Underhill, Ruth M. *Red Man's America: A History of Indians in the United States*. Sixth impression. Chicago: University of Chicago Press, 1960. Surveys origins, history, social customs, material culture, religion, and mythology. Written from the perspective of the first peoples of North America.

See also: Arts and Crafts: Southeast; Beads and Beadwork; Dress and Adornment; Headdresses; Quillwork; Shells and Shellwork.

Architecture: Arctic

Tribes affected: Aleut, Inuit, Yupik

Significance: *Although the domed snow house is the most widely recognized Arctic habitation, a number of other types of structures have been used by groups in the Arctic culture area.*

Throughout the Arctic, housing styles were largely a function of four factors: local weather conditions, availability of raw materials, requirements for mobility, and household size and organization. While the domed snow house (in common parlance, the igloo) is the form of shelter most commonly associated with the Arctic, it actually had a very limited distribution. Many Arctic groups, such as the Yupik of south-western Alaska, the Aleut, and the West Greenlanders, never built snow houses. Rather, there was a wide range of architectural styles, including aboveground plank houses, semi-subterranean log houses, semi-subterranean sod and rock houses, and walrus-skin houses elevated on stilts.

Snow Houses. Without a doubt, the dome-shaped snow house was the most remarkable architectural achievement of Arctic populations. At the time of European contact, the snow house was the primary winter shelter in most areas of the Central and Eastern Canadian Arctic. In these areas, a typical strategy involved building large snow house communities on the ocean ice from which hunters would depart daily to engage in breathing-hole seal hunting. It was essential that the right kind of snow be used: hard-packed, granular snow that was uniformly compressed by blowing winds. The snow house was built by arranging the snow blocks, cut with a large snow knife, in a circular pattern spiraling upward. The spiral ensured that each snow block placed in line had another block to lean against. This made the construction process easier and maximized the structural integrity of the shelter.

Any snow house that was to be occupied for more than one or two nights would have a porch attached to provide storage space and protection from the wind. The entrance generally sloped

The Arctic Culture Area

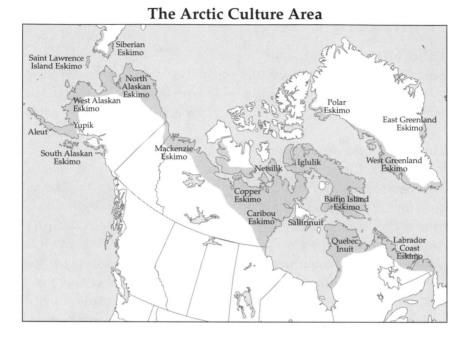

downward so as to create a cold trap. At least half of the interior included a raised sleeping and sitting platform, which provided protection from the cold air on the floor below. Caribou skins or musk ox skins would be placed on the sleeping platform for additional insulation. Often, a small hole would be punched through the roof to provide some air circulation and hence a guarantee against asphyxiation. A piece of ice might also be placed into the wall to provide natural lighting.

Semi-Subterranean Houses. Far more common than the snow house was the semi-subterranean house, found from East Greenland to South Alaska and the Aleutian Islands. Excavated several feet into the ground, these shelters generally consisted of a wood, stone, or whalebone framework covered with insulating sod. Because of the great effort involved in building and maintaining such shelters, they tended to be used by groups with year-round or seasonally occupied villages. In North Alaska, houses were rectangular and constructed of a whalebone and driftwood frame covered by sod. A wood planked floor marked the main living area, which included a raised sleeping platform. Entrance to the house was through a passageway which sloped from ground level downward to a depth of about 4 to 5 feet. On either side of this passageway were side rooms used for storage, cooking, and food preparation. The long tunnel ended under the main living area, which was entered through a trapdoor in the floor. This main living area was usually kept warm by a soapstone lamp, although body heat alone was sometimes adequate to keep it warm. A membrane-covered skylight provided light to the interior.

In the Bering Sea region, easier access to wood resulted in this material being a more significant component in house construction. These houses tended to be slightly larger and were often made with a frame of whole logs covered with sod. The main living areas often had sleeping platforms on all three sides as opposed to the single sleeping platform of the North Alaskan house. A central fireplace fueled by wood and placed under a square smoke hole in the roof was the primary source of heat. Such dwellings occasionally had two entrances: a ground-level entrance for summer use and an underground passageway for winter use. Farther south, among Chugach and Koniag Eskimos, wood was even more evident in house construction. Although these houses were semi-subterranean, they lacked the sloping entranceways characteristic of more northern groups. Even in winter, entry was generally through a ground-level doorway.

The Aleut constructed large semi-subterranean houses which have been documented to range between 70 and 200 feet in length. These houses had log supports and roof frames made of either wood or whalebone. Woven grasses were placed on the roofs, which were then covered with sod. Since the Aleut lived in a far milder climate than most Eskimo groups, an underground passageway was not necessary. Rather, entrance into the house was down one or more notched log ladders positioned under the structure's smoke holes. Since these longhouses generally accommodated a large number of related families, often an entire village of thirty to forty people, each family was assigned a living area along the outside walls. Grasses were woven into partitions to separate the living areas.

Semi-subterranean longhouses were also used in Labrador, West Greenland, and East Greenland, but these generally had underground passageways to function as cold traps. In East Greenland, these longhouses invariably housed an entire village. Given the scarcity of wood, house walls were constructed of stone and sod, while roofs were made of sod placed over driftwood rafters.

In North Greenland, the Polar Eskimo had extremely limited access to wood, so they constructed their semi-subterranean winter houses of cantilevered stone covered by sod and snow. These shelters tended to be small and triangular-shaped, rarely housing more than one nuclear family, and were often dug into a hillside. A similar style of structure, called a *qarmaq*, was used by certain Central Arctic groups. Usually occupied only during transitional seasons, the qarmaq was made of a circular wall of stone, sod, or snowblocks covered over with a skin roof.

Aboveground Wood Houses. Aboveground wood houses had a limited distribution, since they required ready access to timber. They were the dominant form of summer residence among Yupik groups in southwestern and southern Alaska. In the Yukon-Kuskokwim region, for example, these houses were built with horizontally placed logs for the side walls and with vertically placed planks for the front and back walls. The gabled roof was covered with wood planks and bark. Since the houses were occupied only during the warm months of the year, they were built aboveground with ground-level entrances. These houses were typically found at spring and summer fishing camps.

Tents, Stilt Houses, and Men's Houses. Skin tents were ubiquitous throughout the Arctic region. Typically made of caribou or seal skin, they were the primary form of summer residence throughout much of the region, especially among those groups that were highly nomadic in summer. Even the Alaskan Yupik, with their wooden summer houses, used tents while traveling or hunting over long distances.

Perhaps the most unusual houses in the Arctic were the summer stilt houses of King Island, located in the Bering Strait. These small houses were usually erected next to the semi-subterranean winter houses and were boxlike structures with walrus hide walls. Their elevation on wooden stilts was necessary given the steep coastline of the island and the lack of level ground for building.

Ceremonial men's houses constituted an important part of village life throughout most of Alaska. Although large ceremonial snow houses were sometimes built by Central Arctic groups for midwinter games and dances, permanent ceremonial houses were not found anywhere in the Central or Eastern Arctic. Throughout Alaska, ceremonial houses were built in a style similar to regular residences, although somewhat larger. They were regarded as men's houses, but women were allowed to visit and participate in certain ceremonies. In North Alaska, each ceremonial house (*karigi*) was associated with one or more whaling crews. Among the Yupik of southwestern Alaska, the men of the village slept and ate in the ceremonial house (*qasgiq*). These houses were also used for sweatbaths and for important religious ceremonies such as the Bladder Feast. Some of these houses are reported to have been large enough to seat up to five hundred people.

Richard G. Condon and Pamela R. Stern

Sources for Further Study

Crowell, Aron. "Dwellings, Settlements, and Domestic Life." In *Crossroads of Continents: Cultures of Siberia and Alaska*, edited by William Fitzhugh and Aron Crowell. Washington, D.C.: Smithsonian Institution Press, 1988.

Damas, David, ed. *Arctic*. Vol. 5 in *Handbook of North American Indians*. Washington, D.C.: Smithsonian Institution Press, 1984.

Lee, Molly, and Gregory A. Reinhardt. *Eskimo Architecture: Dwelling and Structure in the Early Historic Period*. Foreword by Andrew Tooyak, Jr. Fairbanks: University of Alaska Press with the University of Alaska Museum, 2003.

Nabokov, Peter, and Robert Easton. *Native American Architecture.* New York: Oxford University Press, 1989.

Nelson, Edward. *The Eskimo About Bering Strait.* Eighteenth Annual Report of the Bureau of American Ethnology for the Years 1896-1897. Reprint. Washington, D.C.: Smithsonian Institution Press, 1983.

Oswalt, Wendell H. *Alaskan Eskimos.* San Francisco: Chandler, 1967.

See also: Igloo; Longhouse; Plank House.

Architecture: California

Tribes affected: Achumawi, Atsugewi, Chemehuevi, Chumash, Costano, Cupeño, Gabrielino, Hupa, Juaneño, Kamia, Karok, Kateo, Luiseño, Maidu, Mattole, Miwok, Patwin, Pomo, Quechan, Salinan, Serrano, Shasta, Tolowa, Tubatulabal, Wailaki, Wintun, Wiyot, Yahi, Yana, Yokuts, Yuki, Yurok

Significance: *Indian architecture in California was of a wide variety because of climatic variations throughout the state.*

The Indians of California lived in climates ranging from foggy, damp coastlands in the north to dry desert regions in the south. Using materials available in their natural environment, they constructed homes of earth, wood, brush, sand, or bark. Buildings were used for summer and winter houses, dance chambers, food storage, and sweatbaths.

In the north, large rectangular plank houses were made of cedar, sometimes having several pitched roofs and excavated floors. Sweathouses for male clan members were made of wood and had wood or earth floors. Earth-covered semisubterranean houses were common. These had circular side door openings which had to be crawled through.

The most common form of Indian architecture in the California region, and most characteristic of the central region, was the earth-

The California Culture Area

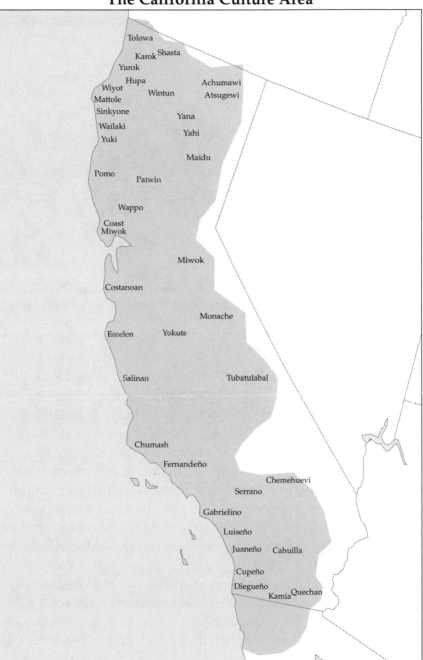

A typical design found in central California was this Mono wickiup-style brush structure. *(Library of Congress)*

lodge. This pit house was a small structure with an excavated earth floor, an earth roof, and a roof smoke hole, which was also used for entry. Ladders ran up the sides of such dwellings in order to gain access to the entry hole. Small slat openings in the lower sides of the earthlodges could be used to crawl through.

Dwellings made of willow poles, tule, brush, or bark had round or cone-shaped roofs and were used by the California region Indian. These structures were covered with bark slabs in winter for greater protection from the cold and could house many families. Ceremonial halls and men's sweathouses were smaller circular or rectangular buildings of the same type.

In the southern regions, dome-shaped brush structures such as the wickiup as well as four-post sand-roofed houses were built. After the arrival of the Spanish, adobe bricks were used and made into mud-thatched one-room homes much like those found in neighboring Mexico.

The roundhouse, largely the result of European contact, was a large, round assembly or dance hall made of wood with metal nails and split shingles.

Diane C. Van Noord

Source for Further Study
Nabokov, Peter, and Robert Easton. *Native American Architecture.* New York: Oxford University Press, 1989.

See also: Adobe; Earthlodge; Grass House; Pit House; Plank House; Wickiup.

Architecture: Great Basin

Tribes affected: Bannock, Gosiute, Kawaiisu, Mono, Numaga, Paiute, Shoshone, Ute, Walapai, Washoe
Significance: *In the sparsely populated Great Basin region, Indians lived in grass huts, wickiups, tipis, or low, flat-roofed houses.*

The Great Basin area north of the Colorado River, basically comprising present day Utah and Nevada, mostly consists of hot, dry desert and continental steppe. The Indians inhabiting this wide area never settled long in one place but constantly moved about in search of fresh food sources. For all but those Indians living along the Colorado River, mobility was a significant factor in the design of their dwellings.

The Paiute made a fiber structure known as the wickiup with small forked branches twisted into the shape of a small cone or dome and then covered with grass and brush with an open door space. This structure was used for sleeping, cooking, and storage, as well as for protection from the sun. The wickiup was either left in place when they moved or carried with them to a new location. In the hot summer, Great Basin Indians also made grass huts with a center ridgepole, slanted roof, open ends, and open side walls made of vertical poles; they looked much like an open-sided tent.

In the winter, frame homes near the foothills were covered with mud thatch for greater protection and warmth.

Those who lived near other geographical regions often borrowed the architectural styles of the neighboring Indian tribes.

The Great Basin Culture Area

Structures included the tipi of the Plains, the earthlodge of California, the adobe of the Southwest, and the pit house of the Plateau.

Along the Colorado River, Indians developed low, flat sand-roofed homes built on poles with excavated floors. The roofs were used for food storage and socializing as well as for protection. These houses also included open ramadas for additional living space.

Diane C. Van Noord

Source for Further Study
Nabokov, Peter, and Robert Easton. *Native American Architecture.* New York: Oxford University Press, 1989.

See also: Architecture: California; Architecture: Plateau; Architecture: Southwest; Grass House; Tipi; Wickiup.

Architecture: Northeast

Tribes affected: Abenaki, Algonquian, Cahokia, Cayuga, Erie, Fox, Huron, Illinois, Iroquois, Kickapoo, Lenni Lenape, Lumbee, Mahican, Maliseet, Massachusett, Mattaponi, Menominee, Metis, Miami, Micmac, Mohawk, Mohegan, Moneton, Montagnais, Montauk, Mountain, Nanticoke, Narragansett, Nauset, Neutral, Niantic, Nipissing, Nipmuc, Nottaway, Ojibwa, Oneida, Onondaga, Ottawa, Passamaquoddy, Pennacook, Penobscot, Pequot, Susquehannock, Tobacco, Wampanoag, Wappinger, Winnebago
Significance: *The woodlands of the Northeast provided basic building materials, such as saplings, brush, and bark, for a variety of buildings, including the wigwam and the longhouse.*

The buildings of the Northeast region Indians were constructed in woodlands, on mountains, along the Atlantic coast, and along inland lakeshores. Architectural styles were versatile, adapting to the particular climate and the social, religious, and economic needs of the particular tribe. Primarily used for protection, architecture also expressed the Indians' way of life.

In the eastern portion of this region, the Iroquois and Huron built long communal buildings which were used year-round by clan groups. The longhouse, which varied in length and accommodated more than a hundred people, could be enlarged to make room for newly married couples. The pole-framed structure had a barrel or vaulted roof. Smoke holes placed about 25 feet apart represented the space given to an individual family. The smoke holes were also sources of light. Sleeping bunks ran along the sides of the building. Doors and storage areas were at each end.

A typical dwelling structure of Northeast region Indians was the wigwam. Its simple construction of a frame and covering could be easily moved. The basic structure of the wigwam was made of sapling frames bent into arches and tied together with fibercord

The Northeast Culture Area

The tipi was among the various structures erected by the Algonquins along the North Atlantic coast. *(National Archives)*

and then covered with rolls of bark or reed mats. A central fire was used for cooking and heating, and smoke escaped through a parting of the mats. There were many different styles of the basic domed wigwam.

The Algonquin used a variety of bark-covered and mat-covered wigwams and barrel or gabled roofs as well as conical tipis using straight poles covered with bark. Along the North Atlantic coast, tipis were made by leaning straight poles vertically together; at the top, these poles met at the center point of a circular shape on the ground, on the circumference of which were positioned the poles' ends. Sapling stringers were lashed to the frame for stability. They were sometimes insulated by laying grass over the frame and covering this with sheets of birchbark. The smoke hole was at the top of the tipi where the poles met, the floor was covered with fir boughs, and an opening in the side provided a doorway.

The Great Lakes region had several basic house types. These were the domed wigwam, used mainly in winter, the conical wigwam, an extension of the domed type by use of a ridge pole, and the summer square bark house, with vertical walls and a gabled roof. Ceremonial lodges and many-sided dance lodges were the largest structures built by the Great Lakes Indians. They were made with poles of cedar, considered to be sacred. A small religious structure called the shaking tent was a single-person hut. Used by the shaman, it was made of a sapling frame covered with bark or canvas, and it shook while the shaman was moving and speaking inside as he performed a rite.

Where the Northeast region came closer to the Plains region, the Indians also used the tipi type of dwelling, often covered with canvas or animal hides.

Diane C. Van Noord

Sources for Further Study

Bushnell, David I., Jr. *Native Villages and Village Sites East of the Mississippi*. Washington, D.C.: Government Printing Office, 1919.

Kubiak, William. *Great Lakes Indians: A Pictorial Guide*. Grand Rapids, Mich.: Baker Book House, 1970.

Morgan, Lewis H. *Houses and House-Life of the American Aborigines*. 1881. Reprint. Salt Lake City: University of Utah Press, 2003.

Nabokov, Peter, and Robert Easton. *Native American Architecture*. New York: Oxford University Press, 1989.

Russell, Howard S. *Indian New England Before the Mayflower*. Hanover, N.H.: University Press of New England, 1980.

See also: Birchbark; Longhouse; Tipi; Wigwam.

Architecture: Northwest Coast

Tribes affected: Chinook, Cowlitz, Haida, Haisla, Kwakiutl, Nisqually, Nootka, Quileute, Salish, Samish, Siuslaw, Snohomish, Tillamook, Tlingit, Tsimshian, Umpqua, other Northwest Coast tribes

Significance: *The abundance of the environment and the ready availability of wood enabled groups in the Northwest Coast area to construct large, permanent plank buildings.*

Primary living quarters for Northwest Coast Indians accommodated large extended families up to fifty or more persons. Family houses served also as meeting halls for clan events as well as theaters for annual performances. Houses faced the shoreline, with a lineage leader's house in the middle and less important family homes on the perimeter. Houses varied in size depending upon the wealth and status of the owner, with the chief having the largest house. Cedar, the prevalent building wood, was hewn into planks to create rectangular, gabled longhouses that regionally varied but could average 60 by 100 feet in area. The commissioning of a house was restricted to the wealthy, and the building of houses was designated to trained specialists, usually of no relation to the owner. Every workman, from skilled craftsman to manual laborer, was paid for each assigned task. Architectural relief carvings or paintings required additional artists and ceremonial feasting at its completion. A potlatch celebration, often including the erection of a totem pole, was expected by the community in order to consecrate the house and the status of the owner. At this time, principal houses were given names that referred to totemic crests of the lineage or to a distinct quality of the house.

Northern House Style. Among the Tsimshian, Haida, Tlingit, and Haisla (the northern Kwakiutl), large houses for wealthy extended families measured up to 50 feet by 60 feet and had gabled roofs and vertical plank walls. The first elements constructed on the site were the corner poles. These were raised into foundation

The Northwest Coast Culture Area

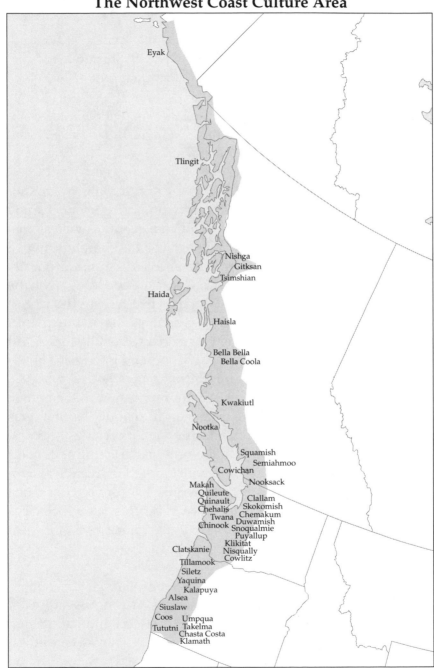

Eyak

Tlingit

Nishga
Gitksan
Tsimshian

Haida

Haisla

Bella Bella
Bella Coola

Kwakiutl

Nootka

Squamish
Semiahmoo
Cowichan
Nooksack
Makah
Quileute   Clallam
Quinault   Skokomish
Chehalis   Chemakum
Twana   Duwamish
Chinook   Snoqualmie
              Puyallup
Clatskanie   Klikitat
              Nisqually
Tillamook   Cowlitz
Siletz
Yaquina
Kalapuya
Alsea
Siuslaw
Coos   Umpqua
Tututni Takelma
        Chasta Costa
        Klamath

holes by pulling and wedging them into position. Tall ridgepoles supported heavy posts at the front and back, which in turn supported the roof planks with a central opening for a smoke hole. The horizontal beams were elevated into the notched holes of the vertical uprights, followed by the elevation of cross beams. Once the structural framework was constructed, the tapered vertical wall planks were put into place. The entrance was an oval or circular doorway cut into the base of the center ridgepole facing the shoreline. The interior contained a planked, platform floor with bench steps (sometimes movable) leading down to a central fire pit located directly below the roof smoke hole, which, often fitted with a movable shutter, allowed directed interior ventilation. The upper platform provided assigned sleeping space for each family, with the lineage head and his family occupying the rear. The center ridgepole, interior vertical support poles, interior planked screen, and the house front typically exhibited elaborate carved and painted totem crests that validated the ancestral legacy of the

Based on a sketch from the 1830's, an engraving of a Chinook lodge in the Oregon Territory. *(Library of Congress)*

house owner. By the nineteenth century, European architectural influences were evident in the introduction of framed doorways and windows in traditional houses, the use of nails instead of notched joints, commercially sawed lumber, and stoves (replacing the central fire pit).

Southern House Style. Two types of house construction differentiate the southern style that dominated throughout the Coast Salish region: the shed roof and the Wakashan. Unlike the northern house style, the walls of horizontal planks created a shell around the house frame. The pitch of the shed roof houses was created by the shoreline vertical poles being taller than the rear support poles. The center-sloping gabled roof of the Wakashan house was created by the center ridge beam being of a larger diameter than the two eave beams. Shed-roof houses averaged about 38 by 80 feet, though they were sometimes much longer when expanded by building end on end. The Wakashan house measured from 36 to 40 feet wide by 40 to 150 feet long.

Secondary Structures. The most common secondary architectural structures included summer houses, sweatlodges, smokehouses, mortuary houses, and decks. Roughly built structures, often without flooring, served to house families during the summer fishing and gathering activities. When summer activities occurred annually in the same place, the framework for these houses was frequently permanent, while the planks and materials for the side and roof were brought by the owners each season. Additionally, a summer house could serve as a drying area for the fish in the absence of a separate drying structure. A smokehouse was a plank framework with horizontal poles functioning as drying racks for smoking fish. Rough, enclosed plank structures on stilt poles served as warehouses for fish storage. Sweatlodges were typically walled with tightly fitted planks or logs supporting a roof of boards and earth. With sand floors, fire pit, and an entrance toward the water, this structure made a controllable interior space for steambaths. Small house replicas (8 feet by 6 feet) or small shed-roof shelters built of logs or planks, with platforms to hold the deceased, functioned as grave houses. Open-deck structures or raised platforms on stilts constructed on the beach provided designated gathering areas in fair weather.

Michael Coronel and Patricia Coronel

Sources for Further Study

Drucker, Philip. *Indians of the Northwest Coast*. Garden City, N.Y.: Natural History Press, 1963.

Emmons, George Thornton. *The Tlingit Indians*. Edited by Fredrica de Laguna. Seattle: University of Washington Press, 1991.

Highwater, Jamake. *Arts of the Indian Americas: Leaves from the Sacred Tree*. New York: Harper & Row, 1983.

Olsen, Ronald L. *Adze, Canoe, and House Types of the Northwest Coast*. Seattle: University of Washington Press, 1991.

Stewart, Hillary. *Cedar: Tree of Life to the Northwest Coast Indians*. Vancouver, B.C.: Douglas & McIntyre, 1984.

See also: Longhouse; Plank House; Sweatlodges and Sweatbaths; Totem Poles.

Architecture: Plains

Tribes affected: Plains tribes
Significance: *Plains tribes used a variety of temporary and permanent dwellings, including earthlodges and grass houses; the best-known Plains dwelling is the tipi.*

Plains Indian architecture is marked by contrasts between mobile and permanent constructions. Evidence suggests that both types of dwelling have a long history in the Plains region. Prehistoric tribes constructed brush-covered lodges supported by stationary cones of branchless trees. They also left "tipi rings," circles of rocks probably used to hold down the sides of small hide-covered dwellings.

The Plains Culture Area

Sarsi

Plains Cree

Blood
Blackfoot
Piegan

Atsina   Assiniboine

Crow   Hidatsa
                Mandan   Yanktonai
                                Sioux
                Arikara
         Teton Sioux   Santee Sioux

Cheyenne   Ponca
                        Yankton Sioux
                Omaha
        Pawnee   Iowa
                        Oto
Arapaho   Kansa   Missouri

                        Osage
        Kiowa

                                Quapaw
Comanche   Apache of   Caddo
            Oklahoma

            Wichita
            Kichai

            Tonkawa

    Lipan Apache

Medicine wheels, circular constructions of boulders with both terrestrial and celestial alignments, were another early architectural achievement. The best-known of these is in the Bighorn Mountains of northern Wyoming. Petroforms, rock designs resembling animal and human figures, suggest a southeastern Indian cultural influence in the Canadian and Dakotan plains.

Along the Missouri River, the typical house type was the earthlodge. From the Dakotas to the northeast, the earthlodges of the prehistoric seminomadic agricultural communities were primarily rectangular and consisted of wooden uprights joined by cross beams and rafters covered with sticks, grass, and sod. Along the upper Missouri, villagers used the terrain to augment defenses consisting of dry moats or log palisades.

Palisades protected the Mandans' earthlodge dwellings, which surrounded plazas dominated by a wooden shrine honoring the mythic hero Lone Man. Mandan post-and-beam construction was overlaid by wooden rafters supporting willow branches, grass, and sod. The rectangular format of the Mandans' sacred Okeepa lodge was a reminder of its prehistoric architectural origins.

A Pawnee family stands outside their earthlodge in Nebraska during the late nineteenth century. *(National Archives)*

The Caddo, Kichai, and Wichita of the southern Plains constructed permanent grass houses of thatch bundles fixed to a wood pole frame. Other permanent Plains structures were the ceremonial Sun Dance lodge (of the Kiowa, Arapaho, Shoshone, and Cheyenne), menstrual huts, funerary platforms, religious structures, and sweathouses, such as the Sioux inipi, made of bent willow saplings covered with buffalo hides.

The tipi, a cone of poles covered by sewn and tanned buffalo hides and staked to the ground, was widely used for temporary shelter and later became a year-round mobile dwelling. Tipis developed from the "tipi ring" shelter and the Northeastern Woodlands three-pole conical tent. With the arrival of horses to serve as transportation, tipis became larger and more elaborate.

William B. Folkestad

Source for Further Study

Nabokov, Peter, and Robert Easton. *Native American Architecture.* New York: Oxford University Press, 1989.

See also: Earthlodge; Grass House; Medicine Wheels; Tipi.

Architecture: Plateau

Tribes affected: Bannock, Gosiute, Kawaiisu, Paiute, Panamint, Shoshone, Ute, Washoe

Significance: *Plateau architecture was characterized by circular pit houses.*

The principal structures within the Plateau culture area were sleeping dwellings, the ubiquitous sweatlodge, isolated menstrual huts, excavated food storage pits, food-drying scaffolds and racks, and temporary lean-to shelters. Though architecture type varied through time and spatial distribution, there were essentially two types of winter dwelling: the circular semi-subterranean pit house and the inverted-V rectangular tule mat lodge. The older pit house

The Plateau Culture Area

was an excavated, flat, circular pit measuring 9 to 15 feet in diameter, with gradually sloping earthen walls of 3 feet. The aboveground shape was achieved by erecting three or four top-forked poles which, when secured, accommodated smaller lodge poles to support cedar planks, which were covered with sewn willow mats. The exterior was made of layered sewn tule mats, with the apex of the structure being open to serve as a smoke hole and entrance up or down a notched log or hafted, runged ladder. Various grasses, old tule mats, and bear skins covered the dwelling floor.

The second type of winter village dwelling was the tule mat-covered, inverted-V-type pole-constructed lodge, usually with no ridge pole. Often the floor was excavated to a depth of one foot. These rectangular structures averaged 30 feet in length and approximately 10 feet in width; they could accommodate three to six extended families. Entrance was usually from both ends, where firewood was kept; food was stored in hemp and pliable root bags suspended from the ceiling. This structure was often used for large gatherings and ceremonial rituals.

A major influence on southern Plateau architecture was the introduction of the horse, permitting greater involvement with Plains culture through trade and bison hunting, as evidenced by the adoption of the tipi. In the mid-1800's, bark, tule, and cattail mats began to give way to canvas as a preferred covering material for sweatlodges, tipi dwellings, and longhouses.

John Alan Ross

Source for Further Study
Nabokov, Peter, and Robert Easton. *Native American Architecture.* New York: Oxford University Press, 1989.

See also: Lean-to; Pit House; Sweatlodges and Sweatbaths; Tipi.

Architecture: Southeast

Tribes affected: Southeast tribes
Significance: *Wattle and daub structures, chakofas, and chickees were among the dwelling types of the Southeast, but the best-known Southeast constructions were large earthen mounds, some of which can still be seen.*

Southeastern tribal architecture is distinguished by a tradition of monumental mound building. Southeastern mound construction may have originated with Mexican Indians who moved to this lo-

The Southeast Culture Area

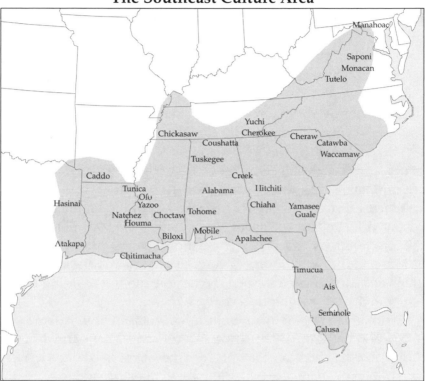

cale to participate in the trade that occurred from the Great Lakes region to Florida. The concentric ridges of shaped soil that define a large central plaza at Poverty Point, Louisiana, are associated with this cultural influence. They date from about 1200 B.C.E.

The Adena culture of the Ohio River valley (1000 B.C.E.-200 C.E.) raised cone-shaped burial mounds. They also built dwellings that were 20 feet to 70 feet in diameter and had clay-covered lattice-work walls, a type of construction called wattle and daub. The dwellings were covered with thatched roofs. Adena effigy mounds, known as geoforms, depicting bears, panthers, reptiles, and birds, survive, from Wisconsin to Louisiana. The Great Serpent Mound (800 B.C.E.-400 C.E.) in southern Ohio is 1,247 feet in length and portrays a serpent clutching an egg in its mouth. The Hopewell cul-

ture's funerary mounds, monumental circles, squares, and pentag-
onal geoforms, found in the Ohio Valley, succeeded the Adena
constructions.

Under the Mississippi tradition (700-1000 C.E.), communities
periodically enlarged their flat-topped trapezoidal mounds. The
Cahokia site (800 C.E.) near St. Louis, Missouri, was the political, religious, and economic center of the Mississippi tradition.
Cahokia's central pyramid is the largest manmade structure north
of Mexico, measuring more than 1,000 feet in length, 700 feet in
width, and 100 feet in height, the result of fourteen different building campaigns over three centuries.

When European explorers first arrived in the Southeast, they
encountered Indian townsites with shaped mounds dominating
the community and its plaza. These mounds supported chieftains'
houses and public buildings or contained burials. The Natchez Indians of Mississippi continued the temple mound building tradition into the early eighteenth century.

Creek and Yuchi Indians built large villages with ceremonial
plazas and ball courts. The Creek chakofa was a communal structure with a thatched conical roof. The Cherokees also built communal structures on low earthen mounds to house sacred fires.

By the nineteenth century, many southeastern tribes had
adopted European-style buildings. One notable exception was in
Florida's southern marshes, where the Seminoles built wide-eaved,
open-sided dwellings with elevated platforms of cypress poles
and palmetto thatch known as chickees.

William B. Folkestad

Source for Further Study

Nabokov, Peter, and Robert Easton. *Native American Architecture*.
New York: Oxford University Press, 1989.

See also: Chickee; Mississippian Culture; Mounds and Moundbuilders; Wattle and Daub.

Architecture: Southwest

Tribes affected: Anasazi, Eastern Pueblo, Hohokam, Hopi, Mogollon, Zuñi, other Southwest traditions and tribes

Significance: *Architecture in the Southwest evolved from the crude pit house to the magnificent stone pueblos of the prehistoric Anasazi, and then to pueblos built in the historic period in the Rio Grande Valley and at Zuñi and Hopi.*

All three prehistoric cultures in the Southwest were pit house builders. The Mogollon constructed circular pit houses grouped in small villages of fifteen to twenty families. The Hohokam built square or rectangular pit houses randomly scattered over a large area (the settlement at Snaketown covers almost a square mile).

Basket Maker and Developmental Pueblo. Basket Maker Anasazi (circa 1-700 C.E.) in the Four Corners area built crude circular subterranean structures with flat roofs, entered by ladder through the smoke hole. Later in this period, three major Anasazi centers developed: Mesa Verde, Chaco Canyon, and Kayenta. In these villages, circular pit houses were as much as 25 feet in diameter and often were divided into ceremonial space and living space.

During the Development Pueblo period (700-1100), the Anasazi evolved building techniques which resulted in structures that were considerably more complex and sophisticated. The pit house continued as a kiva, but dwellings were now aboveground, consisting of slightly curved rows of contiguous flat-roofed rooms, each housing an entire family. The earliest utilization of stone was in "jacal," a method similar to wattle and daub, with the addition of stone slabs placed against the bottoms of walls and held in place with adobe. A true masonry technique evolved from jacal, wherein large, irregular rocks were laid end to end and packed solidly with adobe.

Stone Masonry. Toward the end of this period, the Anasazi shaped sandstone rocks into building blocks, using stone tools not much harder than the sandstone itself. At first, only the load-bearing surfaces were shaped, but eventually both visible surfaces were smoothed as well, producing a wall that was both aesthetically pleasing and strong. This new masonry technique resulted in an increase in both the size and complexity of the pueblos; some were as large as thirty or more contiguous rooms and were two stories high. Stone masonry also affected the kiva, whose walls and floor were now lined with carefully shaped and fitted stone blocks, with a stone bench and stone pilasters to support the flat roof.

During the Classic Pueblo period (1100-1300), the Anasazi refined their masonry further, developing walls built with a three-

The Southwest Culture Area

Taos Pueblo in New Mexico. (Library of Congress)

ply construction: an inner and outer facing of shaped sandstone blocks with an interior filling of loose stones and adobe. Varying the shapes of the blocks created linear patterns, adding visual interest to the walls. Pueblos of this period often rose to as many as five stories, with heavy beams set into the walls to support the floors above ground level. Flat roofs were constructed with beams laid across with poles and brush and covered with several inches of clay and mud. Chaco Canyon, Mesa Verde, and Kayenta continued to be major centers of Anasazi culture; their influence had spread from the upper Rio Grande Valley to Texas and Nevada and to central and southern Arizona.

Pueblo Bonito in Chaco Canyon was the largest pueblo in the Southwest, housing more than one thousand people and covering almost four acres, with eight hundred rooms rising in tiers from a single frontal story to five stories at the back. The Anasazi at Mesa Verde built large stone pueblos on the mesa tops but abandoned them a hundred years later in favor of the cliff dwellings—stone buildings erected in irregularly shaped caves in the cliff faces. They apparently made the move for reasons of defense, because the caves were much less desirable places to live, being without sunlight much of the day, difficult to reach, and limited in size. Even so, some of the cliff dwellings contained as many as two hundred rooms, twenty-three kivas, and both square and round towers. Having been built in haste in a less desirable location, the stonework was not as skillful as that of the earlier pueblos. Keet Seel and Betatakin were the largest pueblos at Kayenta, a center that was never as populous as Chaco Canyon or Mesa Verde, probably because crops grew less abundantly there. Pueblos both in the open and in the cliffs were built with masonry that was inferior to the other sites.

Anasazi Influence. As Anasazi culture spread during the Pueblo period, it transformed the architectural styles of both the Mogollon and the Hohokam. The Mogollon abandoned their pit houses in favor of aboveground masonry structures, such as those at Gila Cliffs in southern New Mexico. There they built forty rooms in five deep caves 150 feet above the canyon floor. The Hohokam were also influenced by Anasazi pueblo architecture, as evidenced by the ruins of Casa Grande in the Arizona desert. Built of caliche, a subsoil with high lime content, Casa Grande has deeply trenched walls 4.5 feet thick at the bottom, tapering to 2 feet at their height. The main two-storied structure was set on a base of earth 5 feet high. A single room atop the building had holes in one wall that lined up precisely with sunset at the equinoxes, suggesting that it may have served as an observatory. Pueblo Grande, on the outskirts of Phoenix, was built of adobe and stone masonry on an earthen platform, providing an unobstructed view of the surrounding countryside. The platform was retained by a massive adobe and rock wall, with a second wall built around the pueblo itself.

About 1300, the Anasazi began to leave their major centers to migrate elsewhere. There are several theories which attempt to explain this, among them drought, invasion, or plague. In any case, Pueblo culture was reestablished in large communities in the Rio Grande Valley from Isleta Pueblo to Taos, in the Zuñi Mountains, along the Little Colorado River, and in the area of the Hopi Mesas. Although construction varied according to time and place, pueblos generally followed the traditions established at Chaco Canyon, Mesa Verde, and Kayenta: large communal structures with hundreds of rooms, often multistoried, built around a central plaza. Some continued the techniques of stone masonry, while others were built with solid adobe or mixed adobe and stone construction. Kivas either were above ground and incorporated into the room blocks or were square or circular subterranean structures located in the plazas.

The Puebloans of the Southwest and many of their pueblos survived the Spanish, the Mexican, and finally the United States' occupation of their lands. The traditions that evolved in the fourteenth and fifteenth centuries formed the basis for the Pueblo cultures that exist in these areas today.

LouAnn Faris Culley

Sources for Further Study

Ambler, J. Richard. *The Anasazi: Prehistoric People of the Four Corners Region.* Rev. ed. Flagstaff: Museum of Northern Arizona, 1989.

Amsden, Charles A. *Prehistoric Southwesterners from Basketmaker to Pueblo.* Los Angeles: Southwest Museum, 1949.

Brody, J. J. *The Anasazi: Ancient Indian People of the American Southwest.* New York: Rizzoli International, 1990.

Frazier, Kendrick. *People of Chaco: A Canyon and Its Culture.* Rev. and updated ed. New York: W. W. Norton, 1999.

Jones, Dewitt, and Linda S. Cordell. *Anasazi World.* Portland, Oreg.: Graphic Arts Center, 1985.

Lister, Robert H., and Florence C. Lister. *Chaco Canyon: Archaeology and Archaeologists.* Albuquerque: University of New Mexico Press, 1981.

Nabokov, Peter, and Robert Easton. *Native American Architecture.* New York: Oxford University Press, 1989.

Stuart, David. *The Magic of Bandelier.* Santa Fe, N.Mex.: Ancient City Press, 1989.

See also: Anasazi Civilization; Cliff Dwellings; Hohokam Culture; Kivas; Pit House; Pueblo.

Architecture: Subarctic

Tribes affected: Algonquian, Beaver, Beothuk, Carrier, Chilcotin, Chipewyan, Cree, Dogrib, Han, Hare, Ingalik, Kaska, Koyukon, Kutchin, Naskapi, Slave, Tanaina, Tutchone, Yellowknife

Significance: *The architecture of the sparsely populated, expansive Subarctic region was primarily wigwams, lean-tos, log houses, and tipis.*

Geographically, the Subarctic region, comprising much of present-day Canada, is a land of mountains, tundra, evergreen forests, lakes, and streams, with cold winters and heavy snow. Raw materials used for dwellings were saplings, bark, brush, planks or logs, and animal skins.

In the Northwest, basically three types of shelters were used. Double lean-tos made of wooden frames were covered with bark, animal skins, or brush. As a result of contact with Northwest Coast Indians, Subarctic Indians made wooden plank houses. Portable

The Subarctic Culture Area

tents for summer and winter were used in the northwest Subarctic with snow piled against the sides for winter insulation.

In the eastern Subarctic region, the cone-shaped wigwam was covered with birchbark rolls. Framed with wooden arched poles, the wigwams were covered with rolls of bark which had been sewn together. The floors were layered with pine boughs, and the larger wigwams had central hearths or family fires. Double walls filled with brush in the wigwams provided cooling in the warm months. Brush-covered conical lodges and tents were also used as summer dwellings, and earth-covered conical structures and log cabins with moss-covered roofs were used in winter.

In the Subarctic, some Indians migrated to warmer climates during the winter. Tipis were used throughout the region by those who moved often because they were quickly built and portable; they were made of wooden poles and animal skins.

A basic need of Subarctic community was safe food storage. A simple log building constructed on poles off the ground provided a place for food to be stored out of the reach of animals.

Diane C. Van Noord

Source for Further Study
Nabokov, Peter, and Robert Easton. *Native American Architecture.* New York: Oxford University Press, 1989.

See also: Birchbark; Lean-to; Tipi; Wigwam.

Art and Artists: Contemporary

Tribes affected: Pantribal
Significance: *Drawing both on antiquity and on the present, Indian artists depict their history, legends, insights, and sorrows.*

Contemporary American Indian art was spawned by the mid-1960's Civil Rights movement and the 1962 founding of the Institute of American Indian Arts in Santa Fe, New Mexico. By the late 1960's, the innovative work of Fritz Scholder (Luiseño) and his student T. C. Cannon (Kiowa/Caddo) had alerted other American Indian artists to new ways of depicting the world. Today's Indian artists balance the traditional and the contemporary, seeing these times as aspects of merging and intersecting cycles.

Individuality. In the new atmosphere created by the Civil Rights movement and its aftermath, artists feel free to pursue their own views and concerns rather than having their lives and traditions expressed, often stereotypically, by others. They are doing this in many different ways. There is no singular position from which to examine American Indian art and artists, no distinctive style, materials, or outlook. Today's American Indians belong to or are descended from hundreds of unique peoples, each with their own culture, language, and history. It can never be assumed that all have a similar history or see themselves unilaterally in relation to European Americans or other American Indians.

Many speak through their art to their individuality, which may be woven from a number of different cultures. In *Kaaswoot* (1982), a self-portrait, Edna Jackson reflects both her Tlingit and European ancestry. Some artists draw on traditions other than their own. Sylvia Lark (Seneca) has been attracted to the arts of Asia. Lark's fellow Seneca, Peter Jemison, on the other hand, continues the Northeast tradition of artful containers by placing his self-portrait on a paper bag (*Aotearoa/Ganondagan*, 1986). Those who redefine the old ways, like Jemison, generally attract more critical attention than those who follow the old ways. Thus, Florence Riggs (Navajo), who weaves the life around her—a circus, a trading post—is distinguished from those who reproduce traditional patterns. Political and social statements are often conveyed through these modern interpretations. Many artists, however, do continue the traditional arts and ideas of their culture and gender; women, for example, continue to weave or sculpt with clay, sometimes drawing on ancient forms and styles. Subscribing to another position are those who define themselves as American rather than American Indian, and who may believe that cultural identity has no place in the definition of their art.

Shared Concerns. While American Indian art can never be funneled into a single definition, many of these artists do share a sense of community resulting in part from a common history. American Indians are sensitized to the past and present manipulation of their land, peoples, religion, culture, and social position at the hands of the politically and economically dominant. As the only group in America who live on and visit their ancestral lands, American Indians are particularly responsive in their work to the loss of their lands and the destruction of the environment. Edgar Heap of Birds (Cheyenne/Arapaho) in *Native Hosts* (1988) put up aluminum signs in New York parks with messages such as NEW YORK TODAY YOUR HOST IS SHINNECOCK to indicate to today's residents whose land they occupy. Part of the text is written backward to force the viewers to face the past. Jean La Marr (Paiute/Pit River) in *They're Going to Dump It Where?* (1984) shows, reflected in the eyeglasses of a Paiute woman, the Diablo Canyon nuclear facility being struck by lightning—a statement against the destruction of sacred sites for the fostering of European American technology. At the same time, some American Indian artists continue, in both traditional and contemporary styles, to acknowledge the land as sacred, intertwined with culture and religion.

Since the earliest days of European conquest, there has been a tendency by European Americans to objectify all American Indians, assuming similarities across social class, education, personal taste, degree of assimilation, and dozens of other factors. The cultures of the Iroquois, Sioux, Hopi, and others have been compressed, standardized, and packaged. Addressing this objectification in *The Good Doctor's Bedside* (1983), Lance Belanger (Maliseet) documents the stitchwork of a physician who closed the operation scar of a native woman with beads. Jimmie Durham (Cherokee), in his installation *On Loan from the Museum of the American Indian* (1986), speaks to the dominant view that anything Indian is worth collecting and displaying; the piece includes "Pocahontas Underwear," which is decorated with feathers, beads, and pottery shards labeled "Scientifacts" and "Real Indian Blood." James Luna (Diegueño/Luiseño) in 1986 took the ultimate step in illustrating this objectification when he put himself on display, with the appropriate labels, as an American Indian artifact (*The Artifact Piece*). Some artists with wry humor turn the tables. T. C. Cannon's *The Collector (or Osage with Van Gogh)* shows an elder in traditional dress sitting in his comfortable Western living room with his European American possession, a Van Gogh painting.

Jaune Quick-to-See Smith (Cree/Flathead/Shoshone) powerfully addresses past maltreatments of her people in *Paper Dolls for a Post-Columbian World with Ensembles Contributed by U.S. Government* (1991), in which sets of dolls' clothes are labeled "Special Outfit for Trading Land with the U.S. Government for Whiskey with Gunpowder in It" and "Matching Smallpox Suits for All Indian Families After U.S. Government Sent Wagon Loads of Smallpox Infected Blankets to Keep Our Families Warm." Other artists address the present conditions of American Indians. Richard Ray Whitman (Yuchi/Pawnee) presents the plight of the urban homeless in a set of photographs entitled *Street Chiefs Series*, 1988. Ron Nogonosh (Ojibwa), on his *Shield for a Modern Warrior or Concession to Beads and Feathers in Indian Art* (1984-1985), makes reference to Plains art and Dada sculpture; but most poignantly, the crushed beer cans in the center speak to the past and ongoing tragedy of alcoholism among native peoples.

Most American Indian artists today, whether they live in a city, on an Indian reservation, or both, speak from two worlds. In works that call on antiquity and the present, they depict their history and their legends, their insights and their sorrows.

Zena Pearlstone

Sources for Further Study

Berlo, Janet Catherine. *Native North American Art*. New York: Oxford University Press, 1998.

Brody, J. J. *Indian Painters and White Patrons*. Albuquerque: University of New Mexico Press, 1971.

Contemporary Native American Art. Stillwater: Gardiner Art Gallery, Oklahoma State University, 1983.

Hammond, Harmony, and Jaune Quick-to-See Smith, curators.

Women of Sweetgrass, Cedar, and Sage. New York: Gallery of the American Indian Community House, 1985.

Lippard, Lucy R. *Mixed Blessings: New Art in a Multicultural America*. New York: Pantheon Books, 1990.

McMaster, Gerald. *Reservation X*. Seattle: University of Washington Press, 1998.

Pinder, Kymberly N., ed. *Race-ing Art History: Critical Readings in Race and Art History*. New York: Routledge, 2002.

Rushing, W. Jackson. "Recent Native American Art." *Art Journal* 51, no. 3 (Fall, 1992): 6-15.

See also: Paints and Painting; Pottery; Symbolism in Art.

Arts and Crafts: Arctic

Tribes affected: Aleut, Inuit, Yupik

Significance: *Art of the Arctic, including prints, basketry, tapestries, and sculpture of stone, bone, and ivory, is exhibited and sold throughout the world; it grew in commercial importance in the years after World War II.*

Visitors to nearly any Canadian city cannot help but notice the ubiquitous small black and gray stone carvings of polar bears, walruses, seals, and fur-clad hunters. These hastily made souvenirs of the Canadian Arctic may be the best-known objects of Eskimo tourist art, but they are hardly representative of the great variety and fine quality of representational art from the Arctic region. Sculptures of stone, bone, and ivory, tapestries of wool and fur, wood and skin masks, baskets, dolls, and prints are widely exhibited in art museums and galleries.

Historical Roots. The manufacture of arts and crafts, first for trade and later for cash sale, can be traced to early contacts between Arctic peoples and European explorers, whalers, and traders. Visitors to the region sought souvenirs of their adventures, and native residents quickly discovered that they could obtain desirable trade goods by providing those souvenirs, often in the form of miniatures of native material culture. In Alaska, this trade accelerated and grew in importance at the beginning of the twentieth century. The export of arts and crafts from the North remained modest until after World War II, when a time of economic hardship existed for Arctic natives because of the dramatic drop in fox pelt prices. In 1948, a young Canadian artist named James Houston traveled to Port Harrison in northern Quebec, where he became entranced by the miniature carvings made by local Inuits. He returned to Montreal, where he organized an exhibition sponsored by the Canadian Handicrafts Guild. Public reaction to the fine carvings was so exuberant that Houston returned to the Arctic the following year to encourage Inuits to produce more of these pieces, which were shipped south for sale. At the same time, the federal government of Canada, concerned about the dire financial situation of most Inuit communities, hired Houston to act as a roving arts and crafts officer. As the volume of arts and crafts exports increased each year, Inuit artists began experimenting with larger carvings made from soapstone and serpentine. Houston was later instrumental in starting the printmaking industry in the Baffin Island community of Cape Dorset.

Throughout the late 1950's and early 1960's, the Canadian government was instrumental in the establishment of arts and crafts cooperatives in most Canadian Inuit communities. An umbrella organization known as Canadian Arctic Producers was established to assist in the purchase of raw materials and the distribution of finished products. Although the organization of arts and crafts production varies somewhat from one northern community to another, in Canada the cooperatives continue to play a vital role in the training of artists and the marketing of their work.

Throughout the Arctic culture area, much of the early tourist or souvenir art consisted of models or miniatures of items of traditional material culture. For generations, natives had manufactured and decorated highly sophisticated utilitarian objects. Thus, the skills necessary to produce artwork were widely distributed.

Scholars generally agree that throughout the Arctic, fine crafts-manship in the manufacture of everyday items was highly valued. The hunting cultures of the region believed that animals preferred to be killed by individuals who took the time to produce beauti-fully designed and decorated weapons. Yupik legend, for exam-ple, relates that seals would give themselves up to men whose wives sewed with skill but would avoid men whose wives were slovenly in their sewing habits.

As natives accepted more southern manufactured goods and produced fewer utilitarian objects, artwork for local consumption became less common. Commercial art, however, grew in impor-tance as people sought the cash with which to purchase the im-ported goods. Consequently, the forms that arts and crafts took were heavily influenced by the demands of the marketplace. It is ironic that natives were often encouraged to produce images de-picting a traditional way of life that, increasingly, they no longer followed. There have been a number of well-known instances in which native-produced art was believed to have been overly influ-enced by Western styles or motifs and was therefore rejected by the market as not native enough.

Contemporary Forms. There is considerable variation in both motifs and materials among the three native groups of the region. On both the eastern and western extremes of the Arctic culture area the art forms draw heavily on spiritual motifs. This is seen most clearly in the *tupilak* sculptures from East Greenland. These small, often grotesque, figurines are generally carved from sperm whale teeth. Although the tupilaks are physical representations of Inuit helping spirits, they have always been produced, not as amu-lets, but for sale. To the contrary, the spirit masks produced by Alaska's Yupik Eskimos were (and to some extent, still are) an inte-gral part of the dance and ceremonies that accompanied the an-nual subsistence cycle. Often made of driftwood, the masks are representations of plants, animals, and helping spirits.

Printmaking is most developed in several Canadian Inuit com-munities, including Holman, Baker Lake, Povungnituk, and Cape

Dorset. Prints are produced in series of fifty per image, and stone block printing, stenciling, and lithography are the most common printmaking methods. Although there are clearly developed community styles, many of these tend to be artifacts of local printmaking techniques. The primary differences in artistic style are those of gender—men tend to produce scenes of hunting and other "male" activities, while women more often depict relationships, families, and spirits.

Sculptures of fossil whalebone and soapstone are produced from St. Lawrence Island in the west to Baffin Island in the east. Most carvers are male and, as with printmaking, many of the images are of animals and hunting. Some notable recent pieces have depicted social concerns such as alcohol abuse. Graceful birds delicately shaped from musk ox horn are also a recent innovation.

Dolls, jewelry, and baskets are also produced in the region. Twined Aleut baskets are among the most delicately woven in the world. Generally woven from wild rye beach grasses, the almost clothlike baskets require great skill, time, and patience. Few Aleut women continue this painstaking activity.

Among the Iñupiat of North Alaska, there are also a few makers of coiled baleen baskets. The first baleen baskets were produced in Barrow around 1914 at the request of the trader Charles Brower. The stiff baleen is extremely difficult to work, and a finely made basket commands a high price. In the Iñupiat community of Anaktuvuk Pass, located in the Brooks Range of North Alaska, residents make a unique caribou-skin mask that is pressed into the shape of a human face and decorated with sealskin and fur for the eyebrows, hair, and beard.

Pamela R. Stern and Richard G. Condon

Sources for Further Study

Black, Lydia T. *Glory Remembered: Wooden Headgear of Alaska Sea Hunters*. Juneau: Friends of the Alaska State Museums, 1991.

Canadian Museum of Civilization. *In the Shadow of the Sun: Perspectives on Contemporary Native Art*. Mercury Series Paper 124. Hull, Quebec: Canadian Ethnology Service, 1993.

Driscoll, Bernadette. *I Like My Hood to Be Full*. Winnipeg, Canada: Winnipeg Art Gallery, 1980.

Goetz, Helga, ed. *The Inuit Print/L'Estampe Inuit*. Ottawa: National Museum of Man, 1977.

Graburn, Nelson H. H. "Inuit Art." In *Arctic Life: Challenge to Survive*, edited by Martina M. Jacobs and James B. Richardson III. Pittsburgh: Carnegie Institution Press, 1983.

Hudson's Bay Company. *Beaver* 298 (1967). Special issue on Canadian Inuit arts.

Iglauer, Edith. *Inuit Journey*. Seattle: University of Washington Press, 1979.

Lee, Molly. *Baleen Basketry of the North Alaskan Eskimo*. Foreword by Aldona Jonaitis. Seattle: University of Washington Press with the University of Alaska Museum, 1998.

Ray, Dorothy Jean. *Aleut and Eskimo Art: Tradition and Innovation in South Alaska*. Seattle: University of Washington Press, 1981.

_____. *Eskimo Art: Tradition and Innovation in North Alaska*. Seattle: University of Washington Press, 1977.

See also: Baskets and Basketry; Sculpture.

Arts and Crafts: California

Tribes affected: Chumash, Cupeño, Fernandeño, Gabrielino, Hupa, Kato, Luiseño, Maidu, Miwok, Modoc, Patwin, Pomo, Salinan, Tolowa, Wintun, Yana, Yokuts, Yurok

Significance: *Californian tribes are known for fine basketry work and rock art.*

California tribes hunted, gathered, and fished, and they were divided into many relatively small groups. Although they neither produced monumental art nor possessed a complex art tradition as did the tribes of the Southwest or the Plains, they were nevertheless masters in basketry. Artistic traditions were divided into three geographical zones within the state of California. The southernmost groups had poorly made pottery, carved stone bowls and figures (including stone effigies), rock art, and basketry. The central groups, especially the Pomo, were master basketmakers. The northern groups were influenced by Northwest Coast arts and crafts and made plank houses, dugout canoes, slat armor, and basketry hats.

A sampling of basketry made by the Northern California Hupa tribe. *(Ben Klaffke)*

Basketry. The preeminent craft of Native Americans in California has been basketry. They used both coiling and twining techniques, with coiling being done by the southern groups and twining by the northern ones. Basketry was used to make most containers and to provide many other functional necessities, including mats, baby boards, and boats. Basketry was also used to make decorative objects such as headdresses, and was a part of religious rituals and the life passage rituals of birth, puberty, marriage, and death.

Basketry has always been a woman's art among the California groups, and it provided the women with their primary means of aesthetic expression. Basket designs, considered to be the property of women, were usually geometric and abstract, including circles, crosses, steps, and parallel line designs. Stylized figures of plants and people were also made. Natural vegetable colors were used to achieve the designs. The aesthetic accomplishment in the finer baskets from this region goes far beyond the functional needs for which the basketry was made.

The finest examples of basketry are the "jewel" or "gift" baskets made by Pomo women. These special baskets incorporated feather mosaics into the design along with clam and abalone shells. Red, white, black, blue, and green feathers were used. In some cases the feathers and shells were used sparingly to heighten the basketry design, but in others they became a second layer which totally covered the basket and formed designs of their own. Shells hung along the rim or sides of the basket as ornamentation.

These "jewel" baskets were not only made by women, but were also made as gifts for other women. They were seen as a special ceremonial gift for a woman at important life passage points in her life, such as birth, puberty, and marriage. These baskets had emotional importance for Indian women, probably forming part of self-identity. They were usually cremated along with the woman at death.

Baskets also play a crucial role in mythology. One story says that the earth did not originally have the light of the sun. The original culture hero and creator discovered a village where there was light which was kept in baskets in a sacred sweatlodge. Able to steal one of the magic sun baskets, he hung it in the sky so that all would have light.

Functional baskets were important to the economy of the California groups. Since most groups did not have pottery, baskets were used for cooking and domestic purposes which included storing, grinding, toasting, and boiling food. Water containers were also made from baskets. Although some groups sealed their baskets with pitch or tar, the Pomo, Patwin, and other groups from central California made coiled baskets so tightly bound that they were naturally waterproof.

Rock Art. Rock art consisted of painting highly personalized dream images onto rocky cliffs or overhangs. The Chumash seem to have been the only group to practice it. This art may have reproduced hallucinogenic images seen by men after the ceremonial taking of datura. Rock art consists of compositions of geometric forms, including circles, zigzags, diamonds, chevrons, and crosses, juxtaposed with figures of animals, plants, and people. The colors normally used were strong, saturated hues of red, yellow/orange, black, white, and blue, and the paints were made from minerals and bonded with vegetable and animal oils. The practice of this art seems to have died out in the late 1800's without the meanings being explained in historical records.

Ronald J. Duncan

Sources for Further Study

Bibby, Brian, ed. *The Fine Art of California Indian Basketry*. Berkeley, Calif.: Heyday Books, 1996.

Szabo, Joyce M., ed. *Painters, Patrons, and Identity: Essays in Native American Art to Honor J. J. Brody*. Albuquerque: University of New Mexico Press, 2001.

See also: Baskets and Basketry; Paints and Painting.

Arts and Crafts: Great Basin

Tribes affected: Bannock, Gosiute, Kawaiisu, Mono, Numaga, Paiute, Paviotso, Shoshone, Ute, Walapai, Washoe

Significance: *The arts and crafts of the Great Basin are primarily baskets and other objects created through basketry techniques, reflecting a material culture adapted to a desert environment.*

The arts and crafts of the tribes of the Great Basin represent the highest degree of dependence on basketry techniques of any of the Native American culture areas. Many different kinds of baskets were made, including carrying baskets, serving baskets, and water jars; basketry techniques were also used for making other items, from clothing to boats and houses. Although most baskets were coil made, some were made by the twining technique.

Decorative Baskets. Some of the earliest baskets collected from the Paiutes in the nineteenth century were decorated, and since that time there has been an evolution in designs. The earliest baskets known from this region used the stacked rod coiling technique, which refers to the plaiting of two or more coils. The early decorated baskets were made with a technique different from the one normally used, which suggests that the early decorative patterns were borrowed from neighboring basket-maker groups; the baskets themselves may even have been made by other groups.

By the 1890's, the Paiutes were making decorated baskets for the Navajo, especially wedding baskets, and this relationship has continued to the present day. In addition to that design, the Paiute basket makers borrowed others from Navajo textiles. The designs on Paiute baskets seem to have been largely borrowed.

The wedding basket is an interesting case of one cultural group doing important ceremonial craftwork for another group. The wedding basket is a tray or open bowl shape of twelve to fourteen inches in diameter; it was used by the Navajo to serve cornmeal mush to the honorees and guests at important ceremonies. It is characterized by a circular band of deep red that is bordered by black triangles along both the inside and outside edges. A break in the encircling band is left to provide an opening from the center of the basket outwards, and it is sometimes called the door. During ceremonial use of the basket, the "door" is pointed eastward. Star or snowflake patterns may be created by the black triangles in the center of the basket if the encircling red band is small and the triangles are large. Wedding baskets are made with coils of three bunched rods of sumac. The sewing splints are narrow, and the rims are finished in a herringbone design with diagonal plaiting.

Decorative trade baskets have also been made by various groups, including the Washoe and the San Juan Paiutes. There was a period of outstanding Washoe decorative baskets during the early part of the century. Since traditional Washoe baskets were undecorated, the styles of California tribes were imitated initially; however, the Washoe baskets were distinctive because of their large size, fine stitching, and red and black decoration. Some Washoe baskets were characterized by bold designs, a style that continued throughout the remainder of the century. The San Juan Paiutes experienced a period of florescence during the latter part of the twentieth century based on the borrowing of design patterns, including the use of Navajo *yei* figures, the Navajo Spider Woman cross, and Havasupai angular designs, among others.

Utilitarian Basketry. The largest utilitarian baskets were the conical burden baskets carried on the back with supplies of nuts, roots, or other foods. They were often about 18 inches high and 16 inches across at the opening, and they were made by coiling or twining. Burden baskets could be made with a tight weave for the carrying of seeds and small nuts or made with an open weave for carrying heavier roots. Although utilitarian baskets were rarely decorated, some burden baskets were made with dyed splints.

Basket bowls and shallow circular trays were used for preparing seeds and nuts for eating; food was sometimes cooked or parched with hot stones in the lined baskets. The trays were also used for winnowing out chaff from eatable food. There were also seed beaters in various shapes, ranging from "snowshoe" to handfan designs. These were used to knock seeds off grasses into a conical carrying basket. Pot-shaped storage baskets with tight weave and small necks were used to protect food; water jars were sealed inside with pitch. Scoops, brushes, toys, and other small objects were also made from basketry techniques.

Cradleboards, Canoes, and Houses. The people of the Great Basin could live in basket-made structures from the cradle to

A late nineteenth century mother holding her baby in the traditional cradleboard. *(Library of Congress)*

death. A cradleboard for a small infant was made completely by basketry techniques, with a curved hood to protect the head and a soft back. The cradleboard for a larger infant was made with a wooden frame onto which a basketry back and hood were woven.

Houses were also made with basketry techniques and were essentially upside-down baskets. A willow frame was made by setting up twelve or more vertical willows that were approximately 10 feet long. They were tied together by other willows running horizontally—just above the ground, midway up, and near the top. The top of the frame was tied inward to form a closed-in shape. Cattail leaf mats were woven around other willows, and the mats were tied into place to form the walls. Long grass could also be used to form the walls.

Small canoes were also made with bulrushes (or tule), similar to reed boats made in Peru. Armload bundles of bulrush were tied together with twisted cattail leaf ropes in such a way that a narrow prow was formed, leaving a broader stern where a person could sit and direct the craft. Bulrush duck decoys were also made.

Ronald J. Duncan

Sources for Further Study

Arkush, Brooke S. "The Great Basin Culture Area." In *Native North Americans: An Ethnohistorical Approach*, edited by Daniel L. Boxberger. Dubuque, Iowa: Kendall/Hunt, 1990.

Berlo, Janet Catherine. *Native North American Art*. New York: Oxford University Press, 1998.

Cohodas, Marvin. "Washoe Innovators and Their Patrons." In *The Arts of the North American Indian: Native Traditions in Evolution*, edited by Edwin L. Wade. New York: Hudson Hills Press, 1986.

Feder, Norman. *American Indian Art*. New York: Harry N. Abrams, 1965.

Wheat, Margaret M. *Survival Arts of the Primitive Paiutes*. Reno: University of Nevada Press, 1967.

Whiteford, Andrew Hunter. *Southwestern Indian Baskets: Their History and Their Makers*. Santa Fe, N.Mex.: School of American Research Press, 1988.

Wroth, William, ed. *Ute Indian Arts and Culture: From Prehistory to the New Millennium.* Colorado Springs, Colo.: Taylor Museum of the Colorado Springs Fine Arts Center, 2000.

See also: Baskets and Basketry.

Arts and Crafts: Northeast

Tribes affected: Algonquian, Cayuga, Fox (Mesquaki), Huron, Iroquois, Kickapoo, Lenni Lenape, Lumbee, Menominee, Miami, Micmac, Mohawk, Narragansett, Oneida, Onondaga, Ottawa, Potawatomi, Sauk, Seneca, Shawnee, Susquehannock, Tuscarora, Winnebago

Significance: *The baskets, quillwork, beadwork, and masks of the Northeast tribes are among the finest in North America.*

The Northeast covers New England, New York, and the eastern Great Lakes region down to the Ohio River valley. The art of Native Americans from the northeastern area of the United States used themes associated with nature, mythology, and the supernatural. It might represent otherworldly themes, such as a quillwork ornament representing a thunderbird which protected the wearer from the panther spirit of the other world. It might also represent everyday themes, such as beadwork showing the multicolored hues of flowers and vines that were a natural part of the flora. Included in this rich array of arts were birchbark boxes, quillwork, beadwork, and wood carvings. Pottery was lost in this region soon after contact was made with European groups who introduced the Indians to metal containers.

Masks. Iroquois-made wooden and cornhusk masks are the most striking art form in this region. Men carve and paint wooden masks, while women braid cornhusk ones. These masks are still worn by contemporary members of the Society of Faces in dances that are intended to cure people and drive disease from their

A Seneca carver, Kidd Smith, at work in the Tonowanda Community House during the twentieth century. *(National Archives)*

homes. Characteristics include strong, staring eyes, heavy wrinkles, and horse-mane hair. Although some have sober, dark colors and small mouths, others are brightly painted and have big ear-to-ear mouths. The features may be distorted.

Wooden masks, made and worn only by men, represent many different spirits, including those of trees, plants, waterfalls, unusual rocks, and other special features of the landscape. They are carved from living trees, and the traditional belief was that they embodied a living spirit. Tobacco was tied into the hair for use by the spirit, and the mask was fed regularly. Cornhusk masks may be made and worn by men or women, and they represent the spirits of vegetation which work to heal people.

Various features of the mask identify the spirit portrayed by it. For example, a broken nose and wide crooked mouth represent a spirit called the "Great Defender" or the "Rim Dweller," who was transformed from a malevolent spirit into one which helped people. Wood carving was also used to make clubs and carved figures for knife handles and other uses. Carvings commonly represented hands, the human body, bears, and horses.

Bark Boxes and Baskets. Bark was a favorite material for making boxes, baskets, and even canoes. Birchbark was used in the Great Lakes area, and elm bark was used by the Iroquois and other groups in the East. These barks are soft and pliable when peeled, which permits them to be shaped into square and round designs for containers. Bark can be bent, rolled, and stitched, and it provides a good surface for drawing or incising. Quillwork was frequently used to decorate the surface. Both covered boxes and open baskets made use of this material. Splint basketry was also made in this area.

Beadwork. Both quillwork and small stone beads were originally used to create designs and decorative bands on clothing. After the introduction of European glass trade beads, this art medium went through a spectacular development. The original work was limited to the muted colors of autumn earth tones, but the glass beads permitted the introduction of the saturated hues of spring flowers and berries. Ribbons were introduced along with beads; combined, they gave many more opportunities for the ornamentation of clothing.

Beads have been used to represent both the geometric designs found in earlier ceramic patterns and the floral motifs with which the eastern groups are identified. The latter may have developed out of an earlier tradition of naturalistic representations. There were also European models for the floral motifs which may have been the ecclesiastical attire of priests, but other floral patterns incorporated later may have referred to local medicinal plants. The idea that there were European sources for the floral patterns is reinforced by the fact that they were commonly used on shoulder-strap bags, adapted from European military pouches, and on European-style deerskin coats. Indigenous belts and trumplines decorated with quillwork later evolved into beaded and beribboned votive belts by which people expressed their devotion.

Ronald J. Duncan

Sources for Further Study

Berlo, Janet Catherine. *Native North American Art*. New York: Oxford University Press, 1998.

Dubin, Lois Sherr. *North American Indian Jewelry and Adornment: From Prehistory to the Present*. New York: Henry N. Abrams, 1999.

See also: Baskets and Basketry; Beads and Beadwork; Birchbark; Masks; Quillwork.

Arts and Crafts: Northwest Coast

Tribes affected: Bella Bella, Bella Coola, Haida, Haisla, Kitamat, Kwakiutl, Makah, Nitinat, Nootka, Tlingit, Tsimshian

Significance: *The people of the Northwest Coast have one of the most recognizable art styles of the world and produced the most important monumental art of the indigenous North American groups.*

The people of the Northwest Coast are identified by their art, especially painted house facades, masks, and the monumentality of the totem poles. They are the outstanding wood carvers of North America, and their art treats the themes of cosmology and origins, social status and prestige, and shamanistic power. Both sculpture and painting are characterized by strong colors and shapes.

Totem Poles. Totem poles stand in front of houses as a statement of the sacred history of the family. The vertical series of figures making up the pole traces the family to the time the lineage was founded in the mythic past. The origin story usually tells about the original ancestor encountering a spirit who gave him and his descendants a special power, as well as the image of the spirit as a heraldic crest for the family. Each family may possess more than one crest; crests are inherited by the children in each generation. Multiple crests may be represented on a pole, and common ones include the bear, mountain lion, eagle, frog, and wolf. The totem pole seems only to have developed during the nineteenth century, but similar poles were carved earlier as the crest poles of houses.

The totem poles were carved and erected as memorials to men of chiefly status who had died, and they were mnemonic devices to record the heritage of the family. The pole became a public proclamation of ancestry and the rights to positions of prestige along with their benefits, obligations, and supernatural characteristics. The carver of a totem pole was expected to be a relative of the man honored. If the man chosen to be the carver did not have the required skill, he could conceptualize the piece and name a skilled carver to execute it. The authorship of a pole was assigned to the one who conceptualized it. The poles were as much as 60 feet tall, and they were carved lying on the ground.

House Facades and Crest Poles. The house itself was the cosmos in a microcosm, with the hearth being the navel of the world; the house posts were the supports of the earth and sky, and the smoke hole was the connection between the earth and the heavenly world, forming a vertical cosmic axis. The facades of chiefly houses could be painted with the images of mythical animals who were the head of the lineage. In the nineteenth century and earlier, the crest poles of houses were carved, and sometimes a large entrance hole was cut into it, which served as the door for the house. The opening was frequently portrayed as the mouth or the vagina of the animal lineage head of the family, and going in and out of the house represented death and rebirth from the lineage totem. In some instances the door hole represented the hole of creation through which the original ancestor passed to enter this world. Another version interpreted it as the hole through which the original shaman passed back and forth to the other world to learn the sacred knowledge, ceremonies, and masks that characterized ritual.

Masks and Hats. Masks have been the most common art form among the peoples of the Northwest Coast. Like the motifs of the totem poles, masks belong to families and were originally given to the founding ancestor because of a victory over an adversary. Masks and the accompanying costumes create a figure who was an actor in a myth; songs and dances are also inherited with the mask to dramatize the myth. Masks represent the shamanic power of transformation from the earthly present to the mythic past or to the supernatural world. In the ephemeral other world of the masks, the heroic exploits of the original people are acted out, and the myths reconfirm the fundamental principles of the cosmos. Masks may represent supernatural animal spirits, shamans, or important people. In addition to being carved, many are painted with strong primary colors. Some have movable parts.

The shaman's quest for spiritual powers is also a common theme of mask-myth performances. The shamanic regalia included special masks, costumes, drums, and rattles. The rattles are especially striking because of their elaborate and complex carving. The basic figure shown in the rattle was frequently a water bird, and the shaman is shown on its back with other animals. The tongue of a goat or a frog may become a bridge through which the shaman transforms the power of that animal into his own.

Carved wooden hats and war helmets were traditionally important, and some are essentially variations on the idea of the masks. War helmets have not been made since the nineteenth century, but they represented ancestors or other effigy beings who could give strength to the warrior. Conical clan hats were also important, and they represent the animal of the family crest. Like masks, these hats sometimes had movable parts. These family crest hats are among the most dramatic pieces of Northwest Coast art, possessing abalone-shell inlays, stylized bodies, and polychrome painting.

Domestic Crafts. Weaving, basketry, and the carving of wooden household utensils were also common crafts. During historical periods woven tunics frequently included the family crest motifs, similar to the totem poles, masks, and hats. Spindle whorls for spinning the thread were elaborately carved in wood. Women were accomplished basket makers, and their twined work with grasses and other fibers were as fine as woven cloth.

Ronald J. Duncan

Sources for Further Study
Berlo, Janet Catherine. *Native North American Art*. New York: Oxford University Press, 1998.
Carlson, Roy L., ed. *Indian Art Traditions of the Northwest Coast*. Burnaby, B.C.: Archaeology Press, Simon Fraser University, 1982.
Furst, Peter T., and Jill L. Furst. *North American Indian Art*. New York: Rizzoli International, 1982.
Holm, Bill. *Crooked Beak of Heaven: Masks and Other Ceremonial Art in the Pacific Northwest*. Seattle: University of Washington Press, 1972.
_____. "The Dancing Headdress Frontlet: Aesthetic Context on the Northwest Coast." In *The Arts of the North American Indian: Native Traditions in Evolution*, edited by Edwin L. Wade. New York: Hudson Hills Press, 1986.
King, J. C. H. *Portrait Masks from the Northwest Coast of North America*. London: Thames & Hudson, 1979.
Shearar, Cheryl. *Understanding Northwest Coast Art: A Guide to Crests, Beings, and Symbols*. Seattle: University of Washington Press, 2000.
Suttles, Wayne, ed. *Northwest Coast*. Vol. 7 in *Handbook of North American Indians*. Washington, D.C.: Smithsonian Institution Press, 1990.

See also: Chilkat Blankets; Masks; Paints and Painting; Sculpture; Totem Poles.

Arts and Crafts: Plains

Tribes affected: Arapaho, Arikara, Assiniboine, Atsina, Blackfoot, Caddo, Cheyenne, Comanche, Cree, Crow, Hidatsa, Iowa, Kiowa, Mandan, Missouri, Omaha, Osage, Pawnee, Ponca, Sioux, Tonkawa, Wichita

Significance: *The beadwork and headdresses of the Plains are a dramatic statement of personal aesthetics, and they are the primary association with Native American art for many people.*

The arts and crafts of the Plains tribes were small in scale and highly transportable because of the largely nomadic Plains existence. The arts had supernatural relationships with the spirit world; for example, beautifying the skin of a slain animal was thought to please its spirit and avert retaliation. Ghost Dance shirts and dresses also demonstrate the close relationship between art and the spiritual world.

Clothing and Bags. Clothing, moccasins, and bags were made of skins, and most were decorated with geometric designs by women using quills, beads, or paint. Plains art is most known for the beadwork on clothing and other personal items and the earlier work with porcupine quills. By the early nineteenth century, colored beads of Venetian glass had been introduced by the Europeans as trade items, and by midcentury they had been replaced by even smaller "seed beads," which led to a new style of beadwork that covered entire surfaces.

The elongated shape of the quill was used to decorate medallions, boxes, and cradleboards, among other items, and resulted in geometric designs or highly stylized figures. Beadwork portrayed such things as floral patterns, the tipi, crosses, the United States flag, and lightning. Dresses, shirts, and parfleches were frequently painted. The parfleche was a thick-skinned, folding bag which was capable of withstanding arrows and lances.

Narrative Art. Narrative paintings were done by men on skins, especially on robes and tipis. These narrated calendrical histories (called wintercounts), important tribal gatherings, personal visions, mythological events, and important battles, raids, and hunts. The calendar drawings have mnemonic value for remembering the major events that occurred in a tribe or band over a number of years. The winter camps were the fixed points between which yearly events were remembered. Battle scenes, as well as raids and hunts, narrate the personal bravery and skill of a specific warrior, and these were usually painted by the same warrior on his personal buffalo robe or on his tipi cover. He would usually portray the most important moment of his triumph. Tribal gatherings were also portrayed in narrative detail, describing features of the landscape, placing of tipis, clothing, and tribal paraphernalia. The describing of personal visions and mythological events was done with less narrative detail; it was left to the imagination of the viewer to complete the story. Vision paintings were frequently done on shields or tipis.

As the independent lifestyle of the Plains people came to an end and the people were settled around forts, the art of skin painting was lost. This happened in part because the personal exploits narrated by the men in battle and hunting no longer happened and in part because the skins were no longer available. In its place, ledgerbook painting was developed among the Southern Plains tribes; among the Northern Plains tribes, men adapted to painting on cloth. Ledgerbook art typically narrates the experience of Native Americans with the European American world. Instead of the horses, tipis, and buffalo of the skin paintings, the ledger paintings portray forts, trains, wagons, and even towns. The most famous collection of ledger art comes from the seventy-two warriors from five Southern Plains tribes who were sent to Fort Marion in Florida after their surrender in 1875.

Pipes as Miniature Sculpture. The pipe was the single most important art object made by the Plains groups, and it explored the relationship between humans and the sacred in the earth and sky, including the concept of the universe. Each man carved his own private ceremonial pipe, and sometimes one would be made as a special gift for another person. The holiest pipes were common property and were considered to be especially powerful. The bowls were usually carved from reddish pipestone, which was considered to be blood colored and therefore to represent life. They were usually plain bowls but could include complex carvings of animals or humans. The stems were also elaborately carved and could be two feet long or more; sometimes they were of greater importance than the bowl itself. Stems were carved in a number of imaginative designs, including spiral stems, mazeway puzzle stems, and stems with figurative carvings of animals and guardian spirits. Since the power of the pipe was activated when the stem and bowl were united, they were usually separated when stored. Pipe bags show some of the most important Plains beadwork and quillwork, which indicates the significance of pipes.

Alice Littleman, a member of the Kiowa tribe, displaying Plains beadwork and skin sewing. *(U.S. Department of the Interior Indian Arts and Crafts Board)*

Gender and Art. Women beautified clothes and other items of domestic use with geometric designs in their media of bead and quillwork, with occasional painting. Craft and skill were definitive of women's work, and they used the geometric signs that communicated the important concepts of nature and the supernatural. Many incorporated the United States flag into their beadwork during the late 1800's, perhaps as a statement of peace. The women's art uses collective designs, and it does not emphasize the individuality of the piece. In contrast, men's narrative art is individualistic and boasts of personal exploits. Craft seems to be less important in the narrative art, which is done with lines that are rigid and awkward. Men's pipe carvings are carefully crafted, however, and rival the quality of the women's beadwork.

Ronald J. Duncan

Sources for Further Study

Berlo, Janet Catherine. *Native North American Art*. New York: Oxford University Press, 1998.

Coe, Ralph T. *Sacred Circles: Two Thousand Years of North American Indian Art*. Kansas City, Mo.: Nelson Gallery Foundation, 1977.

Catlin, George. *Indian Art in Pipestone: George Catlin's Portfolio in the British Museum*. Edited by John C. Ewers. Washington, D.C.: Smithsonian Institution Press, 1979.

Dubin, Lois Sherr. *North American Indian Jewelry and Adornment: From Prehistory to the Present*. New York: Henry N. Abrams, 1999.

Furst, Peter T., and Jill L. Furst. *North American Indian Art*. New York: Rizzoli International, 1982.

Penny, David W. *Art of the American Indian Frontier*. Seattle: University of Washington Press, 1992.

Wade, Edwin L., ed. *The Arts of the North American Indian: Native Traditions in Evolution*. New York: Hudson Hills Press, 1986.

See also: Beads and Beadwork; Dress and Adornment; Headdresses; Quillwork.

Arts and Crafts: Plateau

Tribes affected: Cayuse, Chilcotin, Klikitat, Lillooet, Nez Perce, Shuswap, Umatilla, Walla Walla, Wasco, Wishram, Yakima

Significance: *The arts and crafts of the Plateau effectively preserved traditional design styles and techniques longer than most other Native American culture areas.*

The people of the Plateau have produced bags, basketry, beadwork, and wood carving of excellent quality. Their work reflects the influences from neighboring culture areas and demonstrates the diffusion and acculturation of arts and crafts traditions across culture lines among Native Americans. Contact with European groups occurred later here than in most other areas, and this fact permitted a greater preservation of traditional arts and crafts.

Woven Bags. The Plateau bag is the most distinctive art and craft medium of this culture area. These bags are known for their geometric designs and skillful color patterns. The women makers of these bags are known for their weaving skill, and many of them achieved personal visions of aesthetic excellence in geometric and color composition. Along with Navajo blankets and rugs, these bags represent the finest designs in North American weaving. Plateau people have also made blankets but never with the same sophistication with which they weave bags.

The first European Americans to arrive in the area were Meriwether Lewis and William Clark in 1805, and they mentioned the woven bags made by the Nez Perce. The twined or woven bags are made with the beige background of hemp but then decorated with bear grass and cattails dyed with vegetable colors. After corn was introduced into the area in the early nineteenth century, corn husks were used for the bags; later, yarn was also incorporated. After that they were sometimes referred to as cornhusk bags. They were made in varying sizes, ranging from 8 by 8 inches to 18 by 22 inches. Some large versions of the bag are as much as 36 inches long, and they were usually carried vertically. They were originally used for carrying food that had been collected. After horses arrived in the region, they were used as saddlebags. In the twentieth century they became decorative handbags carried by women.

The designs were traditionally geometric, but figurative motifs were introduced in the late nineteenth century. The bag was continuously woven in the round, with the front side being more elaborate than the back. Triangles and diamond shapes were especially popular, and they were sometimes combined to form star, butterfly, cross, chevron, or arrow designs. Smaller designs were incorporated within or around the larger main design, which added complexity and visual interest. Long straight lines were frequently serrated, also creating more visual interest. Bag designs also emphasize the play between positive and negative spaces so that the viewer must shift his or her vision between the two.

The introduction of figurative designs including plants, animals, and humans reflected European American influences, especially the floral designs of the Victorian period. Since weaving lends itself more to the representation of geometric shapes than to reproducing organic ones, geometric forms continued to be important into the twentieth century. The ability to make organic, figurative shapes was the sign of a skillful weaver.

Baskets and Basketry. Both coiling and twining were used to make basketry items. Twining was used to make soft fiber objects such as hats and bags, as discussed above. Coiling was used to make more rigid basket containers, ranging from small bowls to large storage baskets. A technique of decoration known as "imbrication" is distinctive to the Plateau area. Imbrication is a process of creating a second decorative layer on top of the coil-made basket by stitching it into the surface of the basket. Since the decorative layer has no important structural problems to solve, it can be designed purely for aesthetic purposes. The imbricated layer has a continuous surface not interrupted by the dominant coil lines of the coil-made basket. Mats were also made by some groups and were traditionally used to cover the walls of tipis.

Beads and Beading. Beading was done on clothes, bags, baskets, and horse trappings, among other things, and represents an influence from the Plains tribes to the east. Similar to the Northern Plains people, both men and women of the Plateau used buckskin clothing decorated with beadwork. Originally beads were added to fringes, but later overall beading was used for shirts, cuffs, headbands, belts, and other accessories. Beading was used for horse trappings, including bridles, mane covers, shin straps, stirrup covers, and saddle bags. Beading was also used to cover coiled baskets. The bead designs were geometric during the nineteenth century, but figurative motifs became increasingly important in the twentieth century. The Plateau bead workers used triangles, diamonds, squares, and crosses to create geometric designs, and the figurative patterns incorporate floral motifs, eagles, and the U.S. flag, among many other patterns.

Carving. Figures, grave marker totems, scoops, and small bowls were carved of wood and horn, reflecting influences from the neighboring Northwest Coast peoples. Human figures carved of wood represented ancestral spirits or beings, and shaman's wands included anthropomorphic forms. Small wooden bowls included figures carved in relief on the surfaces as well as decorative patterns of parallel or serrated lines. Occasionally figures were carved in three dimensions on the sides of bowls. The handles of scoops and spoons were carved with animal and human figures. The handles of wood-carving tools were themselves elaborately carved.

Ronald J. Duncan

Sources for Further Study

Berlo, Janet Catherine. *Native North American Art*. New York: Oxford University Press, 1998.

Coe, Ralph T. *Sacred Circles: Two Thousand Years of North American Indian Art*. Kansas City, Mo.: Nelson Gallery Foundation, 1977.

Feder, Norman. *American Indian Art*. New York: Harry N. Abrams, 1965.

Kehoe, Alice B. *North American Indians: A Comprehensive Account.* 2d ed. Englewood Cliffs, N.J.: Prentice Hall, 1992.

Linn, Natalie. *The Plateau Bag: A Tradition in Native American Weaving.* Kansas City, Kans.: Johnson County Community College, Gallery of Art, 1994.

Penney, David W. *Art of the American Indian Frontier.* Seattle: University of Washington Press, 1992.

See also: Baskets and Basketry; Beads and Beadwork; Sculpture; Weaving.

Arts and Crafts: Southeast

Tribes affected: Alabama, Anadarko, Apalachee, Catawba, Cherokee, Chickasaw, Chitimacha, Choctaw, Creek, Guale, Mobile, Natchez, Powhatan, Seminole, Tuskegee, Yamasee, Yazoo, Yuchi

Significance: *The Indians of the Southeast are especially known for baskets, beaded sashes and bags, carving, patchwork, and ribbon work.*

The artists of the Southeast tribes are the heirs to one of the richest artistic traditions in North America, but much of it has disappeared over the last few centuries because of acculturation and the dislocation of tribes. Elaborate earthen mounds, excellent stone-carved sculptures, copper sheets cut like mythical animals, baskets, and painted ceramics were made in the period before contact with Europeans. This early art incorporated motifs that suggested contact with the complex civilizations of Mexico. During the historic period, these tribes have been known for their work in belts and bags, baskets, carving, and sewing.

Belts and Bags. Creek, Cherokee, and Choctaw women, taking advantage of the creative possibilities of small seed beads, made sashes and shoulder bags that were well known for their elaborate flowing designs. These women were exceptional colorists and exploited the many colors made available with glass beads. They fashioned complex sashes with beads worked into the designs, and they made shoulder bags with beaded decoration. These were some of the finest bags produced in North America, and they competed with those of the Great Lakes area for aesthetic and technical excellence.

The double-ended scroll is a characteristic design from the Southeast tribes, and the beaded designs on belts and bags frequently use it. It is a linear design 8 to 10 inches long and 3 to 4 inches wide, consisting of a spiral or circle at each end with a line uniting them diagonally. The cross in a circle design surrounded by emanating sun rays was also used in beadwork, and both this design and the scroll pattern were used in other media, such as ceramics. Another common design pattern is the diamond, used especially by the Choctaws but also by Creeks and Seminoles. Creek sashes line up ordered rows of diamonds embroidered in seed beads, similar to the rows of diamonds that Choctaws sew onto the hems of dresses and onto the decorative bands of shirts. All of these designs were also used by prehistoric groups in the region.

Shoulder bags were made from wool or velvet, backed with a cotton lining and embroidered with seed beads in designs of flowing lines that suggest floral patterns but are in reality abstract. The patterns were bold and asymmetrical and the designs seem more individually expressive than the patterned formality of designs of the Northeast. In some designs the lines seem to meander, following their own will and resulting in amorphous "figures" that give a sense of elegant playfulness distinctive to these pieces.

Baskets. Southeastern basketry is especially known for the use of the split and plaited cane technique, which produces a flexible basket of considerable strength. The altering of colors between the warp and the weft gives ample opportunity for the creation of patterns and decoration. Covered baskets were made as containers for storage and protection, and open baskets were made for gathering and carrying food products. A gathering basket made by various tribes in the region has a square base which changes into a round shape for the top half of the basket. It is known for fitting well to the back, making it easier to carry loads. Common design motifs include the diamond, chevron or zigzag lines, crosses, and angular spirals.

Sewing. Patchwork dresses and shirts and elaborate ribbon-work decoration are also associated with the work of women in tribes of the Southeast. The Seminoles are most known for this type of patchwork, which was borrowed from European patchwork quilting. The patching together of hundreds of small pieces of colored cloth has been appropriated to form an aesthetic which is particular to this area and is now considered traditional. Ribbons have also been used in a similar way to create the patterns. Neighboring groups such as the Choctaws have adopted a similar practice of sewing diamond patch designs on dresses and shirts to give them tribal identity.

Carving. Men's craft consisted of carving, and they made stylized figures in wood and pipestone. Effigy pipes, representing bears and other animals from the region, were carved until the nineteenth century, following long Eastern Woodlands traditions. Other pipes were carved in geometric designs.

Ronald J. Duncan

Sources for Further Study

Berlo, Janet Catherine. *Native North American Art*. New York: Oxford University Press, 1998.

Dubin, Lois Sherr. *North American Indian Jewelry and Adornment: From Prehistory to the Present*. New York: Henry N. Abrams, 1999.

See also: Applique and Ribbonwork; Baskets and Basketry; Beads and Beadwork; Dress and Adornment; Sculpture.

Arts and Crafts: Southwest

Tribes affected: Apache, Navajo, Pueblo (including Hopi, Zuñi)
Significance: *The arts and crafts of the Southwest are a thriving and coherent representation of Native American art that has continuity with its prehistoric cultural roots.*

Southwest Native American art can be traced back to prehistoric groups that lived in the area. The prehistoric groups developed pottery, basketry, weaving, and jewelry making, and the contemporary Pueblo groups have continued the designs and techniques inherited in those media. The Navajos and Apaches have a different history, having entered the area only six hundred to eight hundred years ago. Although they originally practiced basketry, they acquired weaving from the Pueblo people and, later, silversmithing from the Spanish.

Eastern Pueblos. The Eastern Pueblos live on or near the Rio Grande River near Santa Fe, and they were most affected by the Spanish. They have had commercial success with arts and crafts. The Eastern Pueblos have the richest pottery tradition, but they also make jewelry, baskets, and woven goods.

Pueblo pottery is made with the prehistoric techniques of coil building, slip painting, and open-air firing. The pots are elaborately painted, usually iron oxide red, white, or black colors. Pueblo designs may use geometric forms or stylized figures of animals, birds, or plants. Border lines are usually drawn as a frame to define the area to be decorated. The designs frequently play back and forth between positive and negative fields, resulting in complex symmetries, and they are usually subdivided into smaller and smaller units. Women are the traditional makers of pottery, but men may paint it and fire it. The most common types of pots are water jars, dough bowls, and storage pots. Although each type was originally made for functional purposes, in modern times they are made primarily for artistic purposes. The pottery tradition from this area is divided into a number of styles, including blackware, redware, and polychrome ware.

Blackware pottery was traditionally made in the Pueblos north and west of Santa Fe, especially Santa Clara, San Juan, and San Ildefonso, where the tradition was made famous by María and Julián Martínez. Santa Clara Pueblo is famous for both blackware and redware pottery, and it is well known for the deep carving of designs in the surface of pots. Rain serpents and the bear paw are popular designs. Polychrome pottery is most associated with the pueblos located to the south and west of Santa Fe, most notably Zia

Native Americans in Santa Clara Pueblo, New Mexico, making pottery during the early 1900's. *(National Archives)*

and Acoma. The colors are typically red and/or black on a white background. Border lines frame the painted areas of the pots, and within those borders designs may include floral patterns, animal figures (especially deer), birds, and geometric forms. Cochiti is the only pueblo to make figurative pieces, and it is now particularly known for the storyteller figure.

The most traditional jewelry of the Southwest is made by people of the Eastern Pueblos, particularly Santo Domingo, and it characteristically includes strings of turquoise for necklaces and other pieces made of mosaics of turquoise. Although weaving and basketry were traditionally important, they have largely disappeared among these pueblos.

Western Pueblos. The Zuñi and the Hopi were more isolated than the Eastern Pueblos and continued many of their traditions until the twentieth century. These Pueblos make polychrome ware, and Zuñi pottery is distinguished by the motif of the deer with a red heart-line going from the mouth into the torso and the rosette design. Hopi pottery is made primarily on the First Mesa by Hopi-Tewa descendants, and it is noted for the flat, broad shape of its pots. Surface designs are geometric and now largely follow the designs of the Sikytki revival pottery.

The Western Pueblos are most known for jewelry making. The Zuñis do lapidary work and silversmithing, while the Hopis focus primarily on silver work. The Zuñis are famous for carving fetishes in stone which are sometimes made into necklaces of turquoise, coral, and other stones. These fetishes depict bears, mountain lions, foxes, frogs, and owls among other animals. They also set turquoise and other fine stones in silver, sometimes in complex patterns called clusterwork, and they do stone inlay jewelry.

The Hopi make jewelry with overlay designs in silver, sometimes including stones. They are best known, however, for making kachina dolls, which are carved, painted, and dressed. The kachinas incorporate rain and cloud symbols and represent the hope for well-being and plenty, and they are used to teach children about the supernatural. The Hopi also do basketry and weaving.

Navajos and Apaches. Although the Eastern and Western Pueblos do weaving, the Navajos have most excelled in this media. The designs are primarily geometric and include stepped frets, crosses, and butterflies. There are complex patterns of repetition and contrasts of positive-negative fields. A number of regional styles exist throughout the Navajo area. Occasionally, the weaving incorporated designs from sand paintings, which have special ritual and healing significance. The Navajo are also famous for turquoise and silver jewelry, especially the squash blossom necklace. The wide range of Apache baskets includes trays, carrying baskets, and pitch-sealed water bottles. The designs include geometric and highly stylized figures.

Ronald J. Duncan

Sources for Further Study

Berlo, Janet Catherine. *Native North American Art*. New York: Oxford University Press, 1998.

Dubin, Lois Sherr. *North American Indian Jewelry and Adornment: From Prehistory to the Present*. New York: Henry N. Abrams, 1999.

Eaton, Linda B. *Native American Art of the Southwest*. Lincolnwood, Ill.: Publications International, 1993.

Furst, Peter T., and Jill L. Furst. *North American Indian Art*. New York: Rizzoli International, 1982.

Wade, Edwin L., ed. *The Arts of the North American Indian: Native Traditions in Evolution*. New York: Hudson Hills Press, 1986.

Whiteford, Andrew Hunter. *Southwestern Indian Baskets: Their History and Their Makers*. Santa Fe, N.Mex: School of American Research Press, 1988.

Wyckoff, Lydia L. *Designs and Factions: Politics, Religion, and Ceramics on the Hopi Third Mesa*. Albuquerque: University of New Mexico Press, 1990.

See also: Baskets and Basketry; Kachinas; Pottery; Sculpture; Silverworking; Weaving.

Arts and Crafts: Subarctic

Tribes affected: Beaver, Beothuk, Carrier, Cree, Dogrib, Han, Hare, Ingalik, Neskapi, Ojibwa, Ottawa, Sekani, Slave, Tahltan, Tanaina, Tsetsaut, Tutchone, Yellowknife
Significance: *Subarctic artisans were especially known for their quillwork and birchbark baskets.*

The arts and crafts of the Subarctic Indians included quillwork, beadwork, bags, birchbark baskets and boxes, and wood carving, but because of the sparse population and the demands of a hunting and gathering life, this work did not exist in quantity. Most of the arts and crafts from this area are known to be from the Algonquian-speaking tribes (Cree and Ojibwa) who occupied the eastern area and were influenced by the arts of the Northeast and Plains culture areas. Athapaskan-speaking tribes (Beaver, Han, Ingalik, Tahltan, Tanaina, Tutchone, and Sekani) occupied the western Subarctic and were influenced by the material culture of the neighboring Northwest Coast groups as well as the Aleuts and the Eskimos (Inuits).

Quillwork and Embroidery. Porcupine quillwork was particularly well developed among the eastern groups, and it was in wide use at the time of the earliest contact with the Europeans. Women used these techniques to decorate the surfaces of birchbark boxes, moccasins, decorate bands (such as wampum belts), and clothing. Designs were made by plaiting the quills in patterns that may have developed out of basketry techniques, and they were sewn to the surfaces.

Designs were primarily geometric and included diamonds, chevrons, parallel lines, crosses, crossbars, cross-hatching, step design, and the double-ended swirl. The sides and lids of boxes were frequently covered with overall decoration. For example, the side of a box could be covered with various parallel bands of quills and the top with concentric circles. The artists varied the density of the plaiting of the quills to make tightly packed patterns or open-weave patterns, which produced different textures.

Quillwork clothing decoration was also geometric. The Cree copied European-style officers' coats in buckskin, which reached the knees and were decorated with quills and paint. Elaborate designs were placed along the bottom edge and the front borders of the coat. Three or four bands of design were frequently used, and it sometimes took on the compositional look of Plains hide paintings, although there were no figures. The designs on coats tended to be bold and clearly visible from some distance, but the designs on moccasins were smaller, intricate, and tightly finished. The decorative bands and epaulets for coats were similarly more intimate in scale.

Eventually, embroidery and beads replaced quillwork on clothing. Moose-hair embroidery was common in earlier periods, and into the twentieth century women were still doing silk embroidery. The quillwork and embroidery from this area is known for its beauty of line and fine stitching.

Beads and Bags. The Ojibwa (or Chippewa) and the Ottawa developed a rich tradition of decorating shoulder bags, also called bandoleer bags. Early buckskin versions were commonly decorated in geometric patterns with quills, but stylized representations of mythological beings were also used. Later versions were beaded and made of cloth, and they incorporated floral patterns. Especially complex versions of these items were called "friendship bags," and they were worn by men as a demonstration of prestige. In the nineteenth century, floral designs were increasingly used, and floral and geometric designs were sometimes incorporated into the same bag. During this period, geometric designs were adapted to represent floral-like patterns. Fringe was frequently added to bags, and in some cases fringe flaps became narrow bands of pure geometric design.

Birchbark. Birchbark was used to make most containers for normal domestic use. Made by peeling birchbark, folding it into the form desired, and sewing it with spruce root, these containers were used as gathering and storage baskets. Since birchbark was both pliable and strong, it was even used to make canoes and houses. It was because of this material's adaptability that these tribes did not make pottery or many baskets. Birchbark designs could be made by scraping the outside layer of the bark, which was white, to reveal the brown layer beneath. Animal and plant figures from the area were normally shown on birchbark, and in keeping with the quillwork tradition, these figures were highly stylized.

Woodwork. Some Subarctic groups did wood carvings of small objects, such as knife handles and spoons, similar to those of the Northeast culture area. Human and animal figures were carved, and both were highly stylized. Simple sgraffito drawings were also done occasionally on wooden surfaces, showing stylized images from the natural worlds, geometric signs, and pictographs.

Ronald J. Duncan

Sources for Further Study

Berlo, Janet Catherine. *Native North American Art*. New York: Oxford University Press, 1998.

Dubin, Lois Sherr. *North American Indian Jewelry and Adornment: From Prehistory to the Present*. New York: Henry N. Abrams, 1999.

See also: Baskets and Basketry; Beads and Beadwork; Birchbark; Quillwork.

Astronomy

Tribes affected: Pantribal
Significance: *The ancient people of the Americas observed the heavens carefully, and many built structures for observing or measuring the movement of the sun and stars.*

Early Native American knowledge of the heavens ranged from the complex Mayan calendars to more simple markings of the solstices. Throughout North America, references to the sun, moon, stars, and planets occur in creation accounts and other cultural practices.

In Central America, the Mayan calendar influenced civilizations from 100 B.C.E. to the time of the Spanish Conquest (1519-1697). Guatemalan "daykeepers" still use the original astronomical system for divination. The four extant books, or codices, in the hieroglyphic Mayan language are almanacs. The Dresden Codex records the revolution of Venus. Mayans observed the solar year as well as lunar cycles and the movements of stars. The Mayan creation account, the *Popol Vuh*, includes references to the Pleiades, the Big Dipper, and Ursa Minor (Draco). The twin heroes of the Mayan creation story are associated with the sun and moon as well as with Venus.

In the northern plains of Canada and the United States, medicine wheels attest an ancient knowledge of astronomy. The prehistoric wheels are spoked circles outlined by stones, up to 60 yards in diameter. About fifty medicine wheels are known to exist, most of which are on the eastern slopes of the Rocky Mountains. The oldest medicine wheel, in Majorville, Alberta, dates to 4,500 years before the present, and it has a central cairn made of 50 tons of stones. Many medicine wheels mark sunrise points of equinoxes and solstices, while a few mark summer stars. The Bighorn Medicine Wheel in Wyoming has cairns that correspond to paths of Aldebaran, Rigel, and Sirius. These three stars rise a month apart during the summer.

In the Midwest, prehistoric mounds in the Mississippi and Ohio river valleys also reflect astronomical understanding. Hopewellian and Mississippian mounds are often in the shapes of animals or stepped temples, but the Marching Bear mounds in McGregor, Iowa, correspond to the stars in the Big Dipper. At Cahokia, Missouri, where 120 earthen mounds formed a large village, a circle of cedar posts marked sunrise solstices and the equinox. Archaeologists have nicknamed the reconstructed site Woodhenge, after Stonehenge.

Stars had sacred meanings to the Skidi Pawnee, who lived in the river valleys and plains of Nebraska. This band arranged their villages in the pattern of the North Star, evening star, and morning star. They arranged the posts of their earthen lodges in the same pattern, so each home repeated the cosmic arrangement. A painted hide at the Field Museum in Chicago records the Milky Way and many Pawnee constellations.

Ancient Anasazi sites in the Southwest still show the yearly cycle of the sun. A stone house at Hovenweep, Utah, has ports through which sunlight enters during the solstices and equinox. Stars were important to the nomadic Navajos. Their creation account describes how Black God made stars from crystals. He placed constellations in the sky, including First Big One (Scorpio), Revolving Male (Ursa Major), Revolving Female (part of Ursa Minor), Slender First One (in Orion), Rabbit Tracks (near Canis Major), and the Pleiades. Star charts on cave roofs had ceremonial importance.

Denise Low

Sources for Further Study

Bol, Marsha C., ed. *Stars Above, Earth Below: American Indians and Nature*. Boulder, Colo.: Roberts Rinehart, 2000.

Miller, Dorcas S. *Stars of the First People: Native American Star Myths and Constellations*. Boulder, Colo.: Pruett, 1997.

See also: Mathematics; Mayan Civilization; Medicine Wheels; Mounds and Moundbuilders.

Atlatl

Tribes affected: Pantribal
Significance: *The atlatl was an ancient and widespread hunting and warfare weapon throughout the Americas.*

The term "atlatl," applied to many versions of the implement, is derived from Nahuatl, the language spoken by the Aztecs of sixteenth century central Mexico. Synonymous terms include spear thrower and dart thrower. Originating from Old World prototypes and brought to the New World by the earliest paleolithic inhabitants, it was gradually replaced by the bow and arrow as the preferred hunting weapon throughout the Americas by 1100 C.E., except in central Mexico, where the Aztecs still used it along with other weapons in the sixteenth century.

The atlatl was a straight or slightly curved wooden stick averaging 24 inches in length. One end was notched and wrapped with hide for a handle, and the opposite end bore a hook or barb. Different versions included loops for finger holes. While the user gripped the handle, the feathered end of a long dart or spear was mounted against the barb, and the dart was hurled overhand in slingshot fashion, significantly increasing its range and power. Small stones were sometimes attached to the atlatl as weights and balances to increase efficiency. In South America, Moche atlatls were elaborately decorated with painted and carved designs.

Atlatl imagery held great symbolic importance, particularly for warrior cults and hunting societies. Atlatls appear frequently in pre-Columbian paintings and in ceramics and relief sculpture from the United States, central and western Mexico, the Maya area, and Peru. In the American Southwest, atlatl depictions are common in rock art, and actual atlatls were frequently included in Anasazi burials. In the Eastern Woodlands, the atlatl weights, called banner stones, were frequently carved in the form of animals from brightly colored stone. Maya and central Mexican artists frequently depicted ruling elites proudly displaying atlatls as signs of military and social status.

James D. Farmer

Source for Further Study
Taylor, Colin F. *Native American Weapons*. Norman: University of Oklahoma Press, 2001.

See also: Banner Stones; Hunting and Gathering; Lances and Spears; Projectile Points; Weapons.

Aztec Empire

Significance: *The greatest flowering of Mesoamerican culture, a militaristic civilization that stretched from Pacific to Atlantic.*

Legend records that the Nahuatl-speaking Aztecs (or, more accurately, the Culhua Mexica) founded the city of Tenochtitlán in 1325 on a small island in Lake Texcoco (the site of modern Mexico City) and a century later emerged as the last great imperial power of indigenous Mesoamerica. Aztec civilization evolved from the legacy of earlier Mesoamerican groups, especially the Teotihuacán and Tula cultures. A widespread commercial network linked Tenochtitlán with the Maya to the south and extended as far north as what is now the southwestern United States. Through strategic alliances, intimidation, and conquest, the Aztecs dominated central Mexico until the Aztec Empire fell victim to Hernán Cortés and his band of Spanish conquistadores and indigenous allies in 1519-1521.

According to their religious myths, the Mexica wandered southward into the valley of central Mexico, guided by their tribal god, Huitzilopochtli. Along the way, Huitzilopochtli's priests began the rite of tearing palpitating hearts from the chests of sacrificial victims. They eventually reached Lake Texcoco and encountered peoples whose culture was more advanced. In fact, these sedentary peoples despised the Mexica as primitive barbarians, but found them useful as mercenaries. Clashes with the city of Culhuacán forced the Mexica to take refuge in a marshy area of the lake, where they founded Tenochtitlán.

Early Aztec society in Tenochtitlán seems to have been egalitarian, based on clans (*calpulli*) that controlled access to agricultural land. As the city grew, however, the *calpulli* lost importance. The Mexica chose their first supreme ruler (*tlatoani*), Acamapichtli, who ruled from 1372 to 1391. Class divisions emerged, and nobles (*pipiltin*) dominated military leadership and monopolized access to the *calmecac* (a school where priests and pictorial writers were trained). Mexica rulers married into the royal families of Culhuacán and Azcapotzalco. Until the early fifteenth century, the Aztecs were subject to Azcapotzalco, which had a small empire around Lake Texcoco. Meanwhile, they expanded Tenochtitlán, providing it with drinking water and constructing *chinampas* ("floating gardens") to help feed the city. Around 1428, under the leadership of Itzcóatl, they joined with the cities of Texcoco and Tlacopan and defeated Azcapotzalco. After this victory, the Aztecs embarked on their own imperial quest, subordinating their two allies. On Itzcóatl's orders, Aztecs burned the recorded myths and history of the conquered peoples and imposed an official Aztec version of the past.

As lands around the lake fell to Aztec power, the state distributed them to the *pipiltin* and the most distinguished warriors. Expansion thus created a gulf between the elite and the commoners. Earlier, most Mexica were peasants (*macehualtin*), who shared the clan's communal lands. As the Aztec population grew, however, clans no longer possessed enough land to meet their needs. Dependent agricultural laborers (*mayeques*) and slaves became more prevalent, as noble estates proliferated and conquered peoples were incorporated into Aztec society.

Area of the Aztec Empire

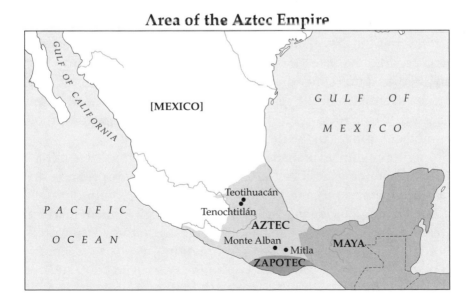

The Aztec Empire stretched from the northern deserts to the strait of Tehuantepec and from the Gulf of Mexico to the Pacific Ocean. Some cities and villages succumbed to Aztec intimidation; others sought to become subordinate allies; some had to be conquered through military force. Only the Tarascans of Michoacán and the Tlaxcalans of Puebla escaped domination. The Aztec Empire was a hegemonic one. The Aztecs allowed the conquered to retain their lands and political leaders, as long as they obeyed imperial decrees and paid tribute. Imperial armies did not occupy conquered territories but exacted harsh vengeance on rebellious cities.

All men in Tenochtitlán were expected to be warriors. From infancy, boys received the physical markings and the training essential to warriors. Each *calpulli* had its young men's house (*telpochcalli*), where warriors taught the military arts. Society accorded great honors and rewards to those who distinguished themselves on the battlefield by capturing valiant enemy warriors. Public humiliation awaited those who showed cowardice on the battlefield.

Other social groups supported these military endeavors. Merchants (*pochteca*) carried out a far-flung trade but also served as spies and intelligence gatherers. At times, they may have purposely provoked hostilities with nonsubject peoples. Priests marched at the head of the army. Girls were raised to be mothers, to bear the next generation of warriors. A woman who died in childbirth had an afterlife status similar to the warrior who perished in battle or on the sacrificial slab. Even the lowliest members of society, the *tamemes* (carriers), served the military cause, transporting food and other supplies to the field of battle.

Environmental explanations have been given for Aztec militarism and human sacrifice (for example, population pressure demanded expansion; cannibalism derived from a protein-deficient diet), but religious ideology played a critical role. Human sacrifice was widespread in Mesoamerica, although not to the extreme practiced by the Mexica. The Aztecs' cosmogony was also Mesoamerican. It held that the earth passed through cycles of creation and destruction. Humanity thus lived in a world doomed to disaster that could be forestalled only by nourishing the gods with human blood. Without human blood, the sun might not rise and preserve humanity. Not only priests but also all people provided blood through ritual self-laceration. Fatalism pervaded Aztec life: One's destiny was determined at birth. It mattered little whether one nourished the gods through self-sacrifice or as the captive victim.

Aztec militarism and religion became increasingly intertwined. The Mexica continued to worship other Mesoamerican deities, such as Quetzalcóatl, Tlaloc, and Tezcatlilpoca, in bloody rituals, but they raised the cult of Huitzilopochtli to an imperial obsession. Wars brought captives to sacrifice. By the mid-1400's, the Mexica staged mock battles ("flowery wars") with rival cities so that both sides could take captives to sacrifice. In 1487, the Aztecs killed at least twenty thousand captives to appease Huitzilopochtli at the dedication of the enlarged Great Temple.

When Moctezuma (or Montezuma) II became *tlatoani* in 1502, Aztec power was at its peak. Tenochtitlán had grown to 150,000 in-habitants, with perhaps 1.5 million living around Lake Texcoco. Social tensions were increasing, because commoners gained little material benefit from the conquests. To enhance his power, Moc-tezuma II claimed to be the incarnation of Huitzilopochtli, creating the ultimate marriage of Aztec militarism and religion.

Moctezuma II proved surprisingly ill-suited to deal with the crisis provoked by the Spaniards' arrival in 1519. More the medita-tive priest than the frenzied warrior, he vacillated, wondering if the strangers were Quetzalcóatl returning, as had long been prophesied. Spanish weapons and horses were superior to Aztec missiles and obsidian-edged swords. Hernán Cortés acquired im-portant indigenous allies by playing upon their hatred of the Az-tecs. Moctezuma II allowed the Spaniards to enter Tenochtitlán, whereupon they took him hostage. He died while in their hands in 1520. The warlike Cuitlahuac replaced him as *tlatoani* but perished from smallpox a few months later. Driven from Tenochtitlán in a bloody rout in June, 1520, the Spaniards and their allies returned in 1521. Their siege destroyed most of the city, and the invaders cap-tured the last *tlatoani*, Cuauhtémoc, as he tried to escape.

The Aztec legacy has provoked controversy. Rival indigenous peoples hated the Mexicas' bloody imperialism, and their human sacrifices and cannibalism horrified the Spaniards. Yet the Spanish invasion brought a demographic holocaust caused by Old World diseases (the empire's population probably declined by 90 percent) and a new oppressive colonialism. Aztec civilization produced a vibrant commerce, an elaborate belief system, and exquisite poetry. The Spaniards compared the splendors of Tenochtitlán to those of Venice, and conquistador Bernal Díaz del Castillo reported that it "seemed like an enchanted vision from the tale of Amadis." Rarely has a culture provoked such contradictory images.

Kendall W. Brown

Sources for Further Study

Berdan, Frances E. *The Aztecs of Central Mexico: An Imperial Society.* New York: Holt, Rinehart and Winston, 1982. A brief overview of Aztec society, religion, and politics.

Broda, Johanna, David Carrasco, and Eduardo Matos Moctezuma. *The Great Temple of Tenochtitlan: Center and Periphery in the Aztec World.* Berkeley: University of California Press, 1987. Interprets the meaning of the Great Temple in Aztec life, emphasizing religion's role as a catalyst for Aztec militarism and human sacrifice.

Clendinnen, Inga. *Aztecs: An Interpretation.* New York: Cambridge University Press, 1991. A sensitive interpretation of Aztec religion and society as a context for understanding the Aztec's reaction to the Spanish invasion.

Coe, Michael D., and Rex Koontz. *Mexico: From the Olmecs to the Aztecs.* 5th ed. New York: Thames & Hudson, 2002. An exhaustive introduction on Mexico's early history and peoples.

Díaz del Castillo, Bernal. *The Conquest of New Spain.* Translated by J. M. Cohen. London: Penguin Books, 1963. The famous narrative by one of Cortés' men.

Hassig, Ross. *Aztec Warfare: Imperial Expansion and Political Control.* Norman: University of Oklahoma Press, 1988. Excessively downplays religious ideology's role in Aztec warfare, but provides useful insights regarding the logistics of expansion.

Sahagún, Bernardino de. *General History of the Things of New Spain: The Florentine Codex.* Translated by Arthur J. O. Anderson and Charles E. Dibble. 13 vols. Santa Fe: School of American Research, 1950-1982. Ethnographic compilation about the religion, politics, society, flora, and fauna of pre-Hispanic Mexico, as reported by indigenous sixteenth century informants.

Smith, Michael Ernest. *The Aztecs.* 2d ed. Malden, Mass.: Blackwell, 2003. An analysis of the cultural, political, and social customs of the Aztec people. The Aztec approach to economics, government, religion, and science, as well as an analysis of the demise of the Aztec empire are also discussed in this informative work.

See also: Ball Game and Courts; Clans; Mathematics; Pochteca; Quetzalcóatl.

Ball Game and Courts

Tribes affected: Aztec, Maya, Olmec, Toltec
Significance: *The "ball game," or* tlachtli, *and the elaborate courts in which it was played constitute one of the most distinctive cultural phenomena of Mesoamerican cultures.*

Originating with the Olmecs ("rubber people") of Veracruz, the ball game was played in every major center as far north as modern Arizona and south to Honduras from 500 B.C.E.-1200 C.E.. The Mayan center of Chichén Itzá had seven courts, including the largest in Mexico—480 by 120 feet.

The I-shaped ball court was enclosed by high vertical or sloping walls on which spectators sat to watch players attempting to knock a solid rubber ball into the vertical stone ring in the center, a rare event which immediately determined the winner. The heavy ball could not be touched with the hands or feet—only knees, elbows, and hips—so players wore protective gloves, knee pads, helmets, and a thick leather belt around their hips. *Tlachtli* was probably a fierce game; injuries, and even death, seem to have been fairly common. In spite of its violence, the game was played with great enthusiasm.

In their recreational games, players from the ruling class made huge bets of their valuable clothing, prized feathers, gold, and even slaves. With such passion for gambling, one could begin the game a rich man and end it a pauper. Also, winners and spectators could claim garments and adornments of their opponents, so feather capes and gold jewelry were often confiscated. Ritual games had even more serious results: death to the losers or, in some cases, the winners. In a culture preoccupied with death, this ultimate sacrifice was the highest tribute one could pay.

The game had social, political, mythological, and religious significance. Mythological and religious meanings of the ball game were revealed during ritual play; the court represented earth, and the ball was the sun or moon. At the Mayan center of Copán, priests divined the future from results of ritual games. Among the Aztecs, chief deities were sky gods who constantly fought a battle between polarities of light and darkness, day and night. The sky was their sacred *tlachtli*, and a star was the ball.

Games were used symbolically to explain natural events. Drought and famine were supposedly the result of a legendary ball game between Huemac, last ruler of the Toltecs, and Tlaloc, the rain god. When Huemac won, Tlaloc offered corn as the prize, but Huemac refused it, demanding jade and feathers. Tlaloc gave them, telling Huemac that leaves of corn *were* precious green feathers and that green corn was more valuable than jade. Huemac got his jade and feathers, but the people starved because the corn would not grow.

Victory was sometimes fleeting, according to the story of Mexican emperor Axayacatl, who played against the lord of Xochimilco, betting his marketplace against this lord's elaborate garden. Axayacatl lost. The next day he sent his soldiers to the palace to honor the winning lord with presents. One gift was a garland of flowers which contained a rope. The soldiers placed it around Xochimilco's neck and strangled him.

Gale M. Thompson

See also: Aztec Empire; Games and Contests; Mayan Civilization; Olmec Civilization.

Banner Stones

Tribes affected: Prehistoric tribes of the Eastern Woodlands
Significance: *Banner stones were part of the technology for casting spears, though their beauty led early archaeologists to imagine them as emblems of chiefly office.*

Early archaeologists in eastern North America discovered a class of ground and polished stone artifacts that were unknown among historic American Indians. These "banner stones" varied widely in shape but shared several characteristics. They usually were made of visually appealing stone such as the banded slate of Hamilton County, Ohio, which was carefully ground and polished to a high luster. Averaging about 3 inches wide and 3 inches long, banner stones were always symmetrical and had a single hole passing through their length, about three-fourths of an inch in diameter. Sometimes found elsewhere, they often were found in graves.

Believing that their beauty had some meaning other than the technological, archaeologists invented the term "banner stone" to reflect their belief that they had been mounted on short handles and held as emblems of office by chiefs. That interpretation was abandoned in the twentieth century, when preserved wooden parts associated with banner stones were discovered. It then became obvious that they were spear-thrower ("atlatl") weights, designed to assist an individual in casting a spear with great power. Their primary period of use was between 1000 B.C.E. and 700 C.E.

Russell J. Barber

Sources for Further Study
Yeager, C. G. *Arrowheads and Stone Artifacts: A Practical Guide for the Amateur Archaeologist*. 2d ed. Boulder, Colo.: Pruett, 2000.

See also: Atlatl; Lances and Spears.

Baskets and Basketry

Tribes affected: Pantribal
Significance: *Basketry was one of the most important utilitarian crafts throughout native North America, and in some areas it was also an important art form.*

Basketmaking is one of the most characteristic crafts of Native American groups, and it is a craft that is considered a woman's activity by most groups. Early Native American people made baskets for thousands of years before ceramics were developed. Basketry techniques were used primarily to make containers, but they were also used for making other objects, ranging from hair brushes to clothes and canoe-like boats. Some early pottery seems to have been shaped around baskets and then fired. Among the historic tribes, the basketry of the West is more widely known than that of the eastern tribes. What is known of basketry today comes primarily from the last two hundred years, and many of the eastern traditions had been lost or significantly acculturated by the late 1700's.

Techniques. Twining and plaiting are related early techniques, while coiling is a later development. Twining is a process similar to weaving in which warp and weft strands are interwoven in various patterns, while plaiting is a simple process of passing a warp and weft alternately over and under each other. In contrast, coiling involves wrapping fibers into coils and stitching them together. To do coiling, a basketmaker gathers a group of fibers, probably grass stems, and wraps them with another long grass stem or yucca fiber. She then wraps the coil in on itself to form a spiral which is stitched together; another bunch of fibers is added and wrapped to lengthen the coil, and so on until the basket is formed. Since the fibers that form the coils are wrapped, a wider range of materials can be adapted to coiling than is the case with twining, and this may be the reason for its popularity. Groups of coils can be stacked one on top of the other, and sometimes two are bunched side by

Examples of Apache basketry from the late 1800's. *(National Archives)*

Known for their basketry skills, a Hopi woman weaving a basket at the beginning of the twentieth century. *(National Archives)*

side as they are stitched; this variation in technique is frequently associated with style differences.

Eastern Woodlands. Twining and plaiting were frequently used basket techniques in the East, and the basketry of this area was especially affected by the easy availability of wooden materials. Birchbark was popular for making basket-boxes among groups that lived across the northern sections of the United States in which the tree grew, and these baskets were frequently decorated with porcupine quills. The Micmac, Montaignais, Cree, and others worked with birchbark. Split-cane techniques were used by the Cherokee, Choctaw, and Chitimacha of the Southeast to make plaited baskets of wood splints, and this technique was borrowed by other tribes. The Cherokee were well known for baskets made of fine, even splints of cream, red, and black colors that were plaited to form interesting visual patterns. Along with more standard shapes, the Cherokee made an unusual shape in which a square base was transformed into a round, bowl-like upper half that was easy to carry as a burden basket.

Southwest. The best basketmakers of the Southwest have been the nomadic peoples living in arid, agriculturally marginal regions—the Apache, Paiute, Hualapai, Havasupai, Pima, and Tohono O'odham (Papago). The Navajo had stopped making baskets by the end of the nineteenth century and now buy baskets made in their own designs from the Paiute. Although the Pueblo peoples are basically pottery makers and produce little basketry, the Hopi are known for basketry. The most successful basketmakers in this region have been the Tohono O'odham, San Juan Paiute, Havasupai, and Hopi.

Twining, plaiting, and coiling are all common basketmaking techniques in the Southwest, but the latter is used most frequently. The basket forms include the tray and open bowl shapes, deep bowl shapes, closed-neck water bottles, conical burden baskets, and vase-shaped baskets. Designs are usually geometric or represent stylized figures. Recurring design motifs include petal designs, butterflies, star or cross, whirlwind, zig-zags, squash blossom, birds, and animal figures.

The most complex designs have been those of the Pima, and they use a complex layering of positive and negative images created by black and beige patterns. Although the Navajo have not been active in basketmaking since the nineteenth century, they are famous for the wedding basket design, which is a band of deep red lined with black triangles around the inside surface of a tray. The band is incomplete, so that a small opening or "door" is left. Traditional Apache baskets include elegant petal and zig-zag designs on open trays, but the most distinctive form is a large pot-shaped basket which may be 30 inches high and almost as broad in diameter.

Great Basin and Plateau. Basketry in this region was largely utilitarian, and it was used for a wide variety of purposes. Large burden baskets were made to be carried on the back for seeds, roots, and other gathered foodstuffs. Carrying bags were made by twining from grasses and other fibers. Winnowing trays and toasting trays were used in the preparation of food. Clothing, housing, and boats were also made using basketry techniques.

Pacific Coast. Some of the finest basketry in North America was produced in California by the Pomo, Tulare, Washo, and Karok. Baskets were made by both coiling and twining; the latter sometimes resulted in baskets of fine woven quality. They made trays, deep bowls, covered baskets, and vase forms and adorned special baskets with elaborate feather designs. The people of the Northwest Coast also made good baskets, but they were not equal to the complexity of their carved art.

Ronald J. Duncan

Sources for Further Study

Berlo, Janet Catherine. *Native North American Art*. New York: Oxford University Press, 1998.

Boxberger, Daniel L., ed. *Native North Americans: An Ethnohistorical Approach*. Dubuque, Iowa: Kendall/Hunt, 1990.

Coe, Ralph T. *Sacred Circles: Two Thousand Years of North American Indian Art*. Kansas City, Mo.: Nelson Gallery Foundation, 1977.

Feder, Norman. *American Indian Art*. New York: Harry N. Abrams, 1965.

Furst, Peter T., and Jill L. Furst. *North American Indian Art*. New York: Rizzoli International, 1982.

Whiteford, Andrew Hunter. *Southwestern Indian Baskets: Their History and Their Makers*. Santa Fe, N.Mex.: School of American Research Press, 1988.

See also: Arts and Crafts: California; Arts and Crafts: Great Basin; Arts and Crafts: Northeast; Arts and Crafts: Plateau; Arts and Crafts: Southeast; Arts and Crafts: Southwest.

Beads and Beadwork

Tribes affected: Pantribal

Significance: *Beadwork is one of the most distinctive decorative techniques used among Native Americans for clothing and other objects of personal and ritual use.*

Beadwork was a popular decorative technique before the arrival of the Europeans, and beads were traditionally made of shell, stone, bone, teeth, hoofs, and seeds. These were used to make necklaces, pendants, fringes, belts, and ornaments on clothing. Quillwork, a related decorative technique, was used in a similar way. Today beads and beadwork normally refer to the glass beads of European origin.

Historical Background. Although glass beads were traded with Native Americans during the eighteenth century, little is known about beadwork from that time. The production of traditional beads was difficult and slow, since each one had to be shaped by hand and then hand drilled. The imported glass beads were preferred because of their color and reflectiveness. About 1800 a large-sized bead made in Venice became available, and beaded artifacts using this type of bead represent the oldest examples of beadwork in collections today. This bead was referred to as the "pony bead" because it was brought by traders on pony pack teams. These beads were one-eighth inch in diameter, and they came in white, sky blue, dark blue, light red, dark red, and beige. They were used to make bands of decoration for clothing, bags, cradles, and moccasins.

About 1840 the smaller "seed bead" that is used today became available; it, too, was made of Venetian glass. It was half the size of the earlier beads and permitted making more delicate designs. Since these beads were partly made by hand, they could be slightly irregular in size and shape. In the 1840's and 1850's they were used to make bands of decoration similar to those made with pony beads.

By 1860 beads were more commonly available, and their smaller size permitted the introduction of a new all-over pattern of beadwork. Indians beaded clothing, bags, horse trappings, and ceremonial objects, among other things. During this period Czechoslovakian (Bohemian) glass beads were introduced; they are darker and more bluish. By 1870 translucent beads had become available, and by the mid-1880's silver- and gold-colored beads were traded. French and British manufacturers also entered the trade, and a wide variety of colors and sizes were available. In the twentieth century the production of beadwork became much more commercialized. Japanese beads entered the market, as did inexpensive Japanese and Chinese reproductions of Native American designs.

Culture Areas. Beadwork has been done in most culture areas. The French fur traders introduced trade beads to the tribes of the Northeast Woodlands in the seventeenth century. The beadwork

A Havasupai girl wearing a beaded necklace. *(National Archives)*

that was to become distinctive of this area displayed the foliate patterns of the Algonquian (Potawatomi, Sauk and Fox, Kickapoo) and Chippewa groups of the western Great Lakes region. The beadwork of the southeastern tribes (especially Creek and Seminole) is related to the floral patterns of the Northeast but is less ordered and symmetrical than that of the north. Plains beadwork has the most complex, detailed patterns, some made with thousands of beads. There is a division between the northern Plains style, which tends to be conservative, and the bolder, more individualized Southern Plains style. Beadwork in the Southwest, Great Basin, and Plateau is usually done by tribes that have had contact with the Plains groups and have borrowed designs from them. In these latter three areas, beading tends to be limited to small-scale work.

Designs. Both geometric and floral designs are given names by the people who use them, and within each culture there is a repertoire of recognized design elements and full design patterns. The fact that the designs were given names has led many students of design to assume they also had symbolic significance. It seems, however, that a given design motif may have been used with a decorative intent by some beadworkers and with symbolic intent by others. Some foliate designs of the western Great Lakes region seem to have represented local flora, perhaps some used for medicinal purposes. Others may have been copied from print designs on manufactured cloth or the designs of vestments of priests. The geometric motifs of the Plains have names that refer to the natural world, such as eye, buffalo, wolves, eagle, turtle, butterfly, centipede, person, and buffalo track.

Techniques. Beads may be embroidered onto a cloth or skin backing, woven to form a beaded band independent of the backing, or attached to fringes. Two basic embroidery stitches are used, the spot stitch and the lazy stitch. The spot, or overlay, stitch means that a beaded thread is attached to the backing by a second thread sewn in an over-and-under stitching pattern. In finely sewn work the overlapping stitch which holds the beaded thread to the backing may come every second, third, or fourth bead. This is especially used with floral designs and curving lines among the Chippewa, Algonquian, and some northern Plains groups.

In contrast, the lazy stitch is used more for overall designs that include straight lines and geometric patterns, and it is used more by the Western Sioux, Cheyenne, Arapaho, Crow, and Kiowa. In this stitching pattern, the thread that carries the beads is itself stitched into the backing, with five or six beads added to the thread between each stitch.

Bead weaving is used to make headbands, armbands, legbands, or belts that do not have backing material. Band weaving is easier and faster than the stitching techniques, but it requires a weaving frame. The warp, or base threads, are wrapped onto the frame, and the weft with beads is woven into it. This technique lends itself best to straight-line geometric shapes; floral designs must be stylized to adapt to it.

Ronald J. Duncan

Sources for Further Study

Coe, Ralph T. *Sacred Circles: Two Thousand Years of North American Indian Art*. Kansas City, Mo.: Nelson Gallery Foundation, 1977.

Dubin, Lois Sherr. *North American Indian Jewelry and Adornment: From Prehistory to the Present*. New York: Henry N. Abrams, 1999.

Furst, Peter T., and Jill L. Furst. *North American Indian Art*. New York: Rizzoli International, 1982.

Lyford, Carrie. *Quill and Beadwork of the Western Sioux*. Edited by Willard W. Beatty. Boulder, Colo.: Johnson, 1979.

Penney, David W. *Art of the American Indian Frontier*. Seattle: University of Washington Press, 1992.

Whiteford, Andrew Hunter. "The Origins of Great Lakes Beaded Bandolier Bags." *American Indian Art Magazine* 2, no. 3 (1986): 32-43.

See also: Arts and Crafts: Northeast; Arts and Crafts: Plains; Dress and Adornment; Quillwork.

Beans

Tribes affected: Pantribal
Significance: *Beans were a significant source of nutrition for agricultural tribes in Mesoamerica, Peru, and North America.*

While fava beans and a few other bean species were domesticated in the Old World, most beans are American. Four major species were domesticated and used by Indians in pre-Columbian times. Common beans (*Phaseolus vulgaris*) are highly variable, including pinto, kidney, navy, black, and many other varieties. This bean was domesticated by 5000 B.C.E. in Mexico and was the most commonly used bean in most parts of the Americas; it was the only bean in most of North America. Tepary beans (*Phaseolus acutifolius*), a small species not used in modern commerce, were domesticated by 3000 B.C.E. in Mexico and used in the American Southwest and western Mexico. Lima beans (*Phaseolus lunatus*) were domesticated separately in Peru (3300 B.C.E.) and Central America (200 C.E.) and were used there and in Mexico. Runner beans (*Phaseolus coccineus*) were domesticated in Mexico by 200 B.C.E. and spread to Peru, Central America, and the American Southwest.

Beans were important for the nutrition of Indian agriculturalists, providing protein and lysine, a critical amino acid lacking in maize, the primary starchy staple. While diffusing to North America separately, beans, squash, and corn were grown together virtually everywhere that crops were cultivated.

Shucked and dried, beans could be stored for a full year and reconstituted by boiling, either with or without presoaking. Most tribes ate beans boiled and mashed, added to soups, or mixed with corn and other ingredients as succotash.

Russell J. Barber

See also: Agriculture; Corn; Food Preparation and Cooking; Squash; Subsistence.

Berdache

Tribes affected: Pantribal
Significance: *An anthropological term denoting the third gender status, which many tribes attributed to individuals who behaved and dressed like members of the opposite sex.*

Although varying widely in their content and elaboration, rules prescribing the behavior and goals for each of the sexes were a sociocultural universal among native North American peoples. From early childhood, Indian boys and girls learned through observation, imitation, and formal training those statuses and roles that their communities deemed proper for the respective genders, so that by the time they reached adulthood most willingly accepted them as major parts of their social identities. However, both

A Zuñi man from the late 1800's dressed as a woman, weaving a belt. *(National Archives)*

ethnohistorical literature and tribal oral traditions provide ample evidence that individuals within many Indian societies veered away from typified gender patterns, assuming modes of behavior and dress generally associated with the opposite sex. Anthropologists and ethnohistorians have commonly employed the term "berdache" (taken from the Persian word *bardaj* and variably translated as "kept boy" or "male prostitute") as a cross-cultural category for males leading such lives. In this regard, it is important to note that because of the gender bias that long characterized anthropological studies, there exists no parallel classification for transgender females.

In many ways the pejorative roots and meanings of the word "berdache" render its application to many Indian communities problematic. Rather than deeming the latter as deviants or misfits, numerous tribes instead ascribed them a third-gender status, frequently attributing their nature and proclivities to spiritual causes. In accord with this spiritual understanding, such individuals were often considered to possess extraordinary sacred power that could be directed toward socially beneficial ends. On the other hand, their assumed spiritual prowess sometimes rendered third gender persons objects of suspicion and fear.

In a collection on Indian gay and lesbian issues, editors Sue Ellen Jacobs, Wesley Thomas, and Sabine Lang, have reported that a number of American Indians and anthropologists consider the term "berdache" demeaning and have suggested that the term "two-spirit persons" be used in its place. They also critique the tendency of some current scholarship to romanticize supposedly "positively sanctioned Pan-Indian gender or sexual categories." Such an idealization, they state, does "not fit the reality of experiences faced by many contemporary gay, lesbian, third-gender, transgender and otherwise Native Americans who have had to leave their reservations or other communities because of the effects of homophobia."

Harvey Markowitz

Sources for Further Study

Jacobs, Sue Ellen, Wesley Thomas, and Sabine Lang. *Two-Spirit People: Native American Gender Identity, Sexuality, and Spirituality.* Urbana: University of Illinois Press, 1997.

Williams, Walter. *The Spirit and the Flesh: Sexual Diversity in American Indian Culture.* Boston: Beacon Press, 1986.

See also: Ethnophilosophy and Worldview; Gender Relations and Roles; Societies: Non-kin-based.

Birchbark

Tribes affected: Tribes throughout the Northeast and Great Lakes areas

Significance: *Birchbark served a wide variety of purposes for the northeastern and boreal Indians, from roofing material to the covering of canoes.*

The image of figures gliding silently along a river in a birchbark canoe, as depicted in thousands of stories and films, is one of the most common images people throughout the world have of American Indians. Indeed, in the Northeast and Great Lakes regions, birchbark canoes were widely used both for personal travel and for transporting goods. The canoes were made by first fashioning a framework of cedar, comprising the keel and the ribs; over this framework, sheets of birchbark, stripped from the trees in seven-foot-long sheets, were stretched tight and bound together with cordage made from the inner bark of the basswood tree. Pitch from evergreens was used to caulk the seams to make the canoe watertight.

Birchbark canoes were highly maneuverable, though it took some skill to navigate them. Because they were so light in weight, a single person could carry one over a portage. They were so ideal for use in northern waters that they were adopted by the French fur traders for use throughout Canada.

Birchbark was also used to cover the tipis of the Algonquian tribes. Four basic framing poles were connected together, and additional "leaner" poles were positioned around them. The whole was covered with sheets of birchbark. Among the tribes that constructed longhouses, birchbark was used, along with elm bark, for the roofing material.

Birchbark was used by northeastern Indians to make a wide variety of containers. Before pottery, cooking pots were made of birchbark. The contents were heated by dropping hot stones into the mixture. Birchbark containers were used by many tribes as tubs to hold dried food to be set aside for use during the winter; sometimes these tubs were buried in underground pits to protect the contents from freezing. The Indians of Maine used small birchbark pouches to carry tobacco; drinking cups were also made of birchbark.

The Iroquois were in the habit of steeping birchbark in boiling water to make a popular drink with medicinal qualities. Birchbark could be fashioned into a kind of whistle that served as a moose caller. It was also used to make floats for fishnets. The Indians of the northern Great Lakes region used birchbark to make fans. These were used to winnow the wild rice they harvested from the swamps. Feathers were attached to the sheets of bark to stir the air. A personal fan could be made by attaching a stick, as a handle, to a piece of birchbark.

In order to ensure a steady supply of birchbark, the Indians would have needed to clear areas and burn the brush, for the birch is a shade-intolerant tree and will only grow in the open sunlight. It is, however, able to tolerate soils that have modest nutritional capabilities. The fact that the Indians could make such great use of birchbark says much about their environmental management. The range of the paper birch extends from the Atlantic Ocean to the Great Bear Lake in western Canada.

Nancy M. Gordon

See also: Boats and Watercraft; Longhouse; Tipi; Transportation Modes.

Black Drink

Tribes affected: Southeast tribes
Significance: *Black Drink was the main ceremonial beverage of Southeastern Indian tribes.*

Black Drink was a ritual beverage consumed by many Southeast tribes before and during important occasions such as certain council meetings. It was called "Black Drink" by the Europeans because of its color, but Indians called it "White Drink," referring to its purity and medicinal properties. Consuming the drink purified men of any pollution, made them hospitable, and served as "symbolic social cement."

Black Drink was made of holly leaves and twigs gathered along the Atlantic and Gulf coasts. Inland tribes traded for the holly plants and transplanted them. Some tribes, for example the Seminole, combined the holly with other medicinal herbs. To prepare Black Drink, the holly plant was dried and roasted in earthen pots to a parched brown. The roasted leaves and twigs were then boiled in water until the liquid was dark brown. It then was strained and generally consumed hot and fresh.

Black Drink was a stimulant, with one cup containing as much caffeine as eighteen to twenty-four cups of coffee. It was also a diuretic and brought on profuse sweating. If an important man in the tribe died, friends would consume Black Drink for eight successive mornings. A practice of the Timucuans was to consume large quantities and after about fifteen minutes cross their hands on their chests and vomit six to eight feet. The Chickasaw would place a little Black Drink into their ceremonial fire to provide social purification for all present.

David N. Mielke

See also: Mississippian Culture.

Black Hills

Tribes affected: Lakota and Teton Sioux
Significance: *The Black Hills have had both economic and spiritual significance to the Sioux; the U.S. Congress took the Black Hills with no compensation in 1877, violating an earlier treaty.*

The Black Hills are located in southwestern South Dakota along the Wyoming and Nebraska borders. Formed in the Pleistocene era, they form a remote ridge of limestone and granite 110 miles long, 40 miles wide, and 4,000 feet high. They provided a panoramic view of the vast prairie of buffalo grass below. The hills themselves were heavily wooded with dark pine and contained abundant animal and plant life as well as numerous springs and small lakes.

The Black Hills were reached in the late 1700's by the Sioux chief Standing Bull and his followers as the Sioux migrated westward. The Sioux called these hills *Paha Sapa* (Black Hills) because they were so heavily wooded with dark pine that from a distance they looked black. The Sioux had expelled the Kiowa from the area by 1814 and extended this border further west in the next few years.

The Black Hills acquired a special significance to the western Sioux and were perhaps the most loved area in the Sioux domain. They provided water and abundant food, lodgepoles for tipis, and medicinal plants for healing. The steep canyons provided protection from the severe winter weather.

Spiritually, the Black Hills were holy. They were the site of vision quests and the home of *Wakan Tanka*, the Great Spirit. According to legend, two-legged animals raced four-legged animals to see who would dominate the earth. The thunder-being proclaimed that the Black Hills were the heart of the earth and that the Sioux would come back some day and live there. The hills were seen as a reclining female figure whose breasts provided life-giving forces and to whom the Teton went as a young child would go to its mother.

White encroachment into Sioux territory led to war in the mid-nineteenth century. The Treaty of Fort Laramie in 1868 ended this war and created the permanent Great Sioux reservation, of which the Black Hills formed a part. The pressures of white settlement and the discovery of gold in the Black Hills, however, led the government to try to purchase or lease them. The Sioux refused. In 1877 Congress ratified the Manypenny Agreement, which took the Black Hills without compensation. This violation of the 1868 treaty was upheld in the 1903 Supreme Court decision *Lone Wolf v. Hitchcock*. In 1911 the Sioux began what was to become a protracted legal process to regain the Black Hills. In 1980 the Supreme Court affirmed a 1979 Court of Claims ruling that the Sioux were entitled to $106 million in compensation for the taking of the Black Hills. Various attempts to have the Black Hills returned to the Sioux, such as Senator Bill Bradley's land return legislation in 1985, have not succeeded.

Laurence Miller

See also: Land Claims.

Bladder Festival

Tribes affected: Yupik (Eskimo)
Significance: *As the major religious event of the traditional Yupik, the Bladder Festival not only expressed the cosmology of the Yupik but also reiterated the social and economic relationships between people and between humans and animals.*

The Bladder Festival, which occurred at the winter solstice, was perhaps the most elaborate and most important of the traditional Yupik religious festivals. Called *Nakaciuq*, meaning "something done with bladders" in the Yupik language, the annual festival consisted of gift giving, feasting, and ritual performances of songs and dances. The festival lasted five or six days, depending upon the community. It culminated with the return to the sea of the bladders of all the seals and walruses harvested in the previous year. In this respect, the Bladder Festival symbolized the close of one subsistence cycle and the start of the next. It was last celebrated in the early part of the twentieth century.

Like other Arctic peoples, the Yupik believed that future hunting success depended upon a hunter's respectful attitude toward the caught game. The Yupik believed that each animal possessed a soul, or *Inua*, that resided in its bladder. These Inuas were finite in number and in order for future seals and other sea mammals to be caught, the Inuas of previously harvested animals must be returned to the sea. Furthermore, the Yupik believed that the game animals whose souls were well treated by humans would willingly give themselves up again to those humans. Good treatment was evidenced by the observance of hunting rituals, the careful and aesthetic use of the animal's pelt, and the public honoring of the animal at celebrations such as the Bladder Festival.

In the months and weeks leading up to the Bladder Festival, new songs were composed, new bowls, ladles, and buckets were carved, and new clothes were sewn. The semi-subterranean men's house, or *qasgiq*, which was the primary site of the festival, was cleaned and purified. Although most of the festival occurred in and around the men's house, everyone in the village—men, women, and children—participated. Each of the bladders was inflated, decorated, and displayed in the *qasgiq*. Ritual meals were served to the inflated bladders, and they, along with the human hosts, were entertained with songs and dances. At the conclusion of the festivities, each hunter removed the bladders of the animals he had killed through the smoke hole in the roof of the *qasgiq* and carried them to the ice. Once on the ice, he speared the bladders to deflate them and dropped them into a hole in the ocean ice. This was done in order to release the Inua and return it to the sea.

The themes of renewal and regeneration were pervasive throughout the festival. Most important was the recognition that human livelihoods were dependent upon maintaining respectful relationships with the natural and supernatural worlds. The Bladder Festival also provided an opportunity for hunters within a community to compare their abilities as providers. Since each man displayed all the bladders of the sea mammals he had harvested that year, each person's hunting success became common knowledge. Thus, the Bladder Festival provided opportunities for the reaffirmation of, or the reordering of, status among hunters.

Pamela R. Stern

See also: Dances and Dancing; Gifts and Gift Giving; Religion.

Blankets

Tribes affected: Pantribal
Significance: *American Indian trade blankets were manufactured by non-Indians and used as a commodity in trade dealings between the U.S. government and Native Americans.*

The earliest known use of European and English commercially made blankets in North America was in the fur trade with American Indians in the late seventeenth century. The use of the trade blanket as payment for treaties between the U.S. government and Native Americans began in 1776. Small manufacturers of blankets were established in the United States by the early 1800's. About the same time, trade stations were being established across the country for the nonprofit exchange of goods between the government and the Indians. By the 1820's, however, private businesses had replaced the government-controlled trade, and the trade blanket became a profit-making commodity. The market for trade blankets continued to expand with the opening of the West by the railroads, bringing more competition among manufacturers and a greater variety of colors and designs.

At the beginning of the twentieth century, there were five major U.S. manufacturers (one of which was Pendleton) that produced only trade blankets. By the end of the twentieth century, Pendleton was the only company still in business producing "trade" blankets.

The finely woven, double-faced blankets were used by Indians as clothing that provided both warmth and a means of expression.

Navajo blankets and rugs, woven on looms such as this, had become valuable trade and sale items by the late nineteenth century.

They replaced the use of robes made of animal hides by the Plains Indians and the hand-woven blankets of the Navajo; they were also used as highly valued gifts. Blankets conveyed different moods, depending on the style in which they were worn. They were thrown over the shoulder, belted at the waist, wrapped around the waist, or worn as a hooded robe. Blankets were also used as infant and child carriers, covers for the bed, and saddle blankets. The blankets also were a measure of wealth or status and could be used as statements of tribal unity or individual identity.

There were six general categories for design in trade blankets. These include the striped, banded, and nine-element designs used in chief's blankets, as well as center point, overall, and framed designs. Bright earth tones plus white, blue, and black were the predominant colors and were often woven into intricate design patterns. Design elements include motifs such as the cross, swastika, arrow, zig-zag, and banding that formed geometric patterns symbolizing mountains, paths, clouds, stars, birds, and the four cardinal directions. Some designs were believed to express stories and myths and were made for Indians by using Indian symbols and colors.

Trade blankets continue to be highly valued by Indians and non-Indians, both as collectibles and as usable blankets. They became known as "Indian blankets" long ago because American Indians made them a distinct part of their lives and cultures.

Diane C. Van Noord

Sources for Further Study

Coulter, Lane, ed. *Navajo Saddle Blankets: Textiles to Ride in the American West*. Santa Fe: Museum of New Mexico Press, 2002.

Friedman, Barry, with James H. Collins and Gary Diamond. *Chasing Rainbows: Collecting American Indian Trade and Camp Blankets*. Boston: Bullfinch Press, 2002.

See also: Chilkat Blankets; Dress and Adornment; Trade; Weaving.

Boarding and Residential Schools

Tribes affected: Pantribal

Significance: *Boarding schools for Indian youth were established by Europeans in the early days of contact, and these institutions resulted in negative consequences for Indian families, disconnection from education, and for some people psychological problems.*

The object of the Indian boarding schools was to separate Indian children from their parents in order to impart Euro-American values and culture. In 2003, Indian boarding continued to operate in the United States; Canada closed all such facilities in 1988.

Early Period. Many of the earliest treaties negotiated between Indian tribes and European nations during the colonial era contained provisions for education. Through this education system, native people expected to retain their own languages and traditions as well as to learn Euro-American ways. However, from the earliest days, the European (later Canadian and American) goal was to use the schools as tools to assimilate Indian youth. Early schools were run by churches that favored the boarding system because in separating Indian children from their families such institutions were able to extinguish tribal knowledge and languages and imprint children with Christian values. As early as 1568, Indian children from Georgia and Florida were placed in Jesuit schools in Cuba.

Government-Sponsored Schools. In 1802 the U.S. Congress appropriated funds to religious groups to establish schools, and in 1819 Congress increased the appropriation with passage of the Indian Civilization Fund Act. As a result, numerous schools, both boarding and day schools, were established by various denominations for the education of Indian youth. Students in these schools were taught basic skills in reading, writing, and mathematics, and emphasis was on vocational education.

In Canada, the government also was obliged, through treaty provisions, to develop schools for the education of Indian youth. The government deemed it more economical to develop and fund existing missionary schools than develop its own infrastructure, so the government contracted for educational services with the Anglican and Catholic Churches. In Canada there were two types of residential schools: Boarding schools, located on reservations, served students between eight and fourteen years old; industrial schools, located off reservations, admitted students up to fourteen years old. The industrial schools sought to prepare students for life off the reserves, and vocational education was a mainstay of the curriculum. Boarding schools were favored in the United States and Canada, because it was believed that they would be the most efficient means to accomplish assimilation.

In the United States, squabbling among Protestants and Catholics led to repeal of the Civilization Fund in 1873, and the federal government assumed a more direct role in operating Indian schools. Religious schools continued, but federal officials were convinced that they could develop schools and more efficiently accomplish assimilation. The federal government continued to endorse removal of children from their homes as the quickest way to achieve assimilation. Carlisle Indian School, the first federally operated boarding school, opened in 1879 with the goal of transforming the Indian into a patriotic American citizen. Indian education, whether sponsored by the United States government, religious organizations, or in partnership, was intended to strip Indian children of their language and culture and change them into mainstream Americans.

Schools in both Canada and the United States mandated English-only and emphasized the acquisition of basic skills in reading, writing, and arithmetic, along with industrial training. Many of these schools were supported by the manual labor of their students. At many schools students spent more time working than

A group of Sioux boys arriving at the Carlisle Indian School in 1879. *(National Archives)*

learning basic skills. Ultimately this became an issue in both Canada and the United States. After unfavorable publicity, both governments insisted on greater balance between basic skills and industrial education. Nonetheless, assimilation continued as the goal of Indian education in Canada and the United States.

Conditions in the school were difficult for the children. Poor health was a continuous problem in boarding schools, and discipline was harsh. Many students attempted to run away from the schools, and though parents often protested sending their children to the schools, they were arrested if they refused.

Reforms to Hasten Assimilation. Canadian residential schools came under attack in the early 1900's, because they were expensive, inefficient, and rife with health and physical and sexual abuse problems. In response, the government assumed more responsibility in running the schools. In 1927 compulsory attendance was strengthened, and on authority of the Indian agent, children could be committed to boarding schools and kept until age eighteen. Once they had completed their education, Indian youth were told they were not to return to their reserves.

In the United States the Meriam Report (1928), a scathing critique of federal Indian programs, was published. It labeled boarding schools as harmful institutions for children and condemned many aspects of Indian education, and as a result, school reforms were instituted. Many boarding schools closed, and children were sent to public schools or day schools located on their reservations. However, school reforms ended with the Great Depression and World War II. After World War II federal policies in Canada and the United States again sought to dissolve the trust relationship with tribes. In the 1950's, as a way to accomplish assimilation once and for all, the U.S. government reopened many off-reservation boarding schools. Similarly, in Canada, concerns surfaced about how to best accomplish assimilation so the government revised the Indian Act in 1951 and integrated Indian children into public schools. Often these children were boarded in government facilities.

Indian-Controlled Schools. In the 1960's and 1970's tribes began to insist that the school system for Indian children had to change, and they asserted their rights to manage the education of their children. American and Canadian Indians lobbied intensely to close boarding schools and put education in the hands of native people. In Canada and the United States a series of education acts permitted tribes to direct education and to enfold tribal languages and cultures into the curriculum. The last federal residential school closed in Canada in 1988. Many boarding schools in the United States closed during the 1970's and 1980's, and those that remain open provide specialized services such as foster care and developmental education to small numbers of youth. The goal is no longer to assimilate but to educate and instill a sense of pride and self-worth in the students. Boarding schools, once considered by both countries the optimal way to educate Indian children, have given way to innovative tribally controlled schools that underscore self-determination and sovereignty. Tribal languages, cultures, and histories are vital parts of the curriculum in these schools.

Carole A. Barrett

Sources for Further Study

Adams, David Wallace. *Education for Extinction: American Indians and the Boarding School Experience*. Lawrence: University of Kansas Press, 2000.

Archuleta, Margaret, ed. *Away from Home: American Indian Boarding School Experiences*. Santa Fe: Museum of New Mexico Press, 2000.

Child, Brenda. *Boarding School Seasons: American Indian Families, 1900-1940*. Lincoln: University of Nebraska Press, 1998.

Johnston, Basil. *Indian School Days*. Norman: University of Oklahoma Press, 1988.

Lomawaima, K. Tsianina. *They Called It Prairie Light: The Story of Chilocco Indian School*. Lincoln: University of Nebraska Press, 1994.

See also: Children; Education: Post-contact; Education: Pre-contact; Missions and Missionaries; Tribal Colleges.

Boats and Watercraft

Tribes affected: Widespread but not pantribal
Significance: *Many native peoples used watercraft for hunting and transportation.*

Native American watercraft generally fall into three basic types: dugout canoes, birchbark canoes, and kayaks. The word "canoe" is a general term that refers to many different types of light, narrow boats with pointed ends that are propelled by paddling. Christopher Columbus first recorded the word *canáoa*, which was used by natives in the West Indies to describe their dugout boats.

Canoes. Because of their heavy weight and the difficulty of overland transport, dugout canoes were primarily used by more stationary tribes or by those who fished or navigated on the oceans and thus needed a very strong craft. The Tlingit, for example, who lived in the area of present-day southeastern Alaska along the Pacific coast, constructed canoes for fishing and coastal voyages out of large red cedar trees, which they felled by building a fire at each tree's base. They then hollowed out the log with a stone axe and sometimes added planks along the sides or fastened two canoes together, side by side, with spars made from sturdy branches for more stability in rough waters. Smaller canoes for two or three per-

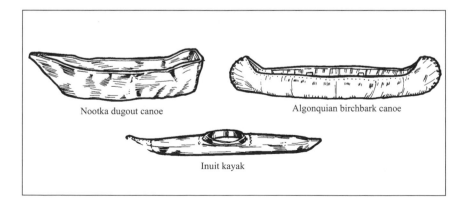

Nootka dugout canoe

Algonquian birchbark canoe

Inuit kayak

sons were fashioned from cottonwood logs and used for river travel and fishing. The larger oceangoing canoes could carry as many as sixty people and measured up to 45 feet in length. A dugout canoe on display in New York City's Museum of Natural History from Queen Charlotte's Island, off the coast of British Columbia, Canada, measures 63 feet long, 8 feet, 3 inches wide, and 5 feet deep; it was cut from a single log. Along the eastern coast of the United States, dugout canoes made from pine, oak, chestnut, or tulip wood were common. It took one man ten or twelve days to make a dugout canoe by lighting a small fire in the center of the log and then chopping out the charred wood with an axe. Dugout canoes were heavy but sturdy, and predominated in areas where birchbark was scarce.

The birchbark canoe was first used by the Algonquin Indians in what is now the northeastern United States and Canada, where birch trees were plentiful. They were extremely buoyant and sturdy, yet light enough to be carried over land, which made them particularly useful for exploration and trade and for hunting and trapping in smaller rivers. The early French missionaries, fur traders, and explorers in North America all used birchbark canoes, and the adoption of the bark canoe by European explorers is in large part responsible for the rapid exploration and development of the continent.

Indian birchbark canoes varied in length from 15 to almost 100 feet for canoes built to carry warriors. The Ojibwa (Chippewa), once one of the largest tribes north of Mexico, were master canoe makers. They would first outline the craft's shape by driving wood stakes into the ground; then thick, pliable sheets of birchbark were placed inside and fastened to wooden gunwales (the upper edge of the canoe). The frame was fortified with cedar ribs, and the bark was sewn with strings made from spruce roots. Finally, the seams were made watertight with sap from spruce trees. Other tribes substituted bark from elm, hickory, spruce, basswood, or chestnut when birch was unavailable, but barks other than birch absorbed water quickly. Often such canoes were built for limited use and then simply abandoned as they became waterlogged and heavy.

Eskimos often used umiaks to carry families and supplies. *(National Archives)*

Kayaks and Umiaks. One of the most significant achievements of the Eskimos (Inuits) was the invention of the kayak, which is perhaps the most seaworthy watercraft ever built. Most were about the size of a small canoe and were made from a frame of driftwood, saplings, or whalebone, over which sealskin was tightly stretched and made waterproof by rubbing it with animal fat. Kayaks were commonly built for one occupant but could be designed for two or three. They were first used as hunting boats for walrus and seals by the Eskimos of Greenland and later also used by Alaskan Eskimos. Some scholars suggest that the design of the birchbark canoes used by tribes in the more southerly areas of North America was adapted from the kayak.

The kayak is completely covered except for a hole in which the paddler sits, which the Eskimos made watertight by lacing their clothing over the rim of the hole. Since they were completely waterproof and highly maneuverable, kayaks could be launched in rough surf and navigated through ice-infested ocean waters that would quickly swamp an open boat. Since the paddler sat low in the center, kayaks were also useful in rivers with swift waters and rapids. Propelled by a double-bladed paddle, a capsized kayak could be righted by a skillful person without taking in any water by rolling full circle.

When pursuing seal or walrus, the hunter would lean forward, concealed behind a small sail-like blind attached to the bow. As he drew close, he would hurl a wooden spear attached to the boat by a line coiled in a tray on the deck.

The Eskimos also used a larger, open boat covered with animal skins called a "umiak," which is Eskimo for "woman's boat," as it was most often piloted by the women in the group. The umiak was used for carrying families and supplies and was propelled by both paddles and oars—the only known instance of the use of oars by Native Americans before the coming of the Europeans. Some of the Eskimo boats may also have been powered by sails; among the other native peoples of the American continents, only the Mayas of the Yucatán Peninsula and the natives of the coast of Peru were known to have used sails before the Europeans arrived. Most Eskimos today have replaced their kayaks with wood or aluminum boats, and their sails and paddles with outboard gasoline motors.

The modern descendants of Native American canoes and kayaks are made from wood, aluminum, canvas, or fiberglass, and are used for sport, recreation, or competition.

Raymond Frey

Sources for Further Study

Adney, Edwin Tappan, and Howard I. Chapelle. *The Bark Canoes and Skin Boats of North America*. Washington, D.C.: U.S. Government Printing Office, 1964.

McPhee, John. *The Survival of the Bark Canoe*. New York: Farrar, Straus, Giroux, 1975.

National Geographic Society. *National Geographic on Indians of the Americas*. Washington, D.C.: Author, 1955.

Oswalt, Wendell H. *This Land Was Theirs: A Study of North American Indians*. 5th ed. Mountain View, Calif.: Mayfield, 1996.

Weyer, Edward Moffat. *The Eskimos: Their Environment and Folkways*. New Haven, Conn.: Yale University Press, 1932.

See also: Birchbark; Transportation Modes.

Booger Dance

Tribe affected: Cherokee
Significance: *The Booger Dance is a major symbolic feature of Cherokee night dances.*

The term "booger," equivalent to "bogey" (ghost), is used by English-speaking Cherokee for any ghost or frightful animal. The Booger Dance originated among Eastern Mountain Cherokee as a way to portray European invaders as awkward, ridiculous, lewd, and menacing. The dance dramatizes hostility and disdain for white culture by mocking elements that cause cultural decay and defeat.

The dance is preceded by a ritual of divination. Should divination devices conclude that an illness was caused by "boogers" (bogeymen), the Booger Dance is then determined to be the means of relief. The dance is conducted to "scare away" the spirit causing the sickness. It is a masked dance, in which masks made from gourds are often garishly painted with hideous designs. The dance is not an independent rite but is a major symbolic feature of Cherokee night dances. Early forms of the Booger Dance were limited to winter performances, as killing frost and bitter cold were associ ated with ghosts. The dance then evolved during the nineteenth century to deal with the appearance of whites. Performed by four to ten men and sometimes two to four women, it incorporates profane, lewd, even obscene dramatic elements.

Glenn J. Schiffman

See also: Dances and Dancing; Medicine and Modes of Curing: Pre-contact.

Bows, Arrows, and Quivers

Tribes affected: Pantribal
Significance: *The bow and arrow was the most important missile weapon used by North American Indians.*

Archery was universal in native North America, and the bow and arrow was by far the most important missile weapon complex in use. The bow and arrow was of tremendous importance in hunting, which was vital to procuring the food supply in all parts of the continent. Archery was also essential in warfare, where it existed, and was rich in symbolism. The making of bows and arrows involved highly valued knowledge and skills. The materials from which archery tackle was made were often important in trade, as were the finished products. The design and scale of bows, arrows, and quivers varied regionally, as did the materials utilized. Both bows and arrows were made in proportion to the archer's body; the formulae used varied with the size of tackle desired.

Bows were of several types. Most common was a selfbow (a bow made of a single piece of wood with no laminating materials) of springy wood tapering toward both ends and sometimes narrowed at the grip. This bow type seems to be virtually the only one definitely recorded for the eastern United States, southeastern Canada, and most of Mexico. In the north and west, wooden bows and generally shorter bows of horn, antler, or bone were reinforced with sinew. In the Arctic, the sinew was commonly attached in the form of many strands of a slender cable laced to the back of the bow so that its tension could be adjusted to suit the archer. Elsewhere the sinew was applied directly to the back of the bow with glue and sometimes with lashings as well. An alternative bow type utilized sinew lashings to reinforce the bow but lacked the sinew backing. In general, bows were longer in the east. Bowstrings were made of sinew, plant fiber cordage, hide, or gut. Bracers were often simple hide straps, but other types were known as well.

Arrows were predominantly of wood, but reed- or cane-shafted arrows with wooden foreshafts into which points might be set were common in the western and southern United States and southward. Arrow points were of many types and were made of bone, antler, hardwood, and other materials as well as stone. Points and fletching were attached with lashings of sinew and sometimes with pitch or glue.

Quivers were generally narrow bags of animal skin that could be conveniently slung over the shoulder for ease in carrying. In the north and west, a common quiver type was a fur bag that sheltered

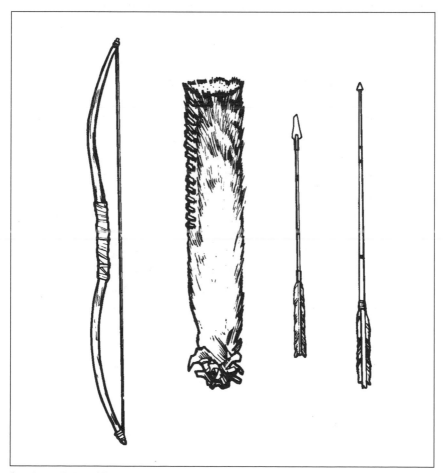

Southern Paiute (Great Basin) hardwood bow, animal skin quiver, and arrows; the left arrow is wooden with an iron point, the right is a cane arrow tipped with stone.

both the bow and its arrows from the weather. In the central United States and neighboring regions a separate case for the bow was sometimes attached to the quiver. Other quivers were simply arrow cases. Accessories, such as sinew and arrow points or a fire drill, were often carried in the quiver or in bags attached to it.

Boys commonly practiced archery from early childhood and began hunting small game while still very young. The bow and arrow was the constant companion of men of all ages. Native archery is said to have been deadly at a distance of fifty yards. The form employed in shooting varied both between and within tribes.

Michael G. Davis

Sources for Further Study

Allely, Steve, and Jim Hamm. *Encyclopedia of Native American Bows, Arrows, and Quivers*. New York: Lyons Press with Bois d'Arc Press, 1999.

Baker, Tim, et al. *The Traditional Boyer's Bible*, Volume 3. New York: The Lyons Press, 1994.

Francis, Leo, III. *Native Time: An Historical Time Line of Native America*. New York: St. Martin's Press, 1996.

Hamilton, T. M. *Native American Bows*. 2d ed. Columbia: Missouri Archaeological Society, 1982.

Harding, David, ed. *Weapons: An International Encyclopedia from 5000 B.C. to 2000 A.D.* New York: St. Martin's Press, 1980.

Laubin, Reginald. *American Indian Archery*. Norman: University of Oklahoma Press, 1980.

See also: Atlatl; Hunting and Gathering; Lances and Spears; Projectile Points; Tools; Warfare and Conflict; Weapons.

Bragskins

Tribes affected: Plains tribes

Significance: *Bragskins are a particular type of pictograph or "picture writing" kept by Plains Indian warriors and painted onto elk hides, buffalo robes, tipi covers and liners, and sometimes men's shirts. They were known as bragskins because a man preserved and recorded his individual exploits and attainments on the battlefield.*

The primary intent of a bragskin was to develop and preserve a personal narrative of accomplishments, particularly deeds connected with warfare. Typically bragskins were made up of a series of pictures which gave the full action of a single event in illustrative style. Taken as a whole, these autobiographical accounts preserved the record of the life of the people; they were conscious historic records which were seen by the people on a daily basis. They were also a constant pictorial reminder of the collective ideals of bravery and fortitude which underscored Plains Indian life.

Men swore that the events depicted on their bragskins were absolutely true and correct as presented. According to tradition, all deeds of bravery or achievement depicted on the bragskins had to have been witnessed by at least two other men who also swore to their veracity. Truthfulness and accuracy were insisted upon or a man would be exposed in public as a liar, and he would bring great dishonor on his family and relations.

Bragskins were more than mere decoration and artistic skill was a minor consideration; their importance lay in communicating facts to their people. The drawings usually consisted of only a few strokes—characters and objects were represented by drawing the single striking feature or characteristic of a person or object. So that they could be read easily by all members of their tribe, pictographic accounts utilized certain conventions. Usually, men represented themselves on their bragskins by drawing the lance, headdress, or some other feature to represent their warrior society; or they would depict the image painted on their shield, which was highly individualized. In this way, each man was the center of his own story and easily identifiable on his own bragskin. Each tribe had conventional ways of representing other tribes, and everyone in camp knew how to read their meaning. For example, in Lakota bragskins the Cheyenne were indicated by drawing hash marks across the arm, because in sign language the Lakota represented the Cheyenne by running the fingers horizontally across the lower arm. In another instance, the Lakota drew Crow men with a knot or bunch of hair at the front of their heads, because this represented that tribe's distinctive hairstyle.

At certain times of the year each men's warrior society would sponsor a feast for tribal members, and at those times, the society members would take out their bragskins and publicly recount their deeds and exploits in warfare. Recitation of war stories was an important way to transmit and model the virtues of fortitude and bravery to young boys and to the tribe in general. Bragskins provided a permanent record of these individual accomplishments in battle and reinforced the warrior ethic among the people.

Carole A. Barrett

See also: Petroglyphs; Pictographs; Shields; Symbolism in Art; Warfare and Conflict; Wintercounts.

Buffalo

Tribes affected: Plains tribes
Significance: *Until the nineteenth century, Plains tribes subsisted largely on the buffalo (or bison); by the 1870's, the combination of the fur trade and white hide hunters had nearly exterminated the herds, forcing Plains tribes to submit to the reservation system.*

From the end of the last Ice Age until the late nineteenth century, the American buffalo, also called the bison, was the dominant species in the Great Plains. While some estimates of the historic bison population have ranged as high as one hundred million, increasingly accurate assessments of the carrying capacity of the grasslands have suggested that the historic bison population in the Great Plains was not more than thirty million. Native Americans hunted bison on foot for thousands of years by surrounding a herd until the animals were within range of bows or by setting a fire to stampede a herd over a bluff.

Following the diffusion of horses into the Great Plains in the first half of the eighteenth century, a number of tribes—among them the Arapaho, Assiniboine, Atsina, Blackfeet Confederacy, Cheyenne, Comanche, Kiowa, Apache of Oklahoma (Kiowa-Apache), and Sioux—became almost exclusively nomadic, equestrian buffalo hunters. Others—among them the Arikara, Hidatsa, Mandan, and Pawnee—maintained their gardens in the river valleys of the Plains while adapting from pedestrian to equestrian buffalo hunting. The nomadic tribes adapted their social organization to the habits of the bison. They assembled as a tribe only during the summer, when the

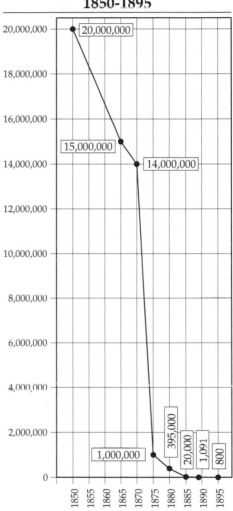

Buffalo Depletion from 1850-1895

Note: In the twentieth century the buffalo population began to rebound from its 1895 low of about 800; in 1983 it was estimated at 50,000.

Source: Data are from Thornton, Russell, *American Indian Holocaust and Survival: A Population History Since 1492* (Norman: University of Oklahoma Press, 1987); Thornton, Russell, *We Shall Live Again: The 1870 and 1890 Ghost Dance Movements as Demographic Revitalization* (New York: Cambridge University Press, 1986).

bison were congregated for the rutting season. During the rest of the year they were divided into bands, reflecting the actions of the herds, which divided to search for winter forage.

In response to the fur trade, Indian hunting of the buffalo accelerated during the nineteenth century. By the 1840's, the Plains Indians were providing between 150,000 and 200,000 buffalo robes each year to European American fur traders along the Missouri River. By the 1850's, Indian commercial hunting had markedly reduced the number of bison in the eastern Great Plains.

White hide hunters delivered the final blow to the herds in the 1870's and early 1880's. As many as two thousand buffalo hunters armed with large-caliber Sharps or Winchester rifles blanketed the southern Great Plains in the early 1870's. The hide hunters were extraordinarily destructive: In the early years of the slaughter, every hide shipped to market probably represented five dead bison. In the late 1870's, having largely extirpated the bison from the southern Great Plains, the hide hunters moved to the north, where they destroyed the remaining herds by 1883. By 1889, there were about a thousand of the animals remaining in remote areas of the Texas panhandle, Colorado, Montana, and Wyoming. Once the herds were destroyed, the Plains Indians were reduced to extreme poverty and had little alternative to the reservation system.

Andrew C. Isenberg

Sources for Further Study

Ewers, John Canfield. *Plains Indian History and Culture: Essays on Continuity and Change*. Foreword by William T. Hagan. Norman: University of Oklahoma Press, 1997.

Pickering, Robert B. *Seeing the White Buffalo*. Boulder, Colo.: Johnson Books, 1997.

See also: Buffalo Dance; Hides and Hidework; Horses; Pemmican; Subsistence; White Buffalo Society.

Buffalo Dance

Tribe affected: Mandan
Significance: *The Buffalo Dance and ceremony were meant to ensure an adequate supply of buffalo for the hunt.*

The Mandan, a hunting people of the northern Great Plains, performed the Buffalo Dance before the yearly hunt to ensure success. A special society, the Bull Dancers, wore buffalo head masks with eye and nose holes. The dancers carried buffalo hide shields and long lances. They had buffalo tails tied around their knees and danced until they fell to the ground from exhaustion. Then they were dragged away by other members of the tribe and symbolically skinned and butchered. According to Mandan tradition, the dance originated when a white buffalo took a shaman to the home of the "buffalo people" in the sky. Here he was taught the dance, and he brought it back to his people. As part of the dance cere-

A Buffalo Dance performed at Hano. *(E. S. Curtis/American Museum of Natural History)*

mony, Mandan women prepare two large kettles of corn meal mush—which buffaloes like very much—and set them out at the edge of the village. Women in the White Buffalo Calf Society then lure buffalo to the camp by putting on buffalo robes and dancing wildly. As the dance ends, the performers say a prayer to the gods thanking them for all they have provided and asking for their help in living as the gods wish. The dancers then eat the mush.

Buffalo dancing had stopped by 1900—the buffalo were gone, so there was no longer a reason to perform the dance. White reservation officials had already banned buffalo dancing because of its "pagan" nature. Only in the 1930's, with buffalo herds restored to a few areas of the Great Plains, was the dance performed again, though mostly for the benefit of tourists.

Leslie V. Tischauser

See also: Buffalo; Dances and Dancing; White Buffalo Society.

Bundles, Sacred

Tribes affected: Pantribal
Significance: *Sacred bundles contain objects that represent the power or medicine of their owner; assembled under the guidance of spirit beings, they are used in ceremonies to assure the well-being of an individual, clan, or tribe.*

Sacred bundles were believed to have supernatural power to cure the sick, win the affections of another, get revenge on an enemy, gain possessions, or even assure long life for an individual or a whole tribe. Wrapped in the hide of a deer or the whole skin of an otter, some tribal bundles were large enough to hold hundreds of items, while personal bundles were often small enough to carry in one hand. (Although the use of sacred bundles is treated as historical here to emphasize their great importance in many traditional American Indian cultures, it is important to note that many practices involving sacred bundles still occur today.)

Sacred bundles required special care. They were considered to be "alive" with supernatural power. Some personal bundles were displayed in the owner's lodge or hung outside the tipi, but the great tribal bundles were secluded from everyday view. Because of their magical quality they were surrounded with taboos. Bundles represented an important link with the past and supernatural beings and could be opened only under prescribed circumstances to benefit the person or the tribe.

Traditionally, a personal bundle was acquired through a vision quest. One went out alone for several days and fasted and prayed until the guardian spirit was encountered. A relationship was established and directions were given for the spiritual path of the seeker. Upon return from the quest, objects were gathered for the medicine bundle as symbols of the experience. An item representing the guardian spirit was usually worn to assure ongoing contact. The primary item in a medicine bundle symbolized the guardian spirit. Tobacco, feathers, fur, stones, or anything of special meaning could become part of the bundle. Often a song was given by the spirits as part of the seeker's medicine.

Something of the vision experience, such as a song, a painting on a shield, a dance, or the telling of a particular incident, was shared with the tribe. In this way others received some of the power that was available as long as requirements were met for keeping the bundle.

In some tribes a bundle could be inherited through the father's lineage, captured during a battle, purchased, or received in exchange for horses. A powerful bundle could be duplicated for one or two others with permission of the spirits. The owner could remake a bundle that was lost or taken in a fight. Unless the bundle, with its power, was willingly given to someone, it belonged to the owner until death.

Personal Bundles. Objects in a sacred bundle filled a definite purpose, either spiritual or practical. A large medicine-pipe bundle belonging to a member of the Blackfoot tribe, for example, contained a decorated pipe stem along with a tobacco cutting board and pipe stokers. Animal spirits were represented by an elk hide, bearskin, mountain-goat headdress, eagle-wing feather, head of a crane, skin of a loon (used as a tobacco pouch), fetus of a deer, and skins of prairie dog, squirrel, mink, muskrat, and owl. Other ceremonial tools were a rattle, a rawhide bag of roots for making smudge (sacred incense), a bag of pine needles, and tongs for placing coals on the smudge. Personal items included necklaces, a wooden bowl for food, a horse whip, a thong lariat, and a painted buffalo robe. A sacred song was also given by the spirits and was sung any time the bundle was displayed. In Blackfoot tradition, the pipe bundle could be opened on four occasions: when the first thunder was heard in the spring; when the bundle was being transferred to a new leader; when tobacco in the bundle was renewed; and when the pipe was used in keeping a vow.

Tribal Bundles. The great tribal bundles, such as the Blackfoot Sacred Pipe bundle or the Pawnee Evening Star bundle, were sometimes displayed at ceremonies, but they were opened only on special occasions. In some Plains tribes bundles were used to "keep the world together." The people believed that the tribe's well-being depended on the proper care and protection of those bundles because the items within them symbolized life itself. The Kiowas had a small stone image resembling a man that was shown to the people only once a year at the Sun Dance.

The Fox of the Great Lakes had forty sacred bundle groups in eleven major categories. For the Pawnee of the Plains, the stars were important in sacred traditions, and the Evening Star bundle was assembled under the direction of that highly revered star guardian. A Cheyenne bundle contained the four Medicine Arrows, and an Arapaho bundle held a special flat pipe, an ear of corn, and a stone turtle.

The summer Green Corn Dance was a time of cleansing and renewal for the Seminole of Florida and Oklahoma. Meeting at sacred places in woods and near creeks, they danced and recited oral history to honor their mystical origin. Just before dawn on the fourth day, the sacred bundle was blessed and opened. Nearly seven hundred items wrapped in buckskin or white cloth contained sacred knowledge and medicine for the health of the tribe. The Seminole believed that this renewal of the sacred bundle assured that the people would not die and the tribe would not disappear.

The power within sacred bundles was regarded with wonder, respect, and sometimes fear. The sacred practitioners who worked with this secret and often dangerous knowledge learned by experimenting with natural forces after much ritual preparation. An untrained person would resist contact with this potent knowledge because, as one individual put it, "the power might come back at me if I exposed myself to it when I was not prepared, or not ready to know about it"; another said, "I wouldn't want to go near those medicine bundles if I didn't know how to act."

Gale M. Thompson

Sources for Further Study

Beck, Peggy V., Anna Lee Walters, and Nia Francisco. *The Sacred: Ways of Knowledge, Sources of Life.* Redesigned ed. Tsaile, Ariz.: Navajo Community College Press, 1992.

Brown, Joseph Epes. *The Spiritual Legacy of the American Indian.* New York: Crossroad, 1982.

Garbarino, Merwyn S. *Native American Heritage.* Boston: Little, Brown, 1976.

Radin, Paul. *The Story of the American Indian.* Deluxe illustrated ed. Garden City, N.Y.: Garden City Publishing, 1937.

Underhill, Ruth Murray. *Red Man's America: A History of Indians in the United States.* Chicago: University of Chicago Press, 1953.

See also: Calumets and Pipe Bags; Ethnophilosophy and Worldview; Green Corn Dance; Guardian Spirits; Medicine Bundles; Religion; Sacred, the; Visions and Vision Quests.

Cacique

Tribes affected: Tribes of Spanish America
Significance: *Originally a term applied to Caribbean tribal chiefs, "cacique" was adopted by the Eastern Pueblo peoples, to whom it designates a religious-secular office.*

In the Caribbean, the Spanish encountered Arawak Indians who applied the term "cacique" to their chiefs. The Spanish subsequently used the term to designate leaders with varying degrees of authority. Among North American Indians, the term has been adopted only by the Eastern Pueblo tribes along the Rio Grande of New Mexico. There, it refers to the male religious-secular leader of a community. The Puebloan cacique is probably an outgrowth of a native office, namely the peace leader of the community, whose title and duties were modified by the Spanish. The modern cacique serves as a representative of the pueblo as a whole and is said to have the duty of "looking after the people." This entails presiding at various religious ceremonies, allocating certain rights to agricultural fields, representing the pueblo in dealings with outsiders, and appointing and training one's successor. The degree of power wielded by a cacique varies with that cacique's personality.

Russell J. Barber

See also: Political Organization and Leadership.

Calumets and Pipe Bags

Tribes affected: Pantribal
Significance: *The calumet (sacred pipe) was the most widely used ceremonial object among North American Indians, and it has been a central symbol of modern Pan-Indian movements.*

Calumet, from the French for reed pipe, refers to pipes with long wooden stems and detachable clay or stone bowls. Widely used for both personal and ceremonial purposes, calumet refers to only the sacred pipes. Archaeological evidence shows extensive use throughout North America that may date back four thousand years. Most tribal groups have myths similar to a myth of the Lakota Sioux in which a sacred being, such as White Buffalo Woman, brings the pipe at the time of the creation of the people, or during a time of hardship. The pipe serves as an ongoing means of communication with the spirit beings.

Ceremonial pipes were understood to have a special power and were kept in bags (bundles) tended by specially trained women and men. The bowl and stem were joined only for ritual use, symbolizing the merger of earth and sky, male and female. In most ceremonies, the lit pipe was offered to the six directions (north, south, east, west, up, and down) and then passed in the direction of the sun to all those gathered. Some pipes were so powerful that only certain sacred persons could smoke them. The bowls were often carved in the images of animals or persons, although *L* shapes and inverted-*T* shapes were also common. Red pipestone was prized material for bowls, and many of the carvers were men with disabilities who could not participate in war. The long wooden stems were usually decorated with feathers or ornaments. The decorations revealed when the pipe was to be used: for healing, before the hunt, before war, to bind together confederacies, or to make peace (the peace pipe). Smoking the pipe was understood to link those present and the spirit beings in a cosmic harmony. After a period of decline, pipe carving has been revived, and sweatlodges and pipe ceremonies have become central symbols in pan-Indian movements such as the American Indian Movement (AIM).

Charles Louis Kammer III

Source for Further Study
Steinmetz, Paul B. *The Sacred Pipe: An Archetypal Theology.* Syracuse, N.Y.: Syracuse University Press, 1998.

See also: Bundles, Sacred; Pipestone Quarries; Religion.

Captivity and Captivity Narratives

Tribes affected: Pantribal

Significance: *Captivity narratives provide cultural data concerning Native Americans and early contacts with Europeans, although these narratives were often biased and many of them perpetuated stereotypes of Indians.*

Captivity narratives are accounts written by Europeans who were captured by Native Americans. They provide informative vignettes of Native American life, since in many cases captives were adopted into families and learned the languages and aboriginal cultures. In this way, cultural outsiders became insiders who were later able to write about their experiences. There is a risk, however, in relying too directly on these captivity accounts for objective information on Native Americans. Many of the captives were taken during hostile interactions between the Europeans and the indigenous peoples, and thus they did not always relish their enforced observation of another culture. In addition, captivity narratives were often published for the purpose of providing moral guidance to the masses (and were generally sensationalized for entertainment value), and this agenda seriously affects some of the data reported. A prime example is an early captivity narrative published by a minister's wife under the title *The Sovereignty and Goodness of God, Together with the Faithfulness of His Promises Displayed: Being a Narrative of the Captivity and Restauration of Mrs. Mary Rowlandson; Commended by Her, to All That Desire to Know the Lord's Doing to, and Dealings with Her* (1682). It may be found in Charles Lincoln's *Narratives of the Indian Wars (1675-1699)* (1913). This genre of literature served to warn erring Christians of the dangers in straying from a religious life; Indians served as the stereotype of extreme waywardness.

The commercial success of the earlier captivity accounts resulted in further publications, and by the nineteenth century hundreds of pamphlets and anthologies were available. Many of these were written by women or featured a female heroine; if the typical plot is to be believed, generally the purity of the protagonist allowed her to overcome the dangerous ordeal and to return unscathed to her former lifestyle. Those with a male hero often had the man being seduced by the freedom of the wilderness and its native inhabitants to become one with his aboriginal hosts. Occasionally, these men attempted, with difficulty, to return to their former societies, as in Edwin James's *John Tanner's Narrative of His Captivity Among the Ottawa and Ojibwa Indians* (1830). A history of captivity narratives appears in Robert F. Berkhoffer, Jr.'s "White Conceptions of Indians" in volume 4 of the *Handbook of North American Indians*, entitled *History of Indian-White Relations* (1988), published by the Smithsonian Institution.

Susan J. Wurtzburg

Sources for Further Study
Hartman, James D. *Providence Tales and the Birth of American Literature.* Baltimore: Johns Hopkins University Press, 1999.
Strong, Pauline Turner. *Captive Selves, Captivating Others: The Politics and Poetics of Colonial American Captivity Narratives.* Boulder, Colo.: Westview Press, 1999.

See also: Adoption; Slavery; Torture; Warfare and Conflict.

Chantways

Tribe affected: Navajo
Significance: *"Chantways" is the term used to refer to the Navajo ceremonial healing system based on creation myths, using a combination of singing, sand painting, prayer, and sacred objects.*

The Navajo ceremonial system is composed of rites, chants, and rituals for restoring balance and harmony to life. Based on Navajo creation myths that explain their understanding of the reciprocity of the natural and supernatural worlds, religious rituals requiring from two to nine days and nights are conducted that are both curative and preventative.

Belief. The Navajo believe that the universe is interrelated. All of creation is maintained by a delicate balance of natural and supernatural elements that results in a state of harmony and well being. The natural and supernatural operate in a system of mutual interchange in order to achieve this ideal state of health.

In this system, it is believed that people become ill as a result of disharmony in the world caused by such things as bad dreams, evil spirits and sorcery, excesses in activities, and the hoarding of property. Navajos adhere to a rule of moderation in living to avoid sickness, injury, and other misfortune. For those who are suffering, the sacred ceremony centering on the sand painting is the means to physical, emotional, and psychological restoration.

Sand Paintings. Sand paintings are freehand drawings which serve three main purposes: to attract "the supernaturals"; to identify the patient with them; and to serve as a medium of exchange, absorbing evil or imparting good. Completed sand paintings obligate the Holy People to come and infuse the sand painting with their power. Because of the sacred and powerful nature of this exchange, complete and accurate sand paintings are always used only in a ritual context.

Sand paintings are a type of ritual altar on the floor of the hogan, and they are the center of activity and power in the Chantways ceremonials. The symbols and images used in sand painting are irresistible for the supernaturals; they are compelled to come to their likenesses in the painting. A painting can take from thirty minutes to ten or more hours to complete, often with several apprentice assistants working on it. The average painting takes about four hours. When the painting is completed it is inspected, sanctified, and used immediately.

Practice. Chantways, so called because of the singing and shaking of rattles during the ceremonials, are organized into ceremonial categories or complexes based on the interrelatedness of procedure and myth. Of twenty-four known complexes, about half are well known, with seven of these performed often. These seven are called Shootingway, Mountainway, Nightway, Flintway, Hand-tremblingway, Navajo Windway, and Chiricahua Windway. They are used to treat such ailments as respiratory disease, arthritis, head ailments, emergencies, nervousness, and heart and lung trouble, respectively. They are regulated by one of three rituals, called Holyway, to attract good, Evilway to drive away evil, or Lifeway, for injuries. Holyway uses the greatest variety of sand paintings and is performed at such events as marriage, childbirth, and the consecration of a new home. Rites included in these rituals are Blessingway rites to ensure peace, harmony, and good and Enemyway rites, used to exorcise evil spirits or ghosts from outside the Navajo tribe. Every ceremonial ends with a Blessingway rite.

Holy People are supernaturals composed of two groups. One is represented by mythological figures such as Sun, Changing Woman, and their twin children, Monster Slayer and Born-for-Water. The other group is called the "Yei"; the Yei are led by Talking God and Calling God (who participate in the Nightway chant wearing masks).

Participants include the singer and his assistants, the patient, family members, a diagnostician, and the supernaturals. Trained singers possess the knowledge of the ritual and have undergone a long apprenticeship. Many singers learn only a few ceremonials, each of which involves songs, prayers, plant medicine, sand paintings, sacred objects, and the correct ritual procedure. The singing must be complete and correct to attract the Holy People. If the Holy People are pleased, they are obligated to come and infuse the sand paintings with their power and restore health and harmony to the patient.

Services are performed when needed. Men are usually the singers. Women are allowed to participate, but extreme care is taken to protect them from contacting and absorbing any evil spirits. Pregnant women are not allowed to participate.

The ceremony is held in the family or relative's home, or hogan, which has been ritually consecrated. A diagnostician determines what has caused the patient's illness or trouble and which Chantway is needed to effect the cure. The sand painting is made, and prayer sticks are placed where the supernaturals will see them and be compelled to come. The patient is prepared for the ritual by being cleansed physically and spiritually; the individual then sits almost naked facing east on a specific part of the painting determined by the singer to relate most directly to the patient's trouble. The patient is touched by the singer and his medicine bundle and is sprinkled with sand from appropriate parts of the sand painting. After the patient leaves, the painting is erased in the order in which it was made, and the sand from the sand painting is deposited at a distance from the hogan. Blessingway paintings, however, may be left on the floor of the hogan to become part of the home's floor, continuing to impart their good.

The Chantway system is unique to the Navajo and reflects a holistic approach to health and healing. In spite of the availability of modern medicine to today's Navajo, they continue to preserve this method of bringing harmony to their world.

Diane C. Van Noord

Sources for Further Study

Circle, Black Mustache. *Waterway*. Recorded by Berard Haile. Flagstaff: Museum of Northern Arizona Press, 1979.

Hausman, Gerald. *Meditations with the Navajo: Prayers, Songs, and Stories of Healing and Harmony*. 2d ed. Rochester, Vt.: Bear & Co., 2001.

Parezo, Nancy J. *Navajo Sandpainting*. Tucson: University of Arizona Press, 1983.

Reichard, Gladys A. *Navaho Religion: A Study of Symbolism*. 2 vols. Princeton, N.J.: Princeton University Press, 1950.

Sandner, Donald. *Navaho Symbols of Healing*. Rochester, Vt.: Healing Arts Press, 1991.

Wyman, Leland C. *Southwest Indian Drypainting*. Santa Fe, N.Mex.: School of American Research Press, 1983.

See also: Hand Tremblers; Religion; Religious Specialists; Sacred Narratives; Sand Painting.

Chickee

Tribes affected: Calusa, Seminole, Timucua, Choctaw, Chickasaw, Chitimacha

Significance: *The chickee, a dwelling on poles or stilts, is well suited to a wet climate.*

The chickee is a type of dwelling that was used in the wetter areas of the Southeast culture area. It consists of a platform built on top of four or more posts. The posts are made of trimmed saplings sunk into the earth. These are reinforced by cross members. Beams are cut and laid on top of the posts, and planks are lashed to the beams with braided cords to create a platform that serves as the floor.

A framework of saplings is lashed together, and poles are laid on top of them to support the roof. The roof is then thatched with

Chickee

fronds of palm or grasses. They are arranged in layers that shed water. The walls are open, as the southeastern climate is usually warm and moist. Woven mats are sometimes used in place of walls; mats are also used to cover the floor.

The chickee was well suited to subtropical environments where seasonal flooding of rivers or marshy lands is common. Often a dugout canoe or other water conveyance was tied to the stilts upon which the dwelling sat to serve as transportation when waters are high.

During floods, the residents could use the chickee as a fishing platform. Families could thus be self-sustaining for long periods of time during the wet seasons. Chickees were often built in groups of several, but they could also be isolated. Similar types of dwellings were built by indigenous peoples throughout the Americas who live in wet environments.

Michael W. Simpson

See also: Architecture: Southeast.

Children

Tribes affected: Pantribal
Significance: *American Indian children, reared with love and gentle guidance to respect nature, their elders, and tribal customs, were an integral part of the community.*

Children born into traditional American Indian societies represented part of the never-ending chain of life, and their births were greeted with community pride. The sometimes dangerous nature of Indian life increased the importance of children and made high birthrates common. Considered a gift from sacred forces, children entered the physical world under the guidance and protection of a spiritual guide, and a child's name reflected the qualities of that guide (an adult name would frequently be taken at puberty or when a major accomplishment was noted).

Paiute children playing "wolf and deer" during the late 1800's in Northern Arizona. *(National Archives)*

Early Years. For most Indian children, the first year of life was spent strapped to a cradleboard. These rigid carriers could be fastened to the mother's back, stuck upright in the ground, or attached to horse packs. Once out of the cradleboard, children were allowed to discover their world freely. Although welcomed and cherished, babies represented a potential danger to the tribe: Crying children might reveal the tribe's position to enemies. Therefore, it became a common practice among some tribes (as among the Cheyenne and Sioux) to pinch babies' nostrils to quiet them. Infants were often nursed up to the age of four, helping to create a strong bond between mother and child.

Children flourished in a world surrounded by love and gentle care. Strong extended-family ties brought loving guidance and stability into the child's life. Toilet training was not stressed; children frequently remained naked until four or five years of age, and in some cases, such as the Algonquian peoples, children were occasionally naked until age ten.

Under the direction of their mothers, Indian children were taught the beauties of nature and a deep respect for their elders. Many hours were spent with their elders, especially grandparents, learning tribal history and myths. Children were the key to the future, and elders sought to instill in them the tribe's ancient traditions. Since survival was directly related to what was available and useful from their surroundings, children were directed from an early age to take only what they absolutely needed from Mother Earth.

Preparing for Puberty. Around the age of five, children began to learn the practical knowledge needed for adult life. Tribal society could not tolerate unproductive members, so even small children contributed by picking berries, hunting small game, and assisting their families in chores. Young girls erected miniature tipis and learned through imitating their mothers' daily routine, such as preparing food, caring for smaller children, and tanning hides. Tending small gardens also helped eastern Indian girls learn to grow crops. After the introduction of the horse into Indian cultures, young boys learned to ride early in life. In addition, competitive sports taught the boys vital warrior qualities such as self-sufficiency, strength, endurance, and accuracy in the hunt. Adults encouraged this education, which would prepare children for their future tribal roles.

Art was also an important element of this stage of childhood. Mothers passed down their talents in beadworking, painting, and weaving. Both sexes grew up around religious and social forms of music. Boys began to learn the drum music associated with tribal ceremonies, while girls learned chants and lullabies. Children were also taught the ceremonial dances of their tribe.

Discipline. Discipline among the Indian people was based on respect. Children were born by the good graces of the spirit world, and physical punishment was rare. Many tribes feared that this form of discipline would cause children's souls to depart from their body and thus harm their personality and health. Instead, discipline typically consisted of verbal reprimands designed to teach a lesson. Even with a societal preference for avoiding corporal punishment, however, some children faced harsh treatment, including beatings, scarring from hot stones, or public lashings for severe offenses.

The responsibility of disciplining children was often undertaken by other family members or tribal elders, who interceded on the parents' behalf. Storytelling and legends were frequently used

Cherokee boy and girl in traditional costume on a North Carolina reservation. *(National Archives)*

to shape the character of young minds and to teach the difference between good and evil. For example, the Apache told of Mountain Spirits that dictated proper behavior, while the Hopi related tales of the Soyoko (a "boogeyman" type of figure) to persuade children to follow a moral code. Some parents used disguised tribesmen to educate children about expected behavior. Often representing supernatural spirits, these dressed-up tribesmen warned, frightened, or, in rare cases, even whipped disobedient children.

Modern Indian Children. Reservation life threatened the existence of American Indian culture. Forced into an unfamiliar, constricted way of life and facing the loss of their freedom, tribe members had to find new means to pass their culture on to the next generation. Tribal elders encouraged children to carry on the ancient rituals (sometimes with revisions) and to maintain the tribal bloodline.

The art of hunting became increasingly difficult to teach, as game was scarce on the reservations; children spent less time in nature and more time in school. The skills and values emphasized during the pre-reservation period, such as self-sufficiency, had to be taught through planned events instead of everyday activities. Many tribes found it hard to maintain their ancient traditions while living in an increasingly modern world. As a result, many tribes lost touch with their heritage. Revivals, however, have created new awareness of tribal traditions and customs.

Jennifer Davis

Sources for Further Study

Coles, Robert. *Eskimos, Chicanos, Indians: Children of Crisis.* Vol. 4. Boston: Little, Brown, 1977.

Driver, Harold E. *Indians of North America.* 1961. Rev. ed. Chicago: University of Chicago Press, 1969.

Erdoes, Richard. *The Sun Dance People.* New York: Alfred A. Knopf, 1972.

Gill, Sam D. *Dictionary of Native American Mythology.* Santa Barbara, Calif.: ABC-Clio, 1992.

Holt, Marilyn Irvin. *Children of the Western Plains: The Nineteenth-Century Experience.* Chicago: Ivan R. Dee, 2003.

_____. *Indian Orphanages.* Lawrence: University Press of Kansas, 2001.

Lowie, Robert H. *Indians of the Plains.* New York: McGraw-Hill, 1954.

White, Jon Manchip. *Everyday Life of the North American Indian.* New York: Holmes & Meier, 1979.

See also: Education: Post-contact; Education: Pre-contact; Games and Contests; Gender Relations and Roles; Hand Games; Missions and Missionaries; Names and Naming; Puberty and Initiation Rites; Toys.

Chilkat Blankets

Tribes affected: Tribes of the Northwest
Significance: *Chilkat blankets represent some of the finest and most visually impressive handwoven Indian artifacts.*

The Chilkat Tlingit were a Northwest Indian tribe. The accumulation and display of wealth was an important aspect of their tribal life. Chilkat chieftains commissioned the finest weavers their clan could afford to prepare ceremonial robes. The robes were worn and displayed to symbolize the wealth and status of the owner. The robes were illustrated with depictions of animals and objects that represented the chief's crests. Some of the most popular designs included ravens, whales, drums, bears, and wolves.

Weavers applied twining techniques used in basketry to craft technically intricate blankets. Goat wool, and later commercial yarn, was dyed white, green, black, yellow, and blue with native dyestuff. Weavers decorated the robes with long fringe sewn onto the bottom and sides. The fringe, crafted of cedar bark and mountain goat wool, was a very important aspect of the robe. When chieftains danced, they lifted and swung their robes so that the fringe swung freely and created an impressive effect.

By the 1980's, only one Chilkat robe weaver, Jennie Thlunaut, continued to produce blankets. However, interest among collectors has been renewed, and the number of weavers has increased.

Leslie Stricker

See also: Arts and Crafts: Northwest Coast; Blankets; Weaving.

Clans

Tribes affected: Widespread but not pantribal
Significance: *In societies with these unilineal descent groups, clan membership provides an individual with social identity and regulates marriage choices; clans sometimes own property, perform ceremonies, and control political offices.*

Clans are unilineal descent groups into which a person is born. In a matrilineal society, one is a member of one's mother's clan; in a patrilineal society, one is a member of one's father's clan. In nearly all societies with clans, the clans function to regulate marriage. Clans may also hold property and perform specific rituals. Clans often have distinctive symbols.

Definitions. Colloquially, "clan" often connotes a clique of kin who avoid contact with outsiders. Among members of American Indian tribes with clans, however, and for anthropologists working with such tribes, the term "clan" has a different connotation: two or more lineages closely related through a common traditional bond, usually belief in a common ancestor. Thus, a clan is a unilineal descent group: a group of people who trace relationship to one another through either the mother's line (matrilineal) or the father's line (patrilineal) but not both. A clan, in which the precise genealogical links among members are unknown, is distinguished from a lineage, in which each individual can trace descent from a known common ancestor.

Some anthropologists, following the work of George Murdock in the 1940's, define a clan as a "compromise kin group" that combines principles of descent and residence. The core of the group is a unilineal descent group, but the clan also includes the in-marrying spouses of descent group members. Today, however, most anthropologists have abandoned Murdock's definition of clan. Moreover, most Indians from groups with unilineal descent groups use the term to refer to the descent group rather than to the residential group. For example, when a Navajo says that her "clan" is "Edgewater," she means that she is related, by matrilineal descent, to all "Edgewater" people regardless of where they reside.

Distribution. There can be lineages without clans; this is the case in most of aboriginal California and among the Bering Sea Eskimo. There cannot, however, be clans without lineages. Groups with bilateral descent systems (in which descent is traced equally through both parents) have no lineages and, hence, no clans. Bilateral descent commonly occurs in Great Basin, Plateau, Plains, Arctic, and Eastern Subarctic cultures.

Hunting and gathering societies usually lack clans. Among the primary exceptions to this generalization are some Northwest Coast cultures and adjacent Athapaskan peoples of the Subarctic, which had matrilineal clans. Each Tlingit clan had a symbol ("crest" or "totem") and unique mythic traditions.

Many agricultural peoples of the East (such as Iroquoians and the Creek) and some in the Southwest (Western Pueblos, Navajo, and Western Apache) had matrilineal clans, as did the Mandan and Hidatsa of the Missouri River. The Crow, close linguistic relatives of the Hidatsa, retained matrilineal clans when they shifted from agricultural pursuits to bison hunting on the Great Plains.

Patrilineal clans were found mainly in two areas of North America: among Prairie farming tribes (such as the Omaha and Mesquakie, or Fox) and the adjacent Subarctic Ojibwa, and in the Southwest among Yumans and Pimans.

Clans and Marriage. The most common clan function involves marriage rules, especially clan exogamy (the requirement that one marry a person of a different clan). Because members of the same clan consider themselves to be closely related, marriage to a member of the same clan would be considered incestuous. Various additional restrictions based on clan relationships may also exist. Many matrilineal societies (Hopi, for example) prohibit marriage into the father's clan, while many patrilineal systems (as with the Omaha) prohibit marriage into the mother's clan. Such rules tend to increase the number of families which are allied by marriage, thereby increasing the network of kinship relations throughout the society.

The Navajo clan system illustrates the operation of marriage rules. There are more than fifty matrilineal clans. Sets of clans are linked into one of eight or nine groups ("phratries"). A Navajo is "born into" his mother's clan and is "born for" his father's clan. Notions of kinship are extended to members of these two clans and, more generally, to linked clans (phratry mates). A Navajo cannot marry someone in either of these two clans or phratries. Beyond marriage rules and the idioms of kinship and hospitality, Navajo clans have few functions.

Clans as Corporate Groups. In many tribes, however, clans have functions in addition to marriage regulation. The Hopi also have more than fifty matrilineal clans grouped into nine phratries. Hopi clan-related marriage rules and hospitality are similar to those of the Navajo, but Hopi clans are also corporate groups which hold land, own houses and sacred property, perform rituals, and maintain clan symbols. The eldest competent female of a clan's highest ranking lineage is the "clan mother." She lives in the clan house and, with her brother or maternal uncle, manages clan property. These two are stewards of clan property and agents of the clan considered as a corporation.

Each Hopi clan has its own migration legend. The sequence of the arrival of the clans in Hopi country is a rough measure of the prestige of the clans. For example, Bear clan, acknowledged as the first to arrive, should provide the village chief and the leader of the important Soyal ceremony.

The Siouan-speaking Winnebago and Omaha have twelve and ten patrilineal exogamous clans, respectively. Each Winnebago clan is associated with an animal that serves as a clan symbol or clan totem. According to ethnologist Paul Radin, individual Winnebagos conceive of the relationship to the clan animal as one "of descent from an animal transformed at the origin of the present human race into human beings." The Omaha conform less well to clan totem symbolism. Some Omaha clans are named after animals; others take their names from human attributes or natural phenomena such as lightning. Winnebago and Omaha clans, like those of the Hopi, have ceremonial property and political functions. For example, Winnebago village chiefs are Thunderbird clan, while Bear clan has disciplinary functions.

Eric Henderson

Sources for Further Study

Barnes, Robert H. *Two Crows Denies It: A History of Controversy in Omaha Sociology.* Lincoln: University of Nebraska Press, 1984.

DeMallie, Raymond J., and Alfonso Ortiz, eds. *North American Indian Anthropology: Essays on Society and Culture.* Norman: University of Oklahoma Press, 1994.

Driver, Harold E. *Indians of North America.* 2d rev. ed. Chicago: University of Chicago Press, 1969.

Drucker, Philip. *Indians of the Northwest Coast.* 1955. Reprint. Garden City, N.Y.: Natural History Press, 1963.

Eggan, Fred. *Social Organization of the Western Pueblos.* Chicago: University of Chicago Press, 1950.

Morgan, Lewis Henry. *Systems of Consanguinity and Affinity of the Human Family.* Introduction by Elisabeth Tooker. Lincoln: University of Nebraska Press, 1997.

Murdock, George Peter. *Social Structure.* 1949. Reprint. New York: Macmillan, 1967.

Radin, Paul. *The Winnebago Tribe.* 1923. Reprint. Lincoln: University of Nebraska Press, 1970. A reprint of part of the 37th Annual

Report of the Bureau of American Ethnology, Smithsonian Institution, 1923.

Schusky, Ernest L. *Manual for Kinship Analysis*. 2d ed. New York: Holt, Rinehart and Winston, 1972.

See also: Adoption; Aztec Empire; Incest Taboo; Kinship and Social Organization; Marriage and Divorce; Societies: Non-kin-based.

Cliff Dwellings

Tribes affected: Anasazi, Western Pueblo tribes (Hopi, Navajo, Zuñi)

Significance: *Cliff dwellings identified with the Southwest's Anasazi culture were constructed between 500 C.E. and the climax of what archaeologists define as the Pueblo III period, between 1100 and 1300.*

The remains of these dwellings, some remarkably intact, have been found over a wide area of the Colorado plateau, but the most notable sites are found in the Four Corners area, where the boundaries of Arizona, Colorado, New Mexico, and Utah meet. The largest and best-preserved (or restored) of these ruins include Betatakin, Cliff Palace, Fire Temple, Oak Tree House, Spruce Tree House, and Square Tower House. Today, the ruins of nearly all cliff dwellings have been incorporated either into National Historical Parks, as at Capitol Reef (Utah), Chaco Culture National Historical Park (New Mexico), and Mesa Verde (Colorado), or into National Monuments, as at Bandelier (Colorado), Canyon de Chelly (Arizona), Gila Cliff Dwellings (New Mexico), Hovenweep (Colorado and Utah), Montezuma Castle (Arizona), Navajo (Arizona), Tonto (Arizona), and Walnut Canyon (Arizona).

A culture based on settled agriculture combined with supplemental hunting and gathering, and distinguished by its versatile and beautifully crafted basketwork, the Anasazi originally lived in pueblos of circular pit houses constructed in communal clusters. From as early as 500 C.E., some of these dwellings were built in the

Restored ruins of Cliff Palace in Mesa Verde, Colorado, built by the Anasazi civilization circa 1100. *(Museum of New Mexico)*

numerous cliff overhangs and caves common to the Colorado plateau, particularly in the Four Corners area. Early Anasazi housing was represented by pit houses lined with stone slabs and with wooden roofs and entrances through the roof or passageways. In time, the construction of these structures was carried above ground, retaining the sunken portions as kivas—sacred rooms for men. Built of stone, mud, and wood, some of them three stories high, cliff dwellings, with their terraced apartments, housed scores of people—more than two hundred in Mesa Verde's Cliff Palace—and included courtyards, storage rooms, and kivas. In these regards they continued the essentials of older pueblo architectural traditions. There is only informed speculation about why the cliff dwellings were abandoned during the 1300's.

The "opening" of the Southwest by white Americans, facilitated in the nineteenth century by the Gadsden Purchase, the discovery of gold in California, and the Mormon settlement of Utah, drew attention to previous occupants of the region, beginning with

Lieutenant James Simpson's descriptions of the cliff dwellings and other ruins in Canyon de Chelly and Chaco Canyon, written while he was fighting the Navajos in 1849. Subsequent archaeological interest was stimulated by the explorations of John Wesley Powell and early archaeological work by Cosmos and Victor Mindeleff in the early 1890's. These studies were expanded by Richard Wetherill, Adolph Bandelier, Gustav Nordensjold, and (most important for preservation of the cliff dwellings) Jesse Walter Fewkes.

Clifton K. Yearley

See also: Anasazi Civilization; Architecture: Southwest; Kivas; Pueblo.

Clowns

Tribes affected: Pantribal but especially the Apache, Navajo, Pueblo, Seminole, Sioux

Significance: *Through their behavior, clowns reinforce a sense of order and the need for personal responsibility; they can also serve as powerful healers.*

Clowns are an important part of Indian mythology and ritual. While there is great variation in costuming, ranging from the famous mud-head clowns of the Hopi and Zuñi to the black-and-white-striped clowns of the Koshare and Apache, clowns perform similar functions in all tribal groups. Most creation stories include the creation of a clown figure. As in the Keresan story of the clown being created from the epidermal waste of the creator, Iatiku, the clown figure usually has unusual beginnings. While sometimes associated in mythology with the sun, clowns are more often associated with water and water rituals, as are the Sioux heyoka, who receive their power from the Thunderbeings. In most tribes, one must be selected to be a clown and receive years of training in one of the clown societies.

Clowns engage in various forms of outrageous behavior. Often, like the Contrary Society of the Cheyenne, clowns will do everything backward—walk backward, ride a horse backward, and wear winter clothing in the summertime. Also common is scatological behavior such as eating dirt or excrement, drinking urine, cavorting naked, and simulating sexual acts in public. They may also, like the Apache Crazy Dancers, follow behind ceremonial dancers, healers, and tribal leaders, mimicking their behavior.

While part of the clown's intent is to entertain and generate laughter, they do have a more serious purpose. Through humor, they are trying to teach important lessons to the tribe. Most important, they reinforce the need for personal responsibility, tribal rules, and tribal order. By doing things backward and by violating rules, they show that chaos develops when rules are not maintained. Additionally, through their humor, they show the danger of human vices such as greed, gluttony, and sexual promiscuity. Finally, clowns serve to keep the powerful in check through their mimicking. They remind the healers and tribal leaders that, despite their special gifts, they are only human. By making them look foolish, clowns demystify their power.

Although clowns are humorous figures, they are viewed as very powerful. Their participation in ceremonies helps to assure fertility, a good harvest, and good health. Because of their association with water, they are especially important in bringing rain and performing cleansing rituals. Like the koshare, who are part of the Acoma Medicine Society, they are often powerful healers as well. The Navajo clown, Watersprinkler, is an important figure in the Night Chant ceremony, one of the tribe's most important healing rituals.

While the clowns are usually men, there have been women clowns in the Pacific Northwest. Like many other aspects of Indian culture, recent decades have seen a recovery and revival of the clown tradition and activities. Clown figures often figure prominently in cartoons in contemporary tribal newspapers.

Charles Louis Kammer III

See also: Humor; Husk Face Society; Societies: Non-kin-based; Tricksters.

Codices

Tribes affected: Aztec, Maya, Mixtec
Significance: *Codices were the books of the pre-Hispanic Aztec, Maya, and Mixtec cultures; they describe events of historical, ritual, or calendrical significance.*

The pre-Hispanic cultures of the Aztecs, Mayas, and Mixtecs of Mexico produced written literature called codices (the singular form is "codex"). Aztec and Mixtec codices were made of either deerskin or agave paper; the Maya made theirs from paper made from tree bark covered with a thin layer of lime. Only three pre-Hispanic Mayan codices still survive, while there are no surviving pre-Hispanic Aztec codices; most codices were destroyed by the Spanish in the sixteenth century. Following the Spanish conquest, however, a number of codices were produced by Hispanicized Aztecs which describe the pre-Hispanic culture; several of these texts also survive.

Codices were folded accordion-fashion and were read from right to left. Surviving codices range in length from 4 to 24 feet. Individual pages range from 4 to 8 inches in width and from 8 to 10 inches in height. Pre-Hispanic cultures in Mexico did not use a phonetic alphabet (in which each written symbol represents a sound). Rather, they used a logographic writing system in which each symbol represented a word or concept, or occasionally a syllable. Logographic writing systems are often called pictographic or hieroglyphic. Literacy was not widespread, and codices were probably read only by a specialized class of scribes, who produced them, and the upper classes, who commissioned them. Someone reading a codex would begin with the logographs pictured in the upper right corner of a page and would then move down one column of figures and up the next. Following the Spanish conquest, some Aztec codex authors began to write their native language, Nahuatl, in a phonetic alphabet borrowed from the Spanish; this new writing was largely confined to place names and personal names.

The content of codices varied greatly. Many described the histories or genealogies of rulers or important nobility. As an example, the most famous surviving Mixtec codex tells the history of a chieftain named Eight-Deer from his birth in 1011 C.E. to his death by sacrifice at age fifty-two, following his capture in battle. The codex describes his rise to power, the expansion of his realm through conquest and strategic marriages, and the birth of his children. Some codices describe rituals and mythology, while others outline calendrical or astronomical events. Some codices apparently served as primers, or teaching devices, for the children of nobility or scribes; these primers described rituals, stories, and etiquette with which the children were to be familiar. Codices were not comprehensive texts. Rather, they provided the main outline of their content; readers had to provide many details of a narrative from their own memories. Aztec, Mayan, and Mixtec codices were destroyed by the Spanish priesthood in order to undermine the pre-Hispanic religions and to encourage the conversion of the Indians to Christianity.

David J. Minderhout

See also: Aztec Empire; Mayan Civilization.

Corn

Tribes affected: Pantribal
Significance: *North American corn was first domesticated in Mexico, and by the seventeenth century it was a staple across much of the North American continent.*

Corn, or maize (*Zea mays*), is currently grown worldwide, but the crop is indigenous to the Western Hemisphere. Only after European contact was maize propagated beyond the American continents. When the Europeans arrived in the Americas, domesticated maize was cultivated from the Canadian Great Lakes region to Argentina. Several varieties of corn were grown in different ecological zones in North and South America, ranging from sea level to high in the Andes and other mountains.

European explorers described maize agriculture among the Aztecs, the Mayas, and the Incas of Latin America and among North America Indians of the Southwest, the Plains, the Southeast, and the Northeast. Indeed, at different times during the early contact period, the survival of European settlers depended on corn and other foods provided by the indigenous peoples of these regions. In many of these corn-growing areas, the new settlers recorded aboriginal oral traditions which emphasized the cultural importance of corn. Such was the case among the Mayas of Central America and the Iroquois of upstate New York.

Archaeological Information. Studies concerning the prehistoric origin, domestication, and use of corn rely upon archaeological investigations. Perhaps as a result of the contact-period accounts of the primacy of corn agriculture, archaeologists of the early 1900's often overemphasized the importance of corn to prehistoric peoples. Generally, it was suggested that prehistoric cultures that possessed traits such as settled villages or impressive architecture (which indicated complicated social organization) depended for their subsistence primarily upon corn agriculture. By the 1990's it was recognized that corn was one of several species that were important for New World agriculturalists and that, in addition, not all complex societies depended on corn for their subsistence. It was also formerly believed that maize domestication was a rapid process which had immediate cultural impact. It is now apparent that the process of maize domestication took place over hundreds of years. Maize probably first served merely to supplement local wild plant foods and only later became an important resource. Gradual genetic changes among the maize plants accompanied these slow cultural adaptations. For example, corn cobs became larger, and the number and size of the kernels increased. These and other changes marked the process of domestication. Some maize cobs, kernels, and other remains can be definitely identified as either "wild" or "domesticated," whereas other plant remains fit somewhere on a continuum in between.

General theories concerning the speed of the development of

Areas of Corn and Cotton Cultivation

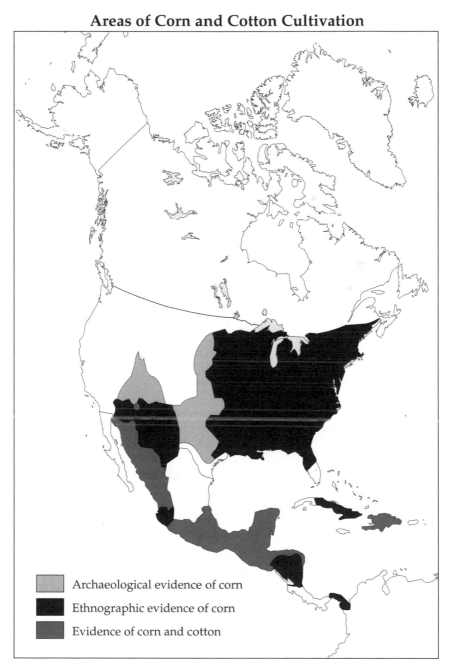

Archaeological evidence of corn

Ethnographic evidence of corn

Evidence of corn and cotton

Source: After Driver, Harold E., and William C. Massey, *Comparative Studies of North American Indians*, 1957.

New World agriculture are based on specific archaeological information concerning ancient subsistence. At some archaeological sites, corn agriculture is well documented by finds of maize plant remains, while at other locations lacking botanical data, researchers may rely on indirect evidence, such as the presence of agricultural implements. For example, ancient use of hoes, milling stones, and storage facilities may indicate a dependence on corn, but archaeologists exercise caution in their inferences, since these tools were also associated with other crops. For this reason, the strongest demonstration of ancient maize agriculture is the discovery of pieces of corn plants, such as stems, leaves, kernels, and cobs. Cobs often provide additional information (such as the corn variety), which contributes to data concerning its origin, domestication, growth, and use. Smaller plant remains, such as pollen or phytoliths (tiny silica bodies within the plant) can also provide evidence for the presence of corn agriculture.

Botanical remains are best preserved under stable environmental conditions which discourage rotting, such as dry heat, cold, or water inundation. They are also more likely to be preserved when burned to a carbonized state. For these reasons, many plant remains left at sites by past peoples are not preserved in the archaeological record. In addition, the preservation of botanical remains does not ensure that they will be carefully and scientifically excavated by professional archaeologists. Unfortunately, site looting and destruction is a major problem throughout North and Central America.

Corn Domestication. Archaeological sites that provide important evidence concerning the earliest domestication of corn have been found in the Tehuacán Valley, Puebla, Mexico. The Tehuacán archaeological-botanical project was directed by Richard S. Mac-Neish, who devoted decades to the search for evidence of early corn domestication. MacNeish excavated the dry caves in the Tehuacán Valley because they would have provided shelter for ancient habitation, and he anticipated good preservation of any botanical remains. The Tehuacán sites date from approximately eleven thousand years ago to the time of the Spanish conquest, and maize pollen and wild maize cobs were excavated from levels dated to about 7000-5000 B.C.E. Cultivated maize was dated to about 5000-3500 B.C.E. This early evidence of corn agriculture is also helpful for determining the ancestral grasses of *Zea mays*. Botanists have argued that corn developed from a wild grass called teosinte, although this has not been definitively demonstrated.

In the 1980's, results from bone chemistry analyses contributed to the archaeological understanding of the Tehuacán Valley. Stable carbon isotope tests of Tehuacán human skeletal remains demonstrated that a chemically distinct group of plants, which included maize, composed 90 percent of the ancient diet from 4500 B.C.E. onward.

Based on the available evidence, it seems that North American maize originated in central Mexico. It may have appeared in the southwestern United States by approximately three thousand years ago. The seasonally occupied sites of the corn-growing Chochise may date to approximately 1200 B.C.E. in southern New Mexico. These people obtained corn (the Chapalote variety of *Zea mays*) and their knowledge of corn agriculture from people in northern Mexico. The Southwest cultures farmed in harsh, unpredictable climatic conditions with the use of highly developed agricultural techniques, ranging from planting strategies to the use of irrigation.

A second variety of corn (Maiz de Ocho, also known as New England flint corn) was introduced later into the Southwest. The earliest use of Maiz de Ocho in this region may date to 1000 B.C.E., but this date is controversial. Generally accepted Maiz de Ocho dates are considerably later. This corn variety was more productive than the earlier Chapalote, and this variety diffused eastward across the continent. Maize agriculture on the Plains dates to approximately 800-900 C.E., while for the Southeast there are a few dates as early as 200 C.E. Agriculture did not provide a substantial contribution to the Southeast diet until 800-1000 and, in some areas, such as the Lower Mississippi, not until as late as 1200. By this time, corn was being grown in regions as diverse as southeast Colorado and upstate New York. Indeed, by 1300, maize agriculture was vital to the Iroquoian economy.

Despite its utility, successful corn agriculture has distinct requirements. Generally, corn plants need adequate moisture and approximately 120 frost-free days to mature. A healthy crop also requires some weeding and care of the developing plants. Maize growing rapidly exhausts the soil's nitrogen stores, and these must be replenished through planting other crops (such as beans, which contribute nitrogen), using fertilizers, or allowing the soil to rest fallow. Corn lacks an amino acid (lysine), essential for humans, and a diet based only on corn is inadequate. Many groups ate beans as well, which provided the missing lysine and resulted in a balanced, healthy diet.

Susan J. Wurtzburg

Sources for Further Study

Cohen, Mark N., and George J. Armelagos, eds. *Paleopathology at the Origins of Agriculture*. New York: Academic Press, 1984.

Creel, Darrell, and Austin Long. "Radiocarbon Dating of Corn." *American Antiquity* 51, no. 4 (1986): 826-837.

Ford, Richard I., ed. *Prehistoric Food Production in North America*. Anthropological Papers 75. Ann Arbor: Museum of Anthropology, University of Michigan, 1985.

Fritz, Gayle J. "Multiple Pathways to Farming in Precontact Eastern North-America." *Journal of World Prehistory* 4, no. 4 (December, 1990): 387-435.

MacNeish, Richard S. "A Summary of the Subsistence." In *Prehistory of the Tehuacan Valley*, vol. 1, edited by Douglas S. Byers. Austin: University of Texas Press, 1967.

Watson, Patty Jo, and Mary C. Kennedy. "The Development of Horticulture in the Eastern Woodlands of North America: Women's Role." In *Engendering Archaeology: Women and Prehistory*, edited by Joan M. Gero and Margaret W. Conkey. Oxford, England: Basil Blackwell, 1991.

Will, George F., and George E. Hyde. *Corn Among the Indians of the Upper Missouri*. Lincoln: University of Nebraska Press, 2002.

Yarnell, Richard A., and M. Jean Black. "Temporal Trends Indicated by a Survey of Archaic and Woodland Plant Food Re-

mains from Southeastern North America." *Southeastern Archaeology* 4, no. 2 (1985): 93-106.

See also: Agriculture; Beans; Corn Woman; Food Preparation and
Cooking; Green Corn Dance; Squash; Subsistence.

Corn Woman

Tribes affected: Apache, Cherokee, Chickasaw, Chippewa, Choctaw, Creek, Iroquois Confederacy, Navajo, Pueblo, Seminole
Significance: *Corn Woman is important in terms of cosmology and religious practices in tribal cultures where maize is the key food source
(Northeast, Southeast, Southwest).*

The domestication of corn had moved north from Mexico to the
Pueblo tribes of present-day New Mexico by 3500 B.C.E. and almost
immediately became the preferred food plant in the region, super-
seding various inferior domesticated plants. Most tribes believed
that corn was a gift from the gods, and this transmission was often
recounted in folktale and song.

Therefore, it was logical that, especially in Keres (a number
of the Pueblo bands, including the Acoma Pueblo and Laguna
Pueblo, speak Keresan dialects) cosmogony, Corn Woman should
serve as a sort of mother goddess—source of life and a staple of
their diet.

The Keres people believed that in the distant past, Ts'its'tsi'nako
(Thought-Woman, or Creating-Through-Thinking Woman) chanted
into life Naotsete and Uretsete, her sister goddesses. In this matrilineal cosmogony, Naotsete served as the cacique, or internal chief,
and Uretsete served as the hotchin, the war chief or outside chief.
Naotsete and Uretsete carried baskets from which came all creatures, plants, and elements of the earth. Uretsete gave birth to twin
boys, one of whom married Naotsete, and their issue became the
Pueblo race. As time progressed, Uretsete became known as Corn
Woman (*Iyatiku*), Mother Corn Woman (*Naiya Iyatiku*), or Earth

Woman. Corn Woman is considered to be the mother of all people, gods, and animals. Some folk myths place Mother Corn Woman as a guardian at the gate of the spirit world.

Richard Sax

See also: Corn; Hako; Mother Earth.

Cotton

Tribes affected: Pima and tribes of Mexico, Central America, South America

Significance: *Cotton, a South American domesticate, spread to the American Southwest and was cultivated by the historic Pima for fiber and food.*

Cotton (*Gossypium herbaceum*) has a highly complex domestication history with independent domestications in both Africa and South America. All cotton in pre-Columbian America descended from that domesticated in coastal Peru sometime before 4,000 B.C.E. Cotton spread northward through Central America and Mexico, finally entering North America in the Southwest. People of the Hohokam archaeological tradition, centered in the Sonora Desert of Arizona and adjacent Mexico, were the first North Americans to use cotton, probably around 100 C.E. They used the fiber for spinning thread from which clothing, bags, and other items were woven; they also used the seed for extracting its nutritious oil. Cotton requires a considerable amount of water for successful growing, and its cultivation probably was a spur to the development of the sophisticated irrigation developed by the Hohokam. The Pima, the Sonoran Desert tribe widely believed to be descended from the Hohokam, were growing irrigated cotton when the Spanish first encountered them in the seventeenth century.

Russell J. Barber

See also: Hohokam Culture; Irrigation; Weaving.

Coup Sticks and Counting

Tribes affected: Primarily Plains tribes, including Arapaho, Assiniboine, Blackfoot, Cheyenne, Crow, Iowa, Kiowa, Omaha, Sioux

Significance: *In warrior cultures, counting coup was a way to prove bravery and merit by touching the enemy; success was rewarded with both signs of honor and tribal status.*

The term "counting coup" comes from the French word *coup*, meaning "to strike a blow." In warrior cultures, bravery was the highest virtue. A way to prove bravery was to touch (count coup) the enemy, whether the enemy was living or dead. More than one warrior could count coup on the same enemy, but "first coup" had higher status than second, and second ranked higher than third. Touching could be done either with the hand or a special stick (a coup stick). Among the Cheyenne, a ceremonial striped stick was used. All acts of coup had to be witnessed.

Acts of coup earned tribal designation, marked by symbolic dress such as wearing a feather, special face paint markings, stripes painted on leggings or on one's horse, or, as among the Crow, wearing a fox tail on the back of one's moccasins. Such markings distinguished among the levels of bravery. First coup might entitle the warrior to wear an eagle feather, while third or fourth coup might earn only a buzzard feather. Groups such as the Kiowa and Crow based tribal ranking and chief status on accumulated acts of bravery including acts of counting coup.

Charles Louis Kammer III

See also: Dress and Adornment; Feathers and Featherwork; Military Societies; Warfare and Conflict.

Culture Areas

Tribes affected: Pantribal
Significance: *Ecological conditions determined tribal methods of material subsistence (food supply, type of shelter) as well as their main cultural patterns.*

No single method of assigning cultural boundaries between different groupings of Native Americans is fully adequate. Persuasive arguments exist for groupings that place primary emphasis, for example, on the most important language groupings (Algonquian, Athapaskan, Siouan, Tanoan, Muskogean, Caddoan, and Shoshonean). Because Native American groupings have undergone a series of displacements from region to region, however, their linguistic origins overlap, a situation which results in an equal amount of overlap in generalizations concerning original cultural traits.

Another mode of assigning culture areas draws on basic forms of technology—specifically on methods of producing household wares such as pottery and basketry. Here again one encounters a phenomenon of cultural overlap because of patterns of borrowing between tribal groupings.

To some degree, essential social indicators of culture can be transferred over time and space, making it difficult to draw boundaries between peoples of clearly distinct traditions. Such sociocultural factors include assignment of leadership, matriarchal versus patriarchal systems, degrees of formalization of kinship ties, and marriage patterns.

Considerations such as these make a division based on geographical/ecological factors the most manageable and, indeed, the most commonly adopted one in the general literature. Such a comparison of Indian culture areas necessarily involves discussion of material and cultural questions shared by all human societies. Among these cultural differences are food subsistence, lodging construction, common artifacts, group organization, and spiritual expression. Each of these elements of Indian life was influenced by the environmental conditions that existed in relatively distinct geographical zones.

Arctic and Subarctic. The northern continental zone running from the Arctic north to British Columbia and eastward to Hudson Bay, while not one culture area, was characterized by a common practice: Natives survived primarily by hunting and fishing. Because the northern Arctic zone is frozen most of the year, Eskimo populations that specialized in sea mammal hunting (especially the Aleuts) stayed in isolated in areas where access to prey was assured. Central Inuit hunters in the interior of Alaska and the Mac-Kenzie Territory, where kayak transportation was limited to a short summer season, reached their prey (usually caribou and moose) on toboggans or snowshoes.

Both Central Inuit and Athapaskan-speaking Dene peoples inhabited the less bountiful Subarctic zone, which forms the interior landmass of northern Canada. Because of the limited density of animal populations, Subarctic hunters relied extensively on trapping devices spread over a vast network, according to the season. Limited food sources limited human population patterns as well, especially deep in the interior. Frequent displacement for subsistence meant that Subarctic tribes maintained semipermanent camps rather than substantial villages.

Like their Eskimo neighbors farther north, Subarctic Indians maintained a network of customs in common that, in good times, helped celebrate nature's bounty. One tribal meeting was the "potlatch," when food-gathering tasks were temporarily suspended and groups from afar could share shelter, gifts, and storytelling, either with distant kin or friendly neighbors.

Religious traditions in these northern areas were usually based on a belief in spiritual forces coming both from the sky and the earth, including living spirits in the form of animals or one's deceased kin.

Northwest Coast and Plateau. Indians in these areas lived more easily off nature's bounty, partially because the climate was less

Culture Areas of North America

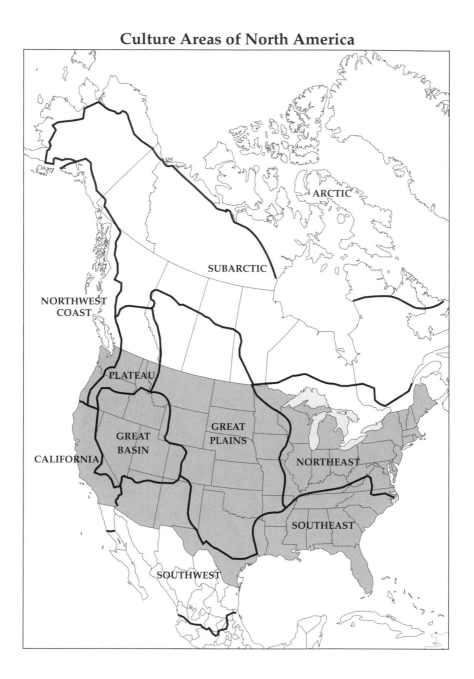

ARCTIC

SUBARCTIC

NORTHWEST
COAST

PLATEAU

GREAT
BASIN

GREAT
PLAINS

CALIFORNIA

NORTHEAST

SOUTHEAST

SOUTHWEST

harsh, facilitating seasonal hunting of deer and bears. Abundant sealife near the coast of Washington and Oregon and easy hunting grounds inland made Northwest Indians such as the Wakashan and Chinook relatively wealthy, in terms of both subsistence and displays of their good fortune.

The Kwakiutl of the Wakashan showed their wealth through large houses of split logs. Their clothing and bodies were decorated with copper and ornate shell jewelry. Frequent public potlatches to commemorate social advancement (such as passage rites for youths and marriages) were paid for by the wealthiest families to attain recognition.

Farther inland was the Plateau, inhabited by tribes of two main linguistic groups: the Sahaptin (including Walla Walla and Nez Perce) and the Salish (Flathead and Wenatchi). In this region, freshwater salmon fishing could be combined with hunting. Plateau river communication networks were less extensive than those of the Northwest, limiting the scope of interaction, even between clans of similar tribal origin. When horses were introduced from the Great Basin Shoshones, some tribes moved seasonally over the mountains into Idaho to hunt bison. Such groups abandoned their traditional pit house structures for portable hide-covered tipis.

California. The Western coast and inland area farther south were more diversified in language groupings, which broke down into the main Penutian and Hokan families (the former including Klamath-Modoc, Miwok, and Central Valley Yokut and Maidu; the latter including Washoe and Yana in the north and in the central eastern zone near Nevada).

Three cultural zones corresponded primarily to ecological subregions. In the northwest corner, dense forests, rugged topography, and the absence of a coastal plain set off isolated (both linguistically and culturally) inhabitants from the fertile core of Penutian-Hokan groups around San Francisco Bay and in the much milder ecological zone of the Central Valley. In this core zone, economic patterns, based on hunting, fishing, and the gathering of available vegetal food sources (including a universal staple, acorn meal), tended to lend similarities to tribal social and cultural patterns. One similarity was the relative lack of formal institutional structures defining tribal organization and authority. Chiefs tended to be heads of the most numerous family among a multitude of generally equal family subdivisions of each clan. One of two main forms of lodging predominated: either the "house pit" scraped out of rolling knolls, or the wickiup, a bark-thatched covering stretched around portable poles. Central California tribes were highly skilled in basketweaving, some (mainly Pomos and Patwins) producing wares sufficiently tightly woven to serve as water containers.

South of the Central Valley, increasing aridity affected not only food-gathering conditions; basic technology (reflected in lodgings and artisanal production, including modes of dress) never attained levels that could be compared with tribes in the central region. Notable degrees of west-east interaction occurred, particularly between the Luiseños of present-day San Diego and Riverside counties (themselves of Shoshone stock) and Nevadan tribes. These contacts were reflected not only in trade of goods, but also in some shared cultural values that set the inland (less than the coastal) southern zone off from the relatively more developed Central Valley region.

Southwest. Beyond California was the inland cultural area of the Southwest. Despite the ecological austerity of these vast expanses, nearly all Southwest Indians practiced some form of agriculture, supplemented by seasonally available wild plant foods. Most also developed technologically advanced cultures, as judged from the remains of their lodging and ceremonial sites (particularly the pueblos) and various artifacts, especially pottery and weaving.

Among the several Indian subgroupings in the Southwest are the Hopi, Navajo, and Zuñi. Their life patterns, although not identical, exemplify the main lines of Southwest Indian culture. Characteristically, Indian villages in the Southwest were constructed in the compact stone and adobe pueblo form, usually located on higher ground or on mesas for purposes of defense. The limited circumstances of dry farming often meant that plantations were located some distance from the pueblo.

In addition to being a dwelling and defense unit, the pueblo was a microcosm for both political and religious life. Particularly among the Eastern Pueblos, different responsibilities, from practical work tasks to ceremonial leadership, were traditionally divided between two fully cooperative factions. Living in different sections of the village, each faction maintained a kiva, or religiously designated meeting place for its elders, and ceremonial dance (kachina) groups, or medicine men, organized in societies. When a particular "season" for representation of the pueblo's ceremonial, political, or administrative needs was recognized, all loyalty was due to the kiva of the designated faction, while others rested from their responsibilities.

Southwest Indian religion and ceremonies were frequently tied to the concept of an "earth mother navel" shrine located in a sacred place within each pueblo. Around this ultimate source of bounty for the members of each tight-knit pueblo community were arranged the symbols of life (seeds and their products). Such symbols, plus other symbols of nature (especially rain) were incorporated into each pueblo's ceremonial dances, according to the season.

Great Basin. In the area wedged between California and the Plateau to the west, and the Southwest and Great Plains to the east, Indian cultures tended to be rather dispersed. Areas of habitation remained highly dependent on the availability of water and vegetation to sustain limited village life. Although broad tribal groupings existed (including Ute, Paiute, and Shoshone), the main activities of Indian life, from food gathering through marital, social, and political alliances, tended to be conducted in smaller bands. Contacts between subtribal bands (the Ute, on both the Colorado and Utah sides of the Rockies, counted some dozen territorial bands) could be only periodic. This rather lower level of tribal cohesiveness relative to Plateau and Southwest Indians, for example, allowed quarreling families from one band to "transfer" over to a band to which they were not tied by kinship; even lines between the tribes (Ute and Paiute, for example) were not that definitely drawn.

Some shared features of cultural existence within and between Great Basin tribes countered this general trend. Although religious consciousness among Great Basin Indians never attained a high degree of ceremonial sophistication, certain symbolic rites, among them the Sun Dance, provided a common cultural symbol in most regions.

Plains. It was among the Plains Indians that the most dramatic subsistence struggle was played out, by tribes such as the Sioux, Cheyenne, Pawnee, and Comanche. Acquisition of the horse from the Spanish after about 1600 transformed the subsistence potential of the Plains, which became the buffalo-hunting domains of competing Indian tribes. Pursuit of the great native herds of buffalo on horseback, beginning in the 1600's, created a situation of Indian nomadism on the Plains. Buffalo hunting affected not only food supply, but also provided raw material for the organization of Plains tribes' movable lodgings and the production of multiple lightweight artifacts. The high degree of mobility of Plains Indians also contributed to another key cultural trait: their tendency to war with rivals over hunting access.

Among the Sioux, the Lakota were drawn into the Plains from the Eastern Prairie region after becoming expert horsemen, well before the French entered the upper Mississippi Valley. Soon their nomadic way of life on the Plains allowed them to subjugate sedentary groupings such as the Arikara and Mandan, who were forced to trade their agricultural goods with the Lakota. The characteristic warring urge of such Plains nomads resulted in serious intertribal disputes, the best known resulting in the reduction and forced relocation of the Pawnee people after multiple encounters with representatives of the Sioux Nation.

The simplicity of the material culture of the Plains Indians was to some degree offset by the complexity of some of their social and cultural patterns. A number of honorary societies, ranging from warrior groups through "headmen" societies (elders who had distinguished themselves earlier as warriors or leaders), provided means for identifying individuals of importance emerging from each family or clan within the tribe. Recognition was also given, among the women, to highly skillful beadworkers, who defined qualification for entry into their "guild" and excluded inferior workmanship from being used in ritual ceremonies.

Another specialized subgrouping, particularly among the Dakota peoples, was the Heyoka, consisting of people who were recognized as possessing some form of supernatural or visionary power. Although not specifically connected to Plains religious beliefs (frequently associated with Sun Dance ceremonies and related celebrations of thanks for bounty, physical endurance, and interclan alliances), Heyoka status implied the ability to communicate with spirits, either good or evil. In some Siouan tribes, such as the Omaha, Heyoka societies were evenly divided into specialized branches, the most notable being one reserved specifically for individuals presumed to have the power to cure diseases.

Northeast and Southeast. In the eastern third of the continent, a higher degree of sedentariness among various tribes prevailed, although this did not necessarily mean that agriculture was more developed. Plantations for food tended to be scattered in the heavily wooded Northeast, with hunting and trapping at least as important in most tribal economies. Another product of the forest, the paperlike bark of the birch tree, served multiple purposes, ranging from tipi-building material to the famous birchbark canoes used to fish or to travel through the extensive river and stream systems of the region.

In general, social organization among the tribes of the Northeast bore two major characteristics. Groups that were known as hunters (such as the Micmacs of New Brunswick and Maine) lived as nuclear families, paramount status being reserved for the hunter-head of closely related kin. Lodgings might be limited to a single family (typically a tipi) or a grouping of families under the single roof of an extended longhouse. In most cases, ascription of chieftainship was determined by a hierarchy that also depended on hunting skills.

A second characteristic of Northeast Woodlands Indian life revolved around political confederations involving several tribes. The best known of these was the Iroquois "Five Nations," but other groups, including the Algonquins and Hurons, formed federations for mutual security against common enemies.

Although the Southeast region of the United States can, like the Northeast, be described as heavily wooded, offering a combination of possibilities for hunting and agriculture, the Indian cultures of this area were substantially different. Some experts argue that there was less communality in cultural development in the Southeast, making distinctions, for example, between peoples who were clearly reliant on the ecology of the first "layer" of the broad coastal plain (called the "Flatwoods," blanketed by conifers and scrub oaks); those inhabiting the so-called Piedmont (further inland, with higher elevations and differing vegetation patterns); and those living in the Appalachian woodlands, with their extensive hardwood forests.

Some experts, noting communality in traits (such as a horticultural maize economy, nucleated villages, and matrilineal clan organization) between key Southeastern tribes such as the Creek, Choctaw, Cherokee, Natchez, and the Iroquois, found farther north, assign a southeastern origin to the Iroquois. A substantial number of differences marked by cultural specialists, however, suggest closer ties between coastal and inland dwellers in the Southeast (especially in linguistic links) than between Southeast Indians as a whole and any of their Northeast neighbors. A series of lesser, but culturally significant, traits justify treating Southeast Indians as a largely homogeneous entity, including modes of processing staple nuts, especially acorns; rectangular, gabled houses with mud wattle covering; an absence of leather footwear; characteristic nested twilled baskets; and varied use of tobacco.

Even among key Southeast tribes, however, parallel traditions (such as matrilineal kinship descent) could be offset by striking differences. The Natchez tribe alone, for example, had a class system dividing tribal nobles (deemed descendants of the Sun), from whom the chief, or "Great Sun" was chosen, and commoners, who could not even enter the presence of tribal aristocrats.

Byron D. Cannon

Sources for Further Study

Catlin, George. *Letters and Notes on the Manners, Customs, and Conditions of North American Indians*. New York, 1841. A recognized classic, including personal observations of Indian ceremonial practices and daily life. Some editions include extremely valuable illustrations, which have gained international fame.

Driver, Harold E. *Indians of North America*. 2d ed. Chicago: University of Chicago Press, 1969. A widely cited textbook organized by subject area (for example, "Rank and Social Class," "Exchange and Trade") rather than geographical location.

Kehoe, Alice B. *North American Indians: A Comprehensive Account*. 2d ed. Englewood Cliffs, N.J.: Prentice-Hall, 1992. Like the Spencer and Jennings book (below), this textbook is divided by geographical region. Less detailed on local conditions of life, it contains useful summary texts within each chapter and a number of translations of original Indian texts.

Ross, Thomas E., and Tyrel Moore, eds. *A Cultural Geography of North American Indians*. Boulder, Colo.: Westview Press, 1987. Contains contributions by specialists dealing with several different geographical themes relating to culture, including "Spatial Awareness," "Land Ownership," and "Migration."

Spencer, Robert, Jesse D. Jennings, et al. *The Native Americans*. 2d ed. New York: Harper & Row, 1977. A very detailed text. Attention is given to diverse patterns of local division of labor, kinship, rites of passage, and so on.

Sturtevant, William, gen. ed. *Handbook of North American Indians*. Washington, D.C.: Smithsonian Institution Press, 1978-2001. The Smithsonian series contains volumes published on the Arctic, Subarctic, Northwest coast, California, Southwest, Great Basin, Plateau, Plains, and Northeast culture areas. It also contains separate volumes on the history of Indian-White relations and languages. The scholarship and coverage are both first rate.

See also: Anasazi Civilization; Aztec Empire; Hohokam Culture; Language Families; Mayan Civilization; Mississippian Culture; Mogollon Civilization; Ohio Mound Builders; Olmec Civilization; Zapotec Civilization.

Dances and Dancing

Tribes affected: Pantribal
Significance: *Among American Indians, dancing has always played a highly significant role in religious ceremonies and other celebrations.*

When white explorers and settlers first came to North America, they were immediately impressed by the amount of dancing in which the native population engaged. Centuries later, some of the significance of tribal ceremonies has been lost, as more and more Indians have accepted white culture and religion. Nevertheless, dancing still plays an important part in American Indian life, whether it represents a true continuation of the original tribal cultures, a celebration of birth, death, or other rites of passage, or merely a performance for non-Indian tourists.

Historical Background. When European explorers and settlers first encountered the native population of what would later become the United States, they found a wide variety of cultures, all of them vastly different from the ones they had left behind. The American Indians had never developed a technological civilization, and the land was much less densely populated than that of Europe. The religious beliefs were like nothing the Europeans had ever encountered.

The first Europeans in North America had no understanding of the native languages they encountered. The usual view of the "red man" was as a savage—inherently inferior to the settlers and potentially dangerous. The two major activities of the Europeans were to conquer the natives and to try to bring to them the Christianity that was virtually universal in Europe at the time.

The result was a long series of wars, in which the Europeans were ultimately victorious. In the process, many native cultures were destroyed altogether, while others were forced to move west. By the late nineteenth century, the last of "Indian territory" had been conquered, and Indians lived on reservations, generally under very harsh conditions.

Gradually, many Indians who survived the early warfare became a part of white culture and accepted its religious beliefs (chiefly Christianity). In the late twentieth century, many Indians began to try to reclaim their ancient heritage, often moving beyond tribal lines and creating a pantribal movement that strove to preserve the Indian cultures from complete assimilation.

As a result of all these factors, it is very difficult to determine the significance of many tribal rituals as they exist today. Some Indians still retain their ancient beliefs and traditions despite centuries of domination. Others may hold on to a tradition for the sake of tradition itself, while at the same time going to Christian churches, speaking English as their primary language, and even living in large cities. For some, the old rituals, including dances, are little more than a way of attracting tourists.

Regardless of this confusion, all the following rituals will be discussed in the present tense, and it will be assumed that the dances still hold their original meaning to the participants. Some of these dances are rarely performed nowadays, while others are making a resurgence as Indians try to regain their lost cultural identity.

Religious Significance. By the time Europeans were settling in the Americas, their own traditions had changed greatly since their days as small tribal groups. It is very likely that the Europeans had once had a culture in which dancing and music were integral to religion, but this had long become a thing of the past. Certain traditions suggested this past; singing is still an important part of many Christian ceremonies and probably always will be. Dances, however, had largely become stylized, social affairs, with no deep religious or cultural significance.

The American Indians, however, had never developed such a differentiation between religious and social climates. To them, the earth and all living creatures on it were possessed by spirits, and these spirits were understood, and to some extent controlled, by a great number of elaborate dances and songs. There were dances for hunting, fishing, rites of passage, rain, and success in warfare.

The many Indian tribes in North America have different religious rituals, including dances. Conditions in different parts of the continent vary, and different spirits must be appeased under different circumstances. The one aspect almost all of these people have in common is a close tie to the earth and the spirits that control it, although different tribes respond to this in different ways.

The Northwest. The Indians of the Pacific Northwest generally perform their dances singly. Both men and women are involved. The dancers are considered to be possessed by spirits, and the dances can become highly frenzied and emotional. The dances are accompanied by drumming and chanting.

An excellent example of Northwest dancing involves the Kwakiutl, who live along the coast of Oregon and Washington. The Kwakiutl have highly formalized dancing, during which various taboos are enforced and dancers are called only by ceremonial names. Even seating arrangements at the festivities are based on dancing societies rather than on families and clans.

The Kwakiutl have three mutually exclusive dancing societies, sometimes called "secret societies." Initiation into one of these societies is highly ritualized, and numbers are limited. The Shaman Society is concerned with violent and dangerous supernatural spirits. The most prestigious dancer is a cannibal/dancer, or Hamatsa. People in the Dluwulaxa Society are possessed by spirits of the sky. The Nutlam are possessed by their mythical ancestors, the wolves.

The Northwest Coast was never very heavily populated by Indians, and it was one of the last areas settled by European Ameri-

Kwakiutl dancers performing during the early twentieth century. *(American Museum of Natural History)*

cans. There are still many Indians who follow tradition as much as possible in the Northwest, but few live on reservations. There is a large American Indian population in big cities such as Seattle, Washington, and Portland, Oregon. Farther inland, where most of the land is mountainous and much is national park and national forest land, the traditions also continue.

The Southwest. The condition in the Southwest is quite different. This area was highly populated by a variety of Indian tribes, then taken over by the Spanish, the Mexicans, and finally the United States government. Climatic conditions vary widely. There are mountain ranges, coastal areas subject to regular flooding, and deserts in which water is the most important consideration for survival. This is the area where the greatest number of Indian reservations exist today and where the greatest proportion of Indians still practice their original rites.

It must be understood that most of the reservations were placed on land the white settlers did not want, and where the climate is harsh. Reservation Indians have both their own problems and their own advantages. There is great poverty, and the social problems that accompany poverty, frustration, and isolation are severe. On the other hand, these Indians are more closely in touch with their origins. The Southwest is probably the best place in the United States to find Indian ceremonies in a state very close to what they were before white people appeared on the scene.

An interesting example of the dancing ceremonies in the Southwest is the kachina dances among the Zuñi of New Mexico. The kachinas are considered to be the spirits of children, lost long ago in the wilderness and transformed into gods who live under a mystic lake. The kachinas wear masks and dance for rain. The dancers impersonating the kachinas "become" rain gods and invoke the spirits who will provide the parched land with much-needed water.

The traditional cultures of the Southwest may be the hardest for white visitors to understand, because many reservations have made tourism a major economic factor. There are certainly many Indians there who still believe in the traditional religions; on the other hand, the great poverty in this area has led many to reenact ceremonies long extinct in order to please tourists.

The Southeast. The southeastern United States is probably the most easily endured climate in North America. While there are hurricanes and other natural disasters, for the most part the people live in a generally warm and hospitable climate, and food is abundant. Hunting is never easy, however, so the spirits must be evoked.

The southeastern tribes were among the first to be encountered by Europeans, a fact which has had two directly opposite results in terms of the study of these cultures. On one hand, these Indians were not opposed to accepting white people as a new tribe moving into the area, and many tribal ceremonies were seen by the explorers in their original state. When Sir Walter Raleigh and his men first set foot on the North Carolina coast, wars between Indians and Europeans were a long way in the future. Therefore, some of the best early descriptions of Indian dances and other rituals date from this era. On the other hand, when the wars did take place, they began on the East Coast. Some cultures were entirely destroyed, and others were forced to move from their home territory. In many cases, there is little but historical evidence on which to draw.

The Southeast Indians use rattles made from gourds and filled with peas, beans, or pebbles; flutes made of reed or cane; and drums made of clay, gourd, or wood, with stretched deerhides for skin, as accompaniments to their dances.

Indians of the Southeast generally dance in large groups, sometimes for many hours at a stretch, with groups of dancers replacing other groups as they grow tired. Masks are often worn, especially in hunting ceremonies, where animal masks are used. The dances are often named after animals.

The Northeast. The Indians of the Northeast also encountered Europeans very early, but the initial meetings were not nearly as friendly as they were farther south. In the Middle Atlantic and New England areas, conditions could be extremely harsh, and good land was not as plentiful as it was in the south. In addition, the northeastern Iroquois were held together by a confederation of six tribes and an alliance with others. Their chief rivals among Indians were the Algonquins, with whom they were often at war. In fact, during the French and Indian War, the Algonquins took the part of the French and the Iroquois that of the English.

White settlers rarely saw Indian ceremonies; in general, these ceremonies tended to be more social and political (and less religious) in nature than those of most North American Indians. Dancing seems to have had less significance here than it did elsewhere. These civilizations are by no means completely gone. There are Indian reservations in New York, for example, where Iroquois live in longhouses and still maintain many of their ancient traditions. The British victory over the French in North America decimated the Algonquins, but there are still many Iroquois in the area.

As in most Indian cultures, many dances have animals as their subjects; the Iroquois, however, are celebrating the animals' lives rather than worshiping their spirits. Dancing involves men, women, and children and is not as clearly structured as it is in the cultures previously described. Since Iroquois dances generally take place inside the longhouses, they cannot be as elaborate or involve as many people as the dances held outside by more southerly tribes.

The Northern Plains. Dance is an integral part of the religious rites of the Indians of the northern Plains. These are performed by both men and women, in large groups, and are highly formalized. Colorful, elaborate costumes are worn. The Plains Indians are the Indians who have been stereotyped in westerns, with feathers, beads, fur, and facial and body paint.

A dance of particular interest is the Sun Dance, a celebration of the cyclical nature of life. The Sun Dance is of interest for several reasons. First, it is still very much in practice, although its nature has changed somewhat. Second, it was elaborately described by Indians in the twentieth century, who saw it in its original form as children. Finally, the Sun Dance was one of the first Indian ceremonies to be banned by the U.S. government, because of its rather violent nature. This ban, never completely successful, was lifted in 1933, after which the ceremony continued in a somewhat curtailed fashion.

In its original form, the Sun Dance is more than a dance. It is a ceremony formed around the building of a lodge. Frenzied singing and dancing accompany the erection of the lodge. After this, young men are initiated into the tribe and become warriors by having their breasts cut by a medicine man and a thong sewn through the cuts. The young men dance and attempt to remove the thongs. Grave injury sometimes results.

Such ceremonies have been curtailed in modern society. The Sun Dance is still practiced, but young men are not as prominently featured in it as they originally were, and the mutilation has been replaced by symbolic sacrifice.

The people now called the Sioux, actually a mixture of related tribes, are strongly dominated by males. Men have traditionally held the central place in dances, as in most other aspects of life. As elsewhere, however, some aspects of the modern world have changed the basic ceremonies. At the beginning of the Sun Dance ceremony, for example, the American flag is raised, and there may be Christian as well as Sioux prayers said.

The Southern Plains. The dances of the southern Plains groups are not very different from those of their northern neighbors in terms of symbolism and theme. One difference is a greater preponderance of war dances. The most important way in which the two areas differ in their ceremonies is in the degree of formality and the exclusiveness of a dance or ceremony to a particular tribe.

In the southern Plains, dances and pow-wows are as much social gatherings as religious rituals. Often, many tribes will participate. Nearly anyone can get up and join in the festivities, and although the costumes can be as elaborate as they are in the north, formalized dress is not required. Today, among the dancers dressed in beads and feathers, one may see others dressed in jeans and flannel shirts.

The southern Plains were the last area in the contiguous states to be taken formally from the Indians, and thus the most traditional ceremonies can often be seen here. Oklahoma, until it was opened to white settlement in 1889, was still considered Indian Territory. Oklahoma has one of the largest proportions of Indian population in the United States.

Marc Goldstein

Sources for Further Study

Bancroft-Hunt, Norman. *People of the Totem*. New York: G. P. Putnam's Sons, 1979. A description of Northwest American Indian culture, including a study of their history, ceremonies, and contemporary conditions.

Buttree, Julia M. *The Rhythm of the Red Man*. New York: A. S. Barnes, 1930. A description of Indian rituals, especially music and dance, including step-by-step instructions for a great number of dances and rituals followed by a variety of tribal groups.

Evans, Bessie, and May G. Evans. *Native American Dance Steps.* Mineola, N.Y.: Dover Publications, 2003. A detailed study of the different dance forms of various Native American tribes.

Hamilton, Charles. *Cry of the Thunderbird: The American Indian's Own Story.* New ed. Norman: University of Oklahoma Press, 1972. A compilation of articles by American Indians about their culture, including memories of childhood, historical beginnings, and contemporary conditions.

Heth, Charlotte, ed. *Native American Dance: Ceremonies and Social Traditions.* Washington, D.C.: National Museum of the American Indian, Starwood Publishing, 1992. An illustrated guide to the dances of many American Indian tribes, with descriptions of specific dances as well as general discussions of dance practices by region.

Spencer, Robert F., Jesse D. Jennings, et al. *The Native Americans.* New York: Harper & Row, 1977. An encyclopedic discussion of American Indian culture, from prehistory to contemporary times.

See also: Deer Dance; Ghost Dance; Gourd Dance; Grass Dance; Music and Song; Pow-wows and Celebrations; Stomp Dance; Sun Dance; Tobacco Society and Dance; White Deerskin Dance.

Death and Mortuary Customs

Tribes affected: Pantribal
Significance: *American Indians have a wide variety of religious traditions and thus a wide variety of practices regarding the disposition of the dead.*

Among the many American Indian tribes studied by modern anthropologists, there is a great variety of practices concerning death, dying, and the disposition of dead bodies. There is a virtually uni-

A depiction of a Native American burial ground from the mid 1800's. *(National Archives)*

versal belief in the existence of a spirit separate from the body which can exist when the body is dead. Since these spirits are considered capable of harming the living, they are often feared. In many Indian cultures death is accepted stoically by individuals, but rituals are considered necessary to provide protection for the living.

Traditional Practices. Unfortunately, many Indian tribal traditions had become extinct before they could be studied by modern scholars, and some puzzling remains have been found. Generally, burial seems to have always been the most common way of disposing of dead bodies, though there is considerable evidence of cremation, as well. In the southwestern United States, mass graves have been found, sometimes consisting merely of piles of heads or headless bodies. In a few cases, burial sites have been found in which only the bones of hands are buried.

In more recent times, Indians have been known to bury their dead in coffins, with ceremonies not greatly different from those of Christians and Jews. There are, however, quite a number of exceptions. On the West Coast, for example, many tribes had the custom of leaving bodies lying in state above ground for as long as a week, after which the remains were buried or cremated. In the far north, among the Eskimos (Inuits), bodies have been left above the ground permanently, usually on a hill far from the village.

Many northern tribes, including the Athapaskans and the Tlingit, begin ceremonies with mourning and wailing and then proceed to have a potlatch, a joyous gathering of tribe members where gifts are exchanged and long, involved feasts take place. A few tribes, including the Mesquakie (Fox) and some Eskimos, traditionally believed that the departing spirit needed a guide and killed dogs for the purpose, which were buried with their former masters. Many tribes surrounded the body with possessions belonging to the deceased.

Beliefs in an Afterlife. Because American Indians have never been a single culture, beliefs vary considerably. There are certain ideas, however, which seem to be almost universal among North American Indians. One of the most common is the belief that the spirit, like the soul of Christian belief, is separate from the body and can leave the body. Many tribes believe that the spirit actually leaves the body during sleep and is capable of wandering in the land of the dead. During this time, the spirit can gain great knowledge of the afterworld and communicate with its ancestors. At death, the separation is final.

The postulated location of the land of the dead also varies. In some cases, it was considered to be very close to the land of the living; such places were dreaded and avoided. Much more often, however, the realm of spirits was placed far from the living lands—in the sky, under ground, beyond the sunset, or over the seas. As a general rule, this land was considered to be very much like the land of the living, with the spirits eating and drinking, hunting, and dancing.

The Current Situation. Many of the practices cited above are unacceptable in the modern world. Leaving a decaying body outside for a week at a time, for example, is considered a clear health hazard. In addition, the majority of modern Indians have accepted Christianity, at least in part. It is not unusual, especially in the more remote areas of the Arctic and Subarctic, for two death ceremonies to be held: one Christian, one traditional. Among the Athapaskans, for example, the body is generally buried in a Christian ceremony presided over by a minister and conducted in English. Afterward, the traditional potlatch is held, conducted in the native language.

Marc Goldstein

Sources for Further Study

Carmody, Denise Lardner, and John Tully Carmody. *Native American Religions: An Introduction*. New York: Paulist Press, 1993.

Ceram, C. W. *The First American: A Study of North American Archaeology*. Translated by Richard Winston and Clara Winston. New York: Harcourt Brace Jovanovich, 1971.

Deloria, Vine, Jr. *God Is Red: A Native View of Religion*. Rev. ed. Golden, Colo.: Fulcrum, 2003.

Oswalt, Wendell H. *This Land Was Theirs: A Study of North American Indians*. 7th ed. Mountain View, Calif.: Mayfield, 2001.

Spencer, Robert F., Jesse D. Jennings, et al. *The Native American*. 2d ed. New York: Harper & Row, 1977.

Wissler, Clark. *Indians of the United States*. Rev. ed. Garden City, N.Y.: Doubleday, 1966.

See also: Ethnophilosophy and Worldview; Feast of the Dead; Mounds and Moundbuilders; Ohio Mound Builders; Religion; Rite of Consolation.

Deer Dance

Tribes affected: Pueblo tribes
Significance: *The Deer Dance was a winter ceremony called by hunters to ensure an increase in game and good luck in hunting.*

In Pueblo culture, all social and religious life revolves around the theme of achieving harmony with the gods of nature to ensure the prosperity of agriculture and hunting. The Deer Dance is performed to achieve harmony with the spirits of the deer to ensure daily survival. Like all game animal dances, the Deer Dance is believed to cause an increase in the deer population and also to enhance the skills of those who hunt them.

In the Pueblo calendrical cycle, agricultural ceremonies are held in the summer, while curing, warfare, and hunting ceremonies occur in the winter. The Deer Dance, along with other game animal dances, is performed in the winter months, when household supplies are at their lowest and families feel the need for spiritual assistance in gathering food. While the ceremony differs from pueblo to pueblo, reciprocity through gift-giving between humans and spirits is an inherent part of the dance. In the Deer Dance, the deer are enticed to the village with cornmeal and are fed; later the deer will feed the people.

Lynne Getz

See also: Dances and Dancing.

Demography

Tribes affected: Pantribal

Significance: *After European contact, most Native American nations experienced dramatic population losses, but today they represent one of the fastest-growing segments of American society.*

When Europeans arrived on the shores of North America, they encountered an estimated 1.2 to 18 million people. They were the "original Americans," descendants of people who journeyed to North America thousands of years before Europeans. Over the millennia, Native Americans evolved hundreds of unique cultural traditions with their own worldviews, perhaps two hundred languages (of several distinct families), ecological adaptations to every environmental situation, and a range of forms of governance. Native North America, prior to the arrival of Europeans, represented one of the most ethnically diverse regions in the world. Tragically, much of this cultural mosaic was extinguished by massive population declines after European contact. Yet Native Americans survived this demographic and cultural onslaught to represent one of the fastest-growing segments of American society today.

Prehistoric Demographic Trends. The colonization of the Americas by Paleo-Indians (an anthropological term for the ancestors of Native Americans) was one of the greatest demographic events in global history. There has been considerable controversy regarding the dates for early migrations to North America. Some scholars have suggested that the earliest migrations occurred as far back as fifty thousand years ago; some have said that migration may also have occurred as recently as three thousand years ago. A more generally agreed-upon time frame for the migrations, however, is between twenty-five thousand and twelve thousand years ago.

Although many Native Americans reject the hypothesis that their ancestors immigrated from greater Eurasia, archaeological evidence suggests that some first Americans may have entered the

Western Hemisphere during the many glacial periods that exposed Beringia, the Bering Strait land bridge. Beringia periodically linked Siberia with the Americas, allowing animals and humans access to both continents. Others may have made the journey using boats, following a maritime route or traveling down a coastal corridor. In any event, these irregular waves of colonizers represented the last great global movement of people into unoccupied land—a migration hallmark in human history.

How many "first Americans" entered the Americas is unknown. Archaeologists note that the Late Wisconsin glacier's recession about fifteen thousand years ago allowed Native American people to migrate southward, eventually colonizing the remainder of the Americas. Prior to that time, the glacier largely prevented further immigration and colonization. What specific routes they took and how rapidly people dispersed across both continents are topics of considerable archaeological debate. There is firm evidence that by 9400 B.C.E. Native Americans had reached southern South America, indicating that Native Americans had dispersed widely across the "New World's" landscape. Despite hypotheses that argue for an accelerated population growth rate, it is likely that during this early colonization period, the Native American population's growth rates were slow to moderate, with cyclical rates of growth and decline. These population fluctuations reflected a complex array of changing social, demographic, and ecological conditions as local populations adapted to regional conditions.

In North America, Native American demographic distribution and redistribution paralleled closely the glacial retreat north, the trend toward regional and climatic aridity that altered local resources, and cultural innovations. The above factors, by 9000 B.C.E., eventually made possible the colonization of every available area on the North American continent. These hunter-gatherers and, later, the cultural traditions known as Archaic societies, developed a greater variety of lifeways, producing marked differences in population size, distribution, and vital events.

Paleopathological evidence indicates that prehistoric Native American populations faced a number of health risks. Documented cases of malnutrition, anemia, tuberculosis, trachoma, trepanematoid infections, and degenerative conditions occurred in pre-Columbian North America. These afflictions, coupled with periodic trauma, accidents, and warfare, affected the demographic structure of regional populations.

A cultural innovation that had significant demographic consequences was the invention and diffusion of agriculture. Sometime before 3500 B.C.E. in Mesoamerica, maize, beans, and squash were domesticated. As this cultural knowledge spread northward, many Native American societies east of the Mississippi River, in the Southwest, and along the major waterways of the greater Midwest adopted agriculture. Demographically, agriculture promoted the development of larger populations, residing in sedentary villages or cities. Near present-day Alton, Illinois, along the Mississippi River, for example, was the urban center of Cahokia. At its height about 1100 C.E., Cahokia extended over 5 square miles and had a population of perhaps thirty thousand people. Although regional population concentrations arose across native North America, by 1300 C.E. many areas containing high population densities began to decline. The causes of the decline and social reorganization in some regions are open to debate. It is clear that in a number of regions, high population densities and size remained until the European encounter.

By the time of European contact, native North America demographically contained a variety of population sizes and densities, ranging from fewer than one person per 10 square miles in the Great Basin to the densely settled, resource-rich regions of the Pacific Northwest, Northeast, Southeast, and Southwest. These areas may have supported from five to more than one hundred people per 10 square miles. By the time Europeans arrived, Native Americans already had undergone a number of profound demographic events.

Historical Demographic Trends. The European colonization of North America launched a series of catastrophic events for Native American populations. Native American societies experienced tremendous population declines. Native American populations periodically experienced mortality increases, decreases in their fertility performance, forced migration, as well as a deterioration of their societal health status.

Of all the factors that affected post-contact Native American societies, the accelerated death rates from the introduction of European diseases remain prominent. Europeans brought smallpox, measles, cholera, and other infections that were foreign to Native American people. It has been estimated that ninety-three epidemics of Old World pathogens affected Native Americans since the sixteenth century. Old World diseases, combined with warfare, genocide, and the introduction of alcohol, forced migration and relocation, and the overall destruction of indigenous lifeways resulted in the demographic collapse of native North America. One Native American scholar called it the "American Indian Holocaust."

Within decades of European contact, Native American populations declined. The colonization of the Spanish, French, and, later, English set in motion significant population changes. Between 1500 and 1820, Native American populations residing east of the Mississippi River declined to approximately 6 percent of their at-contact size. In the southeastern region, for example, the estimated Native American population in 1685 was 199,400. By 1790 their population was approximately 55,900—a decline of 71.9 percent. Paralleling this demographic collapse, the ethnic diversity of indigenous societies residing east of the Mississippi River declined between 25 and 79 percent, as distinct Native American nations were driven to extinction or forced to amalgamate with other Native American nations.

In 1830, the remaining Native Americans in the East were forcibly removed to west of the Mississippi River under President Andrew Jackson's administration. Between 1828 and 1838, approximately 81,300 Native Americans were thus removed. For their relocation efforts, the U.S. government acquired 115,355,767 acres of Indian lands and resources. Furthermore, the Choctaw, Chickasaw, Cherokee, Seminole, and Muskogee lost between 15 and 50 percent of their population during the forced relocation. Other removed Native American tribal nations suffered similar demographic losses. By about 1850, the estimated Native American population stood at 383,000.

As Native American populations declined, the European, African American, and Latino populations grew, occupying the available lands acquired from Native Americans. Aside from losing their land and resources, the increasing contact with non-Indians had other important demographic consequences. Since contact, Native Americans have experienced an increased genetic exchange with European and African populations. The rise of people with Native American-European or Native American-African ancestry, or of all three ancestries, may have had significant implications for tribal survival and demographic recovery. Some scholars suggest that depopulation and the following demographic recovery resulted in certain physical and genetic changes in those groups who survived. The incorporation of Europeans, African Americans, or other Native Americans promoted further those phenotypic and genotypic processes.

As the American population of European descent surpassed twenty-three million by 1850, Native Americans west of the Mississippi River began to experience directly the brunt of colonization and settlement. Prior to that time, western Native American populations had experienced introduced infectious diseases, intermittent warfare with Europeans, and an erosion of their resources. The Mandan, for example, boasted an estimated at-contact population of possibly 15,000. After the 1837-1838 smallpox epidemic, their population collapsed to between 125 and 1,200 individuals, forcing them eventually to merge, culturally and biologically, with the Arikara and Hidatsa. Western indigenous nations, from 1850 through 1880, witnessed continued demographic upheaval. Their population changes during those decades were affected by the dramatic social and economic changes in U.S. society. The United States economy was industrializing, American society was becoming more urban, and the federal government desired a link between the east and west coasts as a completion to its nation-building. In addition, the United States experienced a dramatic influx of European immigrants. In three decades, from 1850 to 1880, the European population increased to 50,155,783. To meet these economic and political demands, western lands and resources were needed. This prompted the federal government to alienate Native Americans from their remaining lands. The continued demographic collapse of many Indian nations occurred under the guise of the nation's rhetoric of Manifest Destiny.

In an attempt to subdue the remaining indigenous populations and force them onto reservations, the U.S. government either negotiated a series of treaties or carried out military expeditions. The combined impact of war, disease, and the continued destruction of their lifeways resulted in further population decline. By the time Native Americans were relegated to reservations or rural communities in 1880, there were 306,543 Native Americans surviving in the coterminous United States.

The indigenous population of the United States reached its nadir in 1890. The 1890 U.S. Census recorded 248,253 Native Americans in the continental United States. Although most infectious diseases experienced during the pre-reservation era began to diminish, these acute infections were replaced with chronic diseases on reservations. Poor sanitation, poor nutrition, and overcrowding resulted in the appearance of tuberculosis, trachoma, and intermittent measles and influenza outbreaks, as well as a rise in infant mortality. As these afflictions reached epidemic proportions, the Native American population between 1900 and 1920 remained rather static. Most Native Americans continued to live on reservations or rural areas, isolated from society. In 1920, only 6.2 percent of Native Americans resided in urban areas.

After 1930, however, Native Americans began to experience a tremendous growth rate. With the passage of the Indian Reorganization Act (1934), cultural oppression lessened, health and sanitation conditions improved, and social programs began to affect Native American demography positively. Native American populations grew because fertility increased, infant survivorship improved, and the death rate fell. The result was a young age-sex structure.

The advent of World War II witnessed a migratory shift away from reservations and rural communities. Attracted by service in the armed forces and urban job prospects, many Native Americans migrated to major cities. The outflow of Native American immigrants to urban centers initiated a demographic trend that continues to the present. The out-migration of Native Americans was stimulated further by the Bureau of Indian Affairs. In the mid-1950's, the federal government instituted a relocation program. The program assisted Native Americans through job training and support services in being placed in urban centers. In 1990, for the first time since indigenous people have been recorded by the U.S. Census Bureau, the census recorded that more Native Americans resided in urban than in rural areas. The Greater Los Angeles metropolitan area, for example, had 87,500 people of Native American descent, an increase of 5 percent over the previous decade.

Since the 1950's, the Native American population has grown tremendously. In 1960, there were 551,636 Native Americans. By 1970, there were 827,273 people who identified themselves as Native American. The 1980 U.S. Census witnessed a 71.1 percent increase. The reasons for this growth are complex and multifactorial. First, after the transfer of the Indian Health Service from the Bureau of Indian Affairs in 1955, Native American health improved dramatically, especially infant and child health care. Second, Native American fertility increased and mortality decreased, adding significantly to the population. Finally, more Americans are identifying themselves as having Native American ancestry.

Demographic Trends. The Native American population of the United States is young and growing: 1.4 million of the total self-identified population of 4.3 million (July 1, 2002) were under eighteen years of age, with less than 300,000 age sixty-five or over. Only 14 percent age twenty-five or over reported having earned at least a bachelor's degree; 75 percent in the same age group reported a high school diploma. A scant 125,000 reported an advanced degree.

As a result, the Native American population suffers from social problems in which demography plays an important role. Native

American health status lags behind that of the United States' general population. Deaths by accidents, violence, suicide, tuberculosis, diabetes, and numerous other conditions exceed national averages. Unemployment, in both rural and urban areas, remains high, although the number of Native American-owned businesses increased by 64 percent between 1982 and 1987 and the introduction of Indian gaming in 1988 made inroads into the socioeconomic problems of poverty. Nonetheless, as reported in a December, 2002, article in *Indian Country Today*, only a few tribes have enjoyed a limited benefit from gaming: 22 tribal casinos account for 56 percent of the nearly $12.7 billion in total Indian gaming revenues. While some members of these tribes are enjoying employment in gaming and tourism industries and a significant improvement in socioeconomic status, poverty continues to plague many Native American families and remains well above the national average.

Population Since 2000. As of July 1, 2002, the U.S. Census Bureau estimated that the number of people who were American Indian and Alaska native or American Indian and Alaska native in combination with one or more other races, was 4.3 million in the United States alone, constituting 1.5 percent of the total U.S. population. Of these, approximately three-quarters (3.1 million) claimed membership in a specific tribe, with Cherokee easily the largest at nearly 700,000 members, followed by Navajo, Choctaw, Blackfeet, Chippewa, Muscogee (Creek), Apache, and Lumbee—all claiming more than 50,000 members. Alaskan tribes with more than 5,000 members were the Tlingit (the largest), followed by the Athabascan, Eskimo and Yupik. The increase in this population over the preceding two-year period (from July 1, 2000) was 2.4 percent.

Native American people reside in every state in the union, with the greatest concentration in California at 683,000—and indeed, the majority of the American Indian population overall is concentrated in the West. Alaska claims the highest percentage of native people (19 percent), followed by Oklahoma and New Mexico (both with 11 percent). The number of American Indians living on reservations or other trust lands was more than 538,000, with nearly one-third of these residing on Navajo lands. The percentage of the American Indian population residing in urban areas was 66 percent, the lowest of any ethnic or racial group in the United States.

Native American Population 1800-1990	
Year	*Population*
1800 [1]	600,000*
1810	—
1820 [2]	471,417*
1830 [3]	312,930*
1840 [4]	383,000*
1850	400,764*
1860	339,421*
1870	313,721*
1880	306,543*
1890	273,607
1900	266,732
1910	291,014
1920	270,995
1930	362,380
1940	366,427
1950	377,273
1960	551,636
1970	827,273
1980	1,420,400
1990	1,959,000

Notes: Dash (—) indicates unavailable information. Asterisk (*) indicates a population estimate. Figures from 1850 to 1990 are U.S. Census figures (1850-1880 figures are estimates). Beginning in 1880, enumeration of Native Americans was affected by changing definitions, including shifting blood-quantum criteria and interpretations of the term "Indian."
1. Office of Indian Affairs estimate (1943).
2. Morse population estimate (1822).
3. Secretary of war estimate (1929).
4. Schoolcraft population estimate (1851-1857).

The phenomenal growth rate among Native Americans exceeds the growth for African Americans and Americans of European descent but not the increase in the Latino or Asian populations. Today, Native Americans and Alaska Natives compose approximately 1 percent of the United States population but continue to represent a higher percentage of the country's cultural diversity.

Native Americans have undergone a number of significant population changes. Initially, their ancestors colonized a continent. Over time, these small groups of hunter-gatherers flourished, their population increased, and some societies constructed large, urban centers. After European contact, as the table "Native American Population, 1890-1990" indicates, the Native American population suffered a devastating demographic collapse that lasted for almost four hundred years.

In spite of the demographic and cultural disruptions, economic and social problems, as well as continued ill health, the twentieth century Native American population made a remarkable recovery. All demographic indicators point to continued population growth into the future.

Gregory R. Campbell, updated by Christina J. Moose

Sources for Further Study

Boyd, Robert T. *Coming of the Spirit of Pestilence: Introduced Infectious Diseases and Population Decline Among Northwest Coast Indians, 1774-1874*. Seattle: University of Washington Press, 1999. An analysis of the role of infectious diseases on the size and structure of the Native American population.

Robertson, R. G. *Rotting Face: Smallpox and the American Indian*. Caldwell, Idaho: Caxton Press, 2001. A comprehensive examination of the smallpox epidemic of 1837-1838 and its impact on the American Indian.

Shoemaker, Nancy. *American Indian Population Recovery in the Twentieth Century*. Albuquerque: University of New Mexico Press, 1999. An examination of the cultural, economic, and social factors that have contributed to the growth of the Native American population.

Stannard, David E. *American Holocaust*. New York: Oxford University Press, 1992. A discussion of Native American population decline in relation to European conquest and colonization.

Verano, John W., and Douglas H. Ubelaker, eds. *Disease and Demography in the Americas*. Washington, D.C.: Smithsonian Institution Press, 1992. A collection of articles assessing the health and demography of pre-contact and post-contact Native American populations.

See also: Disease and Intergroup Contact; Employment and Unemployment; Gambling; Relocation; Urban Indians.

Disease and Intergroup Contact

Tribes affected: Pantribal

Significance: *Within decades after contact with Europeans, Native American societies experienced rapid population declines; although the reasons for the demographic collapse of native North America are complex, a prominent factor in that decline was Old World infectious diseases, introduced by European explorers and settlers.*

After the arrival of Europeans, the estimated aboriginal population of native North America began to decline. The Spanish intrusion first into the Caribbean and then into the Southwest and Southeast, circa 1520, launched a series of lethal epidemics that infected various Native American people. The epidemiological conquest of native North America accelerated after the early seventeenth century with English and French colonization along the Atlantic seaboard. The dramatic population decline of indigenous people continued until the early twentieth century. By 1920, 270,995 Native Americans remained after the epidemiological onslaught of European colonization. They were the survivors of perhaps 1.2 million to 18 million Native Americans who inhabited North America at the time of the arrival of Europeans.

Increased mortality among Native Americans as a result of introduced European diseases such as smallpox is not attributable to a lack of sufficient immunological response to infections in general but to the fact that Native Americans had no prior exposure to these pathogens. The "new" pathogens therefore not only created a high degree of physiological stress but also engendered cultural stress. Epidemic episodes often resulted in a breakdown in the social system, elevating mortality levels.

Although European infectious diseases devastated many Native American societies, pre-contact native North America was not a disease-free paradise. Biological and archaeological evidence documents the fact that pre-contact Native American populations suffered from a number of afflictions. Malnutrition, anemia, and a variety of tuberculoid, trepanematoid, and other degenerative,

North American Epidemics and Regions Affected, 1520-1696

Date of Onset	Epidemic	Regions Affected
1520	Smallpox	All regions
1531	Measles	Southwest
1545	Bubonic plague	Southwest
1559	Influenza	South Atlantic states, Gulf area, Southwest
1586	Typhus	South Atlantic states, Gulf area
1592	Smallpox	North Atlantic states, South Atlantic states, Old Northwest, Great Lakes states, Midwest east of Mississippi River, Southwest
1602	Smallpox	Southwest
1612	Bubonic plague	North Atlantic states, South Atlantic states, Gulf area, Southwest
1633	Measles	North Atlantic states
1637	Scarlet fever	North Atlantic states
1639	Smallpox	North Atlantic states, South Atlantic states, Old Northwest, Great Lakes states, Midwest east of Mississippi River
1646	Smallpox	Gulf area, Southwest
1647	Influenza	North Atlantic states
1649	Smallpox	North Atlantic states, South Atlantic states, Gulf area

chronic, and congenital conditions plagued indigenous populations. The general state of health, in combination with ecological and cultural factors, therefore, greatly affected the post-contact disease experience of Native American societies.

Sixteenth and Seventeenth Centuries. No Old World pathogen was more lethal than smallpox, which was unleashed in the Americas during the Spanish conquest. For four years, 1520-1524, the disease diffused across Central and North America. Whether smallpox reached pandemic proportions is debatable, but in populations with no prior exposure, mortality could be as high as 60 percent. The infected native populations experienced high death

Date of Onset	Epidemic	Regions Affected
1655	Smallpox	Gulf area
1658	Measles, diphtheria	North Atlantic states, Gulf area, Old Northwest, Great Lakes states, Midwest east of Mississippi River, Southwest
1662	Smallpox	North Atlantic states, Old Northwest, Great Lakes states, Midwest east of Mississippi River
1665	Smallpox	South Atlantic states, Old Northwest, Great Lakes states, Midwest east of Mississippi River
1669	Smallpox	North Atlantic states
1674	Smallpox	Gulf area, southern Plains
1675	Influenza	North Atlantic states
1677	Smallpox	North Atlantic states
1687	Smallpox	North Atlantic states
1692	Measles	North Atlantic states, Old Northwest, Great Lakes states, Midwest east of Mississippi River
1696	Smallpox, Influenza	South Atlantic states, Gulf area

Sources: Data are from Dobyns, Henry, F., *Their Number Became Thinned* (Knoxville, University of Tennessee Press, 1983); Thornton, Russell, *American Indian Holocaust and Survival: A Population History Since 1492* (Norman: University of Oklahoma Press, 1987).

rates. Florida's Timucua population may have once had 772,000 people, but by 1524 the group was reduced to 361,000.

Throughout the 1500's and into the next century, twenty-three European infectious diseases appeared in native North America. Smallpox, measles, influenza, and the bubonic plague affected Native American populations largely east of the Mississippi and in the Southwest. European populations grew and expanded geographically as declining indigenous populations relinquished their lands and resources. Those Native Americans who resisted white encroachment were vanquished through genocidal warfare or reduced to mission life.

Eighteenth Century. By the eighteenth century, the European population had reached an estimated 223,000 people. Although Europeans were not the demographic majority, epidemics continued to pave the way for further colonization. Throughout the Atlantic coastal region and into the interior westward, native populations were decimated through genocidal warfare and diseases. In the southeastern region of North America, for example, the estimated Native American population in 1685 was 199,400. By 1790, the population was reduced to approximately 55,900—a decline of 71.9 percent. By contrast, Europeans and African Americans in the region increased their population to 1,630,100 or 31.4 percent.

In sum, European expansion during the three first centuries of colonization produced a demographic collapse of Native American populations. Introduced European infectious diseases, combined with periodic genocidal warfare and the destruction of indigenous lifeways, reduced Native Americans to approximately 600,000. By contrast, the European population grew to more than 5 million.

A patient with tuberculosis surrounded by netting in 1915. *(National Archives)*

Since the Nineteenth Century. During the nineteenth century, twenty-four epidemics affected Native American populations. Smallpox continued to appear every 7.9 years among some segment of the Native American population. Between the smallpox episodes, Native Americans contracted measles and cholera every 22.5 years. According to Henry Dobyns, an anthropologist and authority on Native American historical demography, more epidemics occurred during the nineteenth century, with more frequency, than during any other.

One of the most devastating epidemics during this century was the 1837-1838 smallpox epidemic. The disease diffused across most of native North America, but the northern Plains region was hit especially hard. It is estimated that seventeen thousand Native Americans on the northern Plains died before the epidemic subsided. Such acute infectious diseases continued to plague Native American communities into the early reservation period. Only then did these infections give way to the twentieth century epidemics of influenza, tuberculosis, and trachoma—chronic conditions that would infect Native Americans until the 1950's.

The placement of Native Americans on reservations or in rural communities did not mark the end of epidemics. Acute infectious diseases have been replaced by "diseases of poverty." Many of these afflictions reach epidemic proportions in some Native American communities. Deaths from tuberculosis, type II diabetes mellitus, violence, suicide, accidents, and alcoholism exceed the national average. In addition, Native Americans now have to contend with another epidemic—the threat of human immunodeficiency virus (HIV) infection—a disease that has made its presence felt in some Native American communities.

Gregory R. Campbell

Sources for Further Study

Cook, Noble David. *Born to Die: Disease and New World Conquest, 1492-1650*. New York: Cambridge University Press, 1998.

Robertson, R. G. *Rotting Face: Smallpox and the American Indian*. Caldwell, Idaho: Caxton Press, 2001.

See also: Alcoholism; Demography; Medicine and Modes of Curing: Post-contact; Medicine and Modes of Curing: Pre-contact; Missions and Missionaries; Suicide.

Dogs

Tribes affected: Pantribal
Significance: *Dogs provided hunting assistance, food, and companionship among all Indian groups.*

The first dogs in America were domesticated from wolves in Asia and were brought to the Americas some time between forty thousand and fifteen thousand years ago. There were two major breeds of dog in native North America, one long-legged and the other short-legged. The former resembled a German shepherd in build, and the latter was similar to a beagle, though both were extremely variable in coloring and hair length. There is no evidence of selective breeding to keep breeds separate, and dogs with intermediate characteristics were common.

Both breeds of dog were used primarily as hunting aids, flushing game into the open or treeing it. Some dogs apparently were adept at forcing animals into the open by digging into their burrows, but it is unclear whether any tribes regularly trained dogs for hunting skills. Dogs also were used for hauling travois in the Great Plains, for pulling Inuit dogsleds, and as pets everywhere.

Dogs occasionally were eaten throughout North America, especially in times of food shortage. Some groups, such as the Iroquois, had annual feasts at which the eating of a dog was a central part of the activities. In Western Mexico, dogs were eaten more regularly, and the modern chihuahua is descended from a dog bred particularly for eating. These dogs are depicted in ceramic sculptures in prehistoric shaft tombs, especially in Colima, appearing either as plump animals (indicating bounty) or as gaunt, starving animals with jutting jaws and protruding ribs (representing famine).

Russell J. Barber

See also: Horses; Hunting and Gathering; Transportation Modes.

Dream Catchers

Tribes affected: Pantribal

Significance: *A traditional method employed by Ojibwas and other tribes to block bad dreams, dream catchers are now commonly used by practitioners of New Age spirituality.*

The interpretation of dreams was an important activity among American Indian peoples, most of whom believed that dreaming represented a primary mechanism through which spirits communicated knowledge and their wishes to human beings. One manifestation of the significance attributed to dreams was the traditional use of dream catchers by many tribes of the Northeast and Plains. Among the Ojibwas, who are often credited with originating the tradition, the dream catcher is made of a red willow hoop

A fourth grader, Maysarah Syafarudin, inspects the craftsmanship of a dream catcher she made for a school project. *(AP/Wide World Photos)*

filled with a web of sinew (with a hole at its center) on which feathers and sometimes stones were hung. According to one popular version of their significance, dream catchers were suspended above the sleeping areas of infants in order that the good dreams contained in the night air would pass through their holes and fall onto the children while the bad dreams would become stuck in the webbing and be destroyed in the dawn's light. Variations of this interpretation sometimes include the idea that the lattice represents the web of life, woven by Spider Woman. One occasionally sees dream catchers being worn as pendants in early reservation period photographs of Indian men dressed in their best clothing.

In the late twentieth century, the production of dream catchers became a Pan-Indian phenomenon. This development was the result of the rise of New Age spirituality, which appropriated the tradition, transforming and transvaluing it to coincide with this movement's own assumptions concerning the nature and operation of spiritual power. This appropriation also engendered the fabrication of dream catcher earrings, rings and other forms of jewelry.

Harvey Markowitz

Sources for Further Study

Baxter, Paula A. *Encyclopedia of Native American Jewelry: A Guide to History, Peoples, and Terms*. Phoenix: OBYX Press, 2000.

Dubin, Lois. *Native American Indian Jewelry and Adornment from Prehistory to Present*. New York: Harry N. Abrams, 1999.

See also: Feathers and Featherwork; Kachinas.

Dress and Adornment

Tribes affected: Pantribal

Significance: *Designed for comfort, protection, and utility, American Indian clothing and decoration also often designated group affiliation, social role, and rank; it often conveyed—and still conveys—a spiritual message to both wearer and observers.*

European accounts of early contact vividly describe the wide variety of clothing worn by the original people of North America. Recorded in detail by skilled artists, varied styles of dress emphasized the uniqueness of each group.

Drawings showed Inuit (Eskimo) people of the far north dressed in two-layered outfits of caribou skin, one layer with fur turned out, the other with fur against the body. Sealskin mittens, moccasins, and parkas, all lined with fur, made an insulated cocoonlike outfit designed for survival in the bitterest of Arctic winters. The decorative touch to the male Eskimo's outfit was a carved ivory labret—a disk "buttoned" into his perforated lower lip. Its trade value was twenty-five caribou skins. A ruff of wolverine fur on the hooded parka and eye coverings with narrow slits to protect against the sun's glare on snow left no part of the body exposed to the elements.

In distinct contrast, the men of the Plateau west of the Rockies were shown wearing the simplest of outfits—nothing. Occasionally they wore sandals and a short robe of rabbit skins. Women of nomadic Plateau cultures wore no shirts, only simple apron-skirts and sandals woven of soft fibers. A woman would wear a basketlike hat to protect her forehead from the carrying strap of the basket slung over the back.

Similar modes of dress were seen among other peoples in similar climates. Between these extremes was a vast assortment of styles. Virtually every substance in nature was used in the making of clothing or ornamentation. Materials used ranged from buffalo wool spun on a spindle to the inner bark of cedar trees woven into fabric. It was the custom to use all parts of anything taken from its natural habitat. Furs, skins, feathers, shells, bones, teeth, and claws of animals, birds, and fish were the main materials for clothing or adornment. Fabrics were woven of grasses, tree bark, cotton, and other fibrous plants. Mosses, leaves, and downy plants such as milkweed were used for insulation. Plants were used for making natural dyes.

Clothing of Ancient Peoples. The early people of North America created clothing for comfort and utility. Clothing evolved to suit the climate and the physical, social, and cultural activities of the people. The Hohokam, Mogollon, and Anasazi, ancient peoples in the Southwest, wove clothing and blankets from cotton, animal fur, and feathers, and adorned themselves in turquoise jewelry. Rabbit fur and deerskin were punched with an awl and laced together with thongs. Women's aprons and sandals were made of yucca, a fibrous desert plant.

People of the Adena and Hopewell cultures, ancient Eastern Woodland cultures, fashioned clothing from deerskin, adding leggings and moccasins to the men's shirt and breechcloth. Women wore wraparound skirts and tunics of deerskin. Hopewell people wore copper breastplates, ornate feather cloaks, and headdresses. The Adena wore copper bracelets and rings, stone gorgets (armor for the throat), bone masks, pearl beads, and mica ornaments.

Decoration could be functional as well as attractive. A ceremonial feather cloak could serve as a sunshade or raincoat in a tropical climate. Gorgets protected the vulnerable throat. In later times, when clothing was tailored, fringe helped wet buckskin to dry quickly by wicking moisture away from the body. Beads and quillwork added strength to skins or fabric for longer wear.

Meanings Conveyed by Clothing. Artful adornment created by each group of American Indians expressed both spiritual style and beauty. Clothing and decorations carried meaning, symbolizing the beliefs, values, and intentions of the wearer. A warrior painting his body as he dressed for battle was visibly declaring his purpose and praying for a successful outcome.

Dress and adornment could indicate membership in a particular group, clan, or society, making it possible, even from a distance, to distinguish outsiders from those belonging to the group. In battle, this distinction could mean life or death. An outfit that indicated clan membership could guarantee food and shelter from other clan members for a traveler. Clothing often helped to identify social or familial bonds between people who had just met.

A Sioux man pictured in formal dance attire in 1899. *(Library of Congress)*

Plains People. Among the northern Plains people, clothing and items of adornment for both men and women were carefully planned, patiently made, finely decorated, and functional. In early times animal skins were used; the same designs were rendered later in trade cloth. Motion was expressed in swaying fringe, splashes of bright paint, jingling bells, and beads or elk teeth. The decorations recalled the swaying grasses of the Plains.

Clothing could be packed and transported easily when the nomadic Plains people traveled. The people's mobility helped promote a common style among various Plains groups. Gifts of clothing were exchanged during large seasonal gatherings. Garments worn in successful battles were often copied, both to honor the warrior and to acquire some of his powerful medicine.

The breechcloth, a single panel of plain buckskin or cloth held in place with a thong belt, was the everyday garment for the Native American man of the Plains. A coating of bear grease protected his skin from cold, insects, brush, and germs. For formal wear, the breechcloth was usually beaded or painted. Crow men preferred a two-part apron, with finely beaded floral designs, similar to those worn by Woodlands men. Leggings of elk hide or deer hide were practical for walking or riding through the brush or for sitting on the ground. The ever-present fringe was handy for making repairs or using as cords. If snagged on brush or stone, the fringe would break off, leaving the wearer free and the garment intact.

Men often wore tunic or poncho-style shirts with split sides. Under the shirt a belt held up the leggings and carried weapons, tools, and a pipe bag. In cold weather a decorated robe of buffalo hide or fur completed the outfit.

The war shirt, worn only for ceremony or battle, was richly decorated with fringe, beads or quills, ermine tails, scalps, and other medicine items. Painted with symbols of power, these shirts were believed to be protective for the wearer. When beaded and decorated, the war shirt could weigh as much as forty pounds—an acceptable burden because of its medicine power, which gave confidence and status to the wearer.

The southern Plains groups used rich, dark-green dyes, eagle

Due to the warmer climate, dress in western Arizona was often reduced to loincloths, as worn by these Native Americans in the late nineteenth century. *(National Archives)*

feathers, eagle bone whistles, and medicine bags for decoration. In contrast, the northern peoples—Mandan, Crow, Blackfoot, and Sioux—created ornate shirts with beads and quillwork. When the long northern winter brought a hiatus to war, it provided time for tailoring, repairing, and decorating garments.

Other Regions. In the Southeast, as in most warm climates throughout the continent, the usual outfit for men was breechcloth and moccasins. Algonquian men of the temperate Northeast coastal area spent the summer months in breechcloth and moccasins, and during cooler weather wore skin pants or leggings, skirts, and robes. Men shaved their heads except for a scalp lock, and war paint was worn for ceremonies. Crowns and cloaks of turkey feathers and necklaces made of prized wampum—purple clam shells and white conch shells—made elegant outfits. Women wore sliplike tailored dresses topped with cape-sleeves or the short poncho shirt. They sewed strings of valuable sacred wampum to their deerskin shirts, tied the strings around their waists and in their hair, and wore them as necklaces and bracelets. Leggings and moccasins completed the outfit.

Among the Iroquois of the Woodlands area, men wore deerskin kilts and leggings topped with shoulder sashes of woven fiber. In cooler weather skin shirts and moccasins were added. Women dressed in wrapped deerskin skirts, loose shirts, and moccasins. Elk teeth or cowrie shells adorned the shirts.

The ceremonial dress of the Zuñi woman was a rectangle of black hand-loomed cloth trimmed in dark blue. She tied it over her right shoulder, wrapped a long woven sash around her waist, then covered her shoulders with a white robe.

The valuable Chilkat blanket marked the high point of Northwest weaving art. The Tlingit people made this blanket of goat's wool woven into a cedar bark core in boldly stylized images of clan animals using black, white, yellow, and the prized blue dye. Chilkat blankets originated with the coastal Tsimshian group and were worn by men and women in ceremonial dances.

A wealthy Hupa woman of northern California wore a fringed skirt covered with a full apron of shells. Dozens of shell necklaces covered a sleeveless shirt. Shell hair ties and earrings completed the outfit.

Jewelry and Body Decoration. All peoples of North America used jewelry for decoration and nearly all to indicate status. The earliest jewelry was of shells, feathers, turquoise stones, and easily worked copper. In addition to the purple and white shell wampum in the eastern woodlands, the bear claw necklace was highly prized by warriors. The artisans of the Southwest worked with silver and turquoise to create distinctive jewelry—the Navajo "squash blossom" necklace and concha belt, the Hopi layered silver cutout bracelet, and the Zuñi silver pins inlaid with stone and shell.

Face and body painting was done in most groups, sometimes for decoration, more often for ceremonies. Paint could also take the place of clothing in the summer. Red, black, and white were favored colors. Body piercing for adornment was common and included jewelry such as labrets in the lips, earrings for men and women, and rings, bones, or shells worn in the nose.

Tattooing was done with charcoal, needles, dyed thread or cactus spines, and burned shells. Various styles included: Subarctic (marks on the chin during girls' puberty rites), Haida (crests on arms, legs, chest, and back, especially for the highborn), West Coast people (bands on chin, cheek, or forehead for men or women, with wrist bands and lines on the chest for some women), Teton women (lip and facial tattoos), and Natchez women (across the nose). High ranking men and women wore intricate designs that often completely covered the body.

Hair Styles and Status. Hair was a symbol of strength, individuality, and spirituality. In some groups, women wore their hair long and men wore their hair short. In others this custom was reversed. There was great diversity even among the same people. Styles varied from hair that was never cut (sometimes touching the ground), worn straight or braided, to shaved head with only a small scalplock left on top. Men of the Subarctic tucked their long hair under a turban. Some Plains men wore as many as eight long braids. Aztec commoners kept their long hair uncovered, and Creek men shaved the sides of their heads, leaving a center strip from forehead to the nape of the neck. Natchez men shaved one side of the head and wore their hair long on the other.

Women's hair styles included shoulder length with bangs for Western Apache, side buns of the "squash blossom" style for Hopi maidens, a middle part with two long braids for Jicarilla Apache, braids woven with ribbons and wrapped around the head for Aztec commoners, several braids for Natchez women, a topknot with ribbons for Creek, and hair brought up and forward in bonnet shape (creating a natural sun visor) for Seminole women.

In complex societies with various status levels, hair and head-dressings designated a person's role or rank. More valuable materials and more ornate designs denoted higher status. The Aztecs defined four levels: commoner men and women wore their hair long and uncovered, chiefs wore leather headbands with multi-colored tassels or gold and turquoise crowns, warriors had large feather headdresses, and the priestly wore elaborate outfits with headdresses representing gods and goddesses.

Effects of European Contact. European contact influenced the clothing of almost every group, in style, fabric type and color, and adornment. Earlier garments of natural colored fiber, fur, and hides were replaced with wool and other red or blue fabrics richly decorated with beads or quillwork. Additions of ribbonwork and appliqué to basic styles were most elegantly done by East Coast people, especially Iroquois of the north and Seminole of the south. Satin dresses took the place of coarse woven fiber outfits. Western Apache women adopted the European full skirt of bright calico topped with a belted hip-length blouse.

Zuñi men replaced their short cotton kilts with European-style loose white cotton shirts worn over white pants. Leather concho belts with silver disks and hard-soled sandals set a style eventually copied by Europeans. In the North, caribou and buffalo robes were replaced with woolen coats or the hooded "capote"—a cloak made from the colorful Hudson's Bay Company trade blanket.

Gale M. Thompson

Sources for Further Study
Billard, Jules B., et al. *The World of the American Indian.* Washington, D.C.: National Geographic Society, 1974. More than 440 illustrations, maps of culture areas, poems and chants, tribal location supplement with keys to back-pocket maps, index, and acknowledgments.

Brown, Joseph Epes. *The North American Indians: A Selection of Photographs by Edward S. Curtis*. New York: Aperture, 1972. Images selected from thousands of photographs in the Curtis collection. Features people of many groups west of the Mississippi River, with excellent examples of clothing and headdresses. Songs, quotations from well-known traditional people of North America, historians, and anthropologists, captions and detailed notes on photographs.

Mails, Thomas E. *Mystic Warriors of the Plains*. Garden City, N.Y.: Doubleday, 1972. An in-depth study of Plains people: social customs and religion, arts and crafts, clothing, warriors' regalia and weapons, buffalo and horse. Hundreds of drawings by the author, including a diagram of the buffalo showing uses for every part of the animal.

Maxwell, James A., et al. *America's Fascinating Indian Heritage*. Pleasantville, N.Y.: Reader's Digest, 1978. Comprehensive account of all culture areas, prehistory (including Mesoamerican), cultural, political, and social issues of early twentieth century, paintings, color photographs, and drawings, descriptions of ceremonies, list of museums, historic villages, and archaeological sites.

Sturtevant, William, gen. ed. *Handbook of North American Indians*. Washington, D.C.: Smithsonian Institution Press, 1978-2001. The scholarship and thoroughness of the Smithsonian volumes are exemplary, and they include considerable information on (and illustrations of) modes of dress.

Underhill, Ruth M. *Red Man's America: A History of Indians in the United States*. Chicago: University of Chicago Press, 1953. Surveys origins, history, social customs, material culture, religion, and mythology. Written from the perspective of the first peoples of North America.

See also: Applique and Ribbonwork; Beads and Beadwork; Blankets; Feathers and Featherwork; Headdresses; Moccasins; Quillwork; Shells and Shellwork; Tattoos and Tattooing; War Bonnets.

Drums

Tribes affected: Pantribal

Significance: *Drums and other percussion instruments are an almost universal part of Indian music; they are also used in nonmusical tribal ceremonies and have served as a means of communication.*

Drums are used for a variety of purposes in almost every American Indian culture. Most often drumming accompanies singing, although the singers do not necessarily follow the rhythm of the drums.

Drums come in a variety of types. The hand drum is carried by an individual and can be played while dancing. The most common material for this type of drum is hollowed wood, but woven baskets and hollowed gourds are often used as well. There are also large drums around which several people sit and play together. Water drums are made from hollow logs and are partially

The drumheads used by this early twentieth century Eskimo dance orchestra were made from whale stomachs. *(National Archives)*

filled with water. The water greatly increases resonance, and such drums can be heard for miles.

Drums are often decorated elaborately. Much of American Indian singing has religious significance, and the proper gods and spirits must be evoked. One way of doing this is to paint the proper pictures on the body of the drum. Drumsticks are sometimes given much more significance than they have been accorded in European cultures. For some ceremonies, drumsticks are decorated according to their particular ceremonial meaning, and the possession of such sticks may be a sign of prestige. Apart from the more common types of drums, in some area poles or planks may also be beaten. Elsewhere, stretched hides, without any attached drum body, are used.

As well as providing musical accompaniment, drums were used as a form of long-distance communication. A sort of "Morse code" system was used, and it was different for every tribe. Since the signals produced were kept as secrets within a particular tribe, drumming can be seen as a very secure form of communication.

Marc Goldstein

See also: Dances and Dancing; Music and Song; Pow-wows and Celebrations.

Earthlodge

Tribes affected: Plains tribes
Significance: *Earthlodges were among the earliest forms of shelter devised by cultures living on the Plains.*

Earthlodges are circular dome-shaped structures roofed by earth and entered by a covered passageway. Earthlodges appeared around 700 C.E., housing the earliest farm cultures on the Plains. Semi-nomadic villagers constructed earthlodges in three areas of the Plains. In the Dakotas, the Mandan, Hidatsa, and later the Arikara erected villages along the Missouri River. The Pawnee built earthlodge villages in the central Plains of Kansas and Nebraska. To the northeast the Omaha, Oto, and Ponca also constructed earthlodges.

All these people built their lodges in similar fashion. Four or more central posts—usually cottonwood—were set in the ground and were connected by cross beams. A slanted sidewall of smaller posts marked the circumference. A wheel of roof rafters radiated from the central smoke hole and extended to the central posts. The walls and roof were covered alternately with layers of willow branches, grass thatching, a shingling of sod, and a final coat of wet earth that dried like plaster. The average earthlodge was 11 to 13 feet in height and 40 to 50 feet in diameter. Earthlodges lasted from seven to ten years and were the property of the women, who provided much of the labor in building.

Inside arrangements included a sacred area, platform beds along the wall, food platforms, a fencelike wooden fire screen, storage (cache) pits, and often a horse corral. The fireplace was in the center of the earthlodge, and an opening in the roof vented smoke. In the Upper Missouri a bullboat was inverted over the

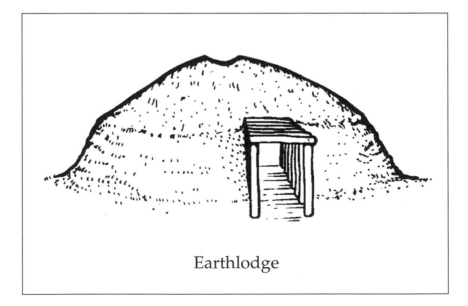

Earthlodge

hole to shut out moisture and regulate downdrafts. When the people went on large summer buffalo hunts they utilized tipis; however, their primary residence was the earthlodge.

Carole A. Barrett

See also: Architecture: Plains; Tipi.

Education: Post-contact

Tribes affected: Pantribal
Significance: *Since 1568, three major groups—Christian missionaries, the federal government, and public school systems—have assumed responsibility for educating American Indians under policies that often have devastated tribal well-being.*

As more and more European settlers entered that part of the Americas now known as the United States, education was seen as a way of assimilating young Native Americans into the dominant white culture. The history of Europeanized Indian education over four centuries tells a story of cultural genocide.

Missionary Activity and Paternalism, 1568-1870. The first school specifically founded for the education of Indian youth in the New World was established by the Jesuits in Havana, Florida, in 1568. For the next three hundred years, Catholic and Protestant religious groups dominated non-Indian attempts to educate Indians. In 1617, King James asked Anglican clergy to collect money for building "churches and schools for ye education of ye children of these Barbarians in Virginia." One of the earliest of these religious schools was founded by the Reverend John Eliot in 1631 in Roxbury, Massachusetts. He developed a plan to bring Indians together in small, self-governing "Indian prayer towns" where they could be instructed in Christian ethics and arts. In order to become accepted by the Puritans in these prayer towns, Indians had to give up their old way of life completely, including long hair for men and short hair for women.

Another example of colonial religious schools was Moor's Charity School, founded in 1755 by Eleazar Wheelock, a Congregationalist minister. This Connecticut school concerned itself with the academic training of Indian youngsters and included reading, writing, arithmetic, English, Greek, and Latin in its curriculum. The school operated until 1769 and enrolled as many as 150 Indian youth.

A common method of providing educational assistance during this period was by treaty stipulation. From the first treaty in 1778 until 1871, when treaty making with the Indians ended, the United States entered into almost four hundred treaties, of which 120 had educational provisions. The terms usually called for teachers, material, and equipment for educational purposes.

The first specific appropriation by Congress for Indian education was the Act of March 30, 1802, which allowed $15,000 per year "to promote civilization among the aborigines." The money went mostly to missionary groups. In 1819, Congress established a civilization fund, which lasted until 1873, to provide financial support to religious groups and other interested individuals who were willing to live among and teach Indians. The Act of March 3, 1819, which established this fund, also gave the president complete authority over Indian education and remained the basic authorization for the educational activities carried out by the government on behalf of Indian people.

Manual labor schools had their beginnings during the period when the tribes were being moved out of the East and Northeast. Usually these were located in Indian country or at a site convenient to several tribes and, for that reason, were agreeable to the Indians. They also drew support from the government, which believed that it was a waste of effort to provide only academic training. The first manual labor school, the Choctaw Academy, was organized in 1837 by Colonel Richard Johnson in Scott County, Kentucky. This school, and others that came later, offered religious, academic, and practical instruction. Six hours were spent daily in the classroom and six at work on farm and shop detail. By 1840, the U.S. government was operating six manual labor schools with eight hundred students and eighty-seven boarding schools with about twenty-nine hundred students.

Several Indian tribes, with the help of missionaries and educators, built and supported their own schools. The Mohawks did this as early as 1712 under the influence of the Reverend Thomas Barkley, an Anglican missionary. This school, with one temporary suspension, operated until the end of the American Revolution. The Choctaws and Cherokees, before their removal from their original homelands, had instituted common schools, supported with funds obtained from the United States for land cessions. After the removal of these tribes to lands west of the Mississippi, the Cherokees, in 1841, and the Choctaws, in 1842, reestablished their schools. (A number of states had not yet provided for a system of common schools in 1842.) The Cherokee system, by 1852, included twenty-one elementary schools and two academies. The enrollment in that year was given as 1,100. The Choctaws had nine schools, of which seven experimented with teaching reading and writing to adults. Teachers were brought from the East to be in charge of advanced academic work, and the course of study included music, astronomy, Latin, botany, algebra, and elocution. Within ten years, however, the majority of their teachers had changed from eastern-educated missionaries to locally trained teachers. The Chickasaw, Creek, and Seminole tribes, also members of the "Five Civilized Tribes," followed the example of the Cherokees and Choctaws within a few years and established school systems. In all cases, the schools were tribally supported, and they operated without federal supervision until 1906, when the tribal governments of these five tribes were destroyed by an act of Congress.

In 1851, the period of reservation settlement began and did not end until the 1930's. Schools established on reservations were designed to devalue the traditional culture and religion of Indian people. One of the most significant ways of undermining Indian culture was the government's attempt to suppress native language. In 1880, the Indian Bureau issued regulations that "all instruction must be in English" in both mission and government schools under threat of loss of government funding. In 1885, some teachers and administrators, recognizing the small utility of standard educational training and methods, suggested that special materials be created for Indian children. No special textbooks were developed, however, until well into the twentieth century.

Government Control and Dependence, 1870-1923. After studying conditions among some of the western tribes, a congressional committee suggested that "boarding schools remote from Indian communities" would be most successful in solving the "Indian problem." President Ulysses S. Grant, believing that the only solution lay in "the civilization" of Indians into white culture, supported the move. In 1878, the boarding school system was launched when the Carlisle Indian School in Carlisle, Pennsylvania, was founded by General Richard Henry Pratt. Pratt, alarmed at the "gross injustices to both races [Indians and blacks]" which he had observed, believed that true equality could come to the Indians only if they learned to feel at home in the white world, where they deserved both "the opportunities and . . . safeguards of our Declaration and Constitution." At Carlisle, which enrolled children from the midwestern and western tribes, students were required to speak, read, and write English and to assume the clothing and customs of white people. They were taught skills which would later help them become employed in trades such as blacksmithing, carpentry, tailoring, and farming. Girls were taught domestic skills. After completing school, students were placed with white families for three years; they worked in exchange for their upkeep. The families were paid fifty dollars a year to cover costs of clothing and health care. This practice came to be called the Carlisle Outing, which Pratt proclaimed to be the "right arm" of the school.

Forts no longer needed by the army were converted into boarding schools. Between 1889 and 1892, twelve such boarding schools were established. Little attention was paid to tribal differences in language and customs. It was assumed—rightly—that if children could be taken at a young enough age and moved far enough away from the influences of family and tribe, the odds against their ever again becoming a part of their original environment were remote.

Boys from the Carlisle Indian School pictured in their cadet uniforms circa 1880. *(National Archives)*

Children as young as five years old were sent to the boarding schools. The shock, fear, and loneliness which these children faced upon being uprooted from everything familiar and known can only be imagined. Pratt, operating under the noblest of intentions, had unwittingly contributed to one of the saddest chapters in Indian history.

By 1887, Congress was appropriating more than a million dollars a year for Indian education. About half the appropriations went to missionaries who were contracted to educate Indians. Feuding between Protestants and Catholics, however, aggravated because the Catholics were much more successful in establishing schools, led the Protestants to support funding only government-run schools. With the appointment in 1889 of General Thomas J. Morgan, a Baptist minister, as commissioner of Indian affairs, the Republicans made a systematic effort to stop government funding of all missionary schools. By 1900 all direct funding to these schools was ended. Tribes continued to receive a portion of the dollars which the federal government had previously provided the churches for funding of the mission schools. Some tribes maintained these schools in spite of the reduced resources; most used the funds for other needs.

Moves to Reform Indian Education, 1924-1944. As the new century began, the continued inability of boarding schools and English-only education to transform Indians into white people led to disillusionment and lowered expectations for Indian education. Increasingly, Indians were viewed in the same light as blacks at that time: as a permanent underclass for whom an inferior, nonacademic, vocational education was appropriate and adequate.

At the same time, because of the staggering loss of land and the inefficiency of education, the total Indian situation was growing progressively worse. In 1902, the Bureau of Indian Affairs (BIA) was operating twenty-five boarding schools in fifteen states for 9,736 students. By 1912, there were more Indian children in public schools than in government schools. As government schools lost ground, efforts to increase Indian enrollment in public day schools did not include examining the ability of these schools to meet Indian needs.

In 1924, a "Committee of One Hundred Citizens" was called together by the secretary of the interior to discuss how Indian education could be improved. The committee recommended better school facilities, better trained personnel, an increase in the number of Indian students in public schools, and high school and college scholarships. These recommendations helped establish reservation day schools up to the sixth grade and reservation boarding schools up to the eighth grade.

In 1928, a government-sponsored study (the Meriam Report) claimed that the Bureau of Indian Affairs was providing poor-quality services to Indians; it particularly pointed to the shocking conditions found in boarding schools. The committee recommended that elementary children not be sent to BIA boarding schools at all. Shortly after publication of the study, John Collier, one of the BIA's leading critics, became commissioner of Indian affairs and immediately sought to implement the recommendations of the Meriam Report. The Johnson-O'Malley Act (1934) allowed the federal government to pay states for educating Indians in public schools.

The Termination Era, 1945-1970. In the 1950's, under President Dwight Eisenhower, six "termination" bills were passed. They were intended to end all federal involvement with the Indians, leaving policy issues in health, education, and welfare up to the states. Conditions improved little as states, for the most part, failed to provide adequate services in any of these arenas. Another program aimed at "relocation" helped Indians move from reservations to cities, where, presumably, educational and employment opportunities were better. Indian children in cities showed improved academic achievement, but many felt displaced and unhappy.

Between 1967 and 1971, Robert J. Havighurst of the University of Chicago directed a research project entitled the National Study of American Indian Education. Their recommendations called for greatly increased Indian participation in goal setting and in implementation of programs. During this same period, a report compiled by a Senate subcommittee on Indian education revealed that Indian school dropout rates were twice the national average, that Indian students lagged two to three years behind white students in school achievement, that only 1 percent had Indian teachers, that one-fourth of teachers of Indian students preferred not to teach them, and that "Indian children more than any other minority group believed themselves to be 'below average' in intelligence."

During this time, Indian educators had become increasingly active, and, by the end of the decade, the National Indian Education Association had been formed. In 1968 the first tribally controlled college, Navajo Community College, was founded, and in 1971 the Coalition of Indian Controlled School Boards was established.

The Move Toward Self-Determination Since 1970. The Senate report on the plight of Indians led to the passage of the Indian Education Act in 1972. This act provided for special programs benefiting Indian children in reservation schools as well as those attending urban public schools. It was amended in 1975 to require that Indian parents be involved in the planning of these programs. The amended version also encouraged the establishment of community-run schools and stressed culturally relevant and bilingual curricular materials. The Office of Education, after a two-year study, recommended that tribal history, culture, and languages be emphasized, using students' own tongue as the language of instruction. During 1977, President Jimmy Carter created the new post of assistant secretary of the interior for Indian affairs and named a member of the Blackfoot tribe, Forrest J. Gerrard, to the position.

In spite of efforts to improve educational opportunities for Indians, Indian students still struggle for visibility in the education market. High-school dropout rates for Indian students continue to be the highest for all minority groups, with fewer than 50 percent completing a high school education. Some reservation schools reported a yearly teacher turnover rate of 90 percent. In 1990, bachelor's degrees earned by Indians comprised less than 0.5 percent of all degrees conferred. Doctorates earned by Indians between 1980 and 1990 actually dropped, from 130 to 102.

In the 1990's, two urban public school districts with relatively large Indian populations began to experiment with schools that focus on Indian culture along with traditional academic curricula. The American Indian Magnet School at Mounds Park All-Nations School in the St. Paul, Minnesota, public school system declared the goal of "placing education into culture instead of continuing the practice of placing culture into education." Three centuries of national educational policy must take at least partial responsibility for the tragic decline of tribal cultures in the United States, but perhaps it will also take the lead in providing a vehicle for the land's original citizens to assume their rightful place in American society.

Dorothy Engan-Barker, assisted by Bette Blaisdell

Sources for Further Study

Cahn, Edgar S., and David W. Hearne. *Our Brother's Keeper: The Indian in White America.* New York: New American Library, 1975. A collection of writings and pictures compiled by the Citizens'

Advocate Center in Washington, D.C.; chronicles the plight of American Indians and actions of the Bureau of Indian Affairs.

Collier, John. *Indians of the Americas.* New York: W. W. Norton, 1947. The author, a former U.S. commissioner of Indian affairs, writes about four centuries of Western European impact on American Indian cultures.

Embree, Edwin R. *Indians of the Americas.* 1934. Reprint. New York: Collier Books, 1970. Embree, writing in opposition to the trend that sought to "integrate" the Indian, revived world interest in the unique lifestyles of North, Central, and South American tribes; focuses on customs, manners, and mysteries of their religion.

Fey, Harold, and D'Arcy McNickle. *Indians and Other Americans: Two Ways of Life Meet.* Rev. ed. New York: Harper & Row, 1970. History of the European influence on the culture of the American Indian; includes first-person accounts by Indians from diverse tribes who shared common experiences regarding attempts by whites to "civilize" them.

Fischbacher, Theodore. *A Study of the Role of the Federal Government in the Education of the American Indian.* San Francisco: R & E Research Associates, 1974. Chronological account of the role of the federal government in the education of American Indians living within the territory of the United States as disclosed in the government's official records.

Fuchs, Estelle, and Robert Havighurst. "Boarding Schools." In *To Live on This Earth.* Garden City, N.Y.: Doubleday, 1972. Summarizes events leading up to and including the establishment of Indian boarding schools, including a discussion of those still operating in the 1960's.

Josephy, Alvin M., Jr. *Red Power: The American Indian's Fight for Freedom.* 2d ed. Lincoln: University of Nebraska Press, 1999. A collection of excerpts from speeches, articles, studies, and other documents providing a documentary history of the critical decade of the 1960's.

Pratt, Richard H. *Battlefield and Classroom: Four Decades with the American Indian, 1867-1904.* Edited by Robert M. Utley. New Haven, Conn.: Yale University Press, 1964. The memoirs of General Richard Henry Pratt, chronicling his work in the establishment of Indian boarding schools; includes photographs from the period.

Riney, Scott. *The Rapid City Indian School, 1898-1933*. Norman: University of Oklahoma Press, 1999. An examination of the daily life of Native American children who attended a BIA boarding school.

Szasz, Margaret Connell. *Education and the American Indian: The Road to Self-Determination Since 1928*. 3d ed. Albuquerque: University of New Mexico Press, 1999. An analysis of the history of edcuation and Native Americans.

U.S. Congress. Senate. Committee on Labor and Public Welfare. Special Subcommittee on Indian Education. *Indian Education: A National Tragedy, a National Challenge*. Washington, D.C.: Government Printing Office, 1969.

See also: American Indian Studies; Children; Missions and Missionaries; Tribal Colleges.

Education: Pre-contact

Tribes affected: Pantribal
Significance: *Pre-contact education did not anticipate great changes in existing lifestyles and therefore centered on the maintenance and preservation of the tribe's culture and way of life.*

Education or socialization of the young is an important concern in all societies, including American Indian societies in the pre-contact period. With the exception of the "high cultures" of Peru and Mexico, however, education did not occur in formal schools. Instead, education of the young was a shared function of families and communities. Owing to the diversity across native cultures, the content of such education varied. In general, both sex and age differences were observed.

Learning Role Skills. One focus of education was the learning of skills necessary for adult roles. Such skills were learned through imitation, often involving play activities, as well as through direct instruction. Among those peoples who subsisted by hunting and gathering, fathers and other older male relatives taught boys the skills of the hunter. Among these same peoples, mothers and other older female relatives served as teachers of girls in gathering plant foods as well as processing and preparing both game and plant foods. Among native peoples who subsisted by farming, fathers and male relatives served as primary teachers of boys, while mothers and female relatives served as primary teachers of girls. Similarly, children received much instruction from adults in learning such skills as weaving, pottery making, tanning, tool making, and the decorative arts. These, too, were differentiated according to gender.

Moral Education. Another major focus of education was the learning of attitudes and values appropriate to the culture. In addition to role modeling, direct instruction was involved. The advent of puberty, with a girl's first menses, was generally marked with advice and instruction on the girl's new status and responsibilities. Older female relatives, and sometimes a shaman and older male relatives, played a part in this. In those native societies that had sodalities, initiates were instructed in the character requirements as well as in the songs, prayers, and powers associated with them.

A major device in instilling proper attitudes and values in children was storytelling. There were not only stories of the sacred, traditions, and events but also stories of culture heroes. The latter, in particular, played a major part in moral education. The storytellers were most often older members of the family or community who were highly regarded for their storytelling skills.

Discipline Strategies. American Indians were noted for their love and mild treatment of children. Discipline was generally marked by an absence of corporal punishment. Instead, children were most often teased and cajoled into proper behavior by their parents and elders. In some of the matrilineal societies, much of the responsibility for discipline was taken on by the mother's brother. Cultural "frighteners" were also known but were not usually flagrantly used.

A Dakota (Sioux) Example. Being primarily a hunting and gathering people, the Dakota had no need for an extensive program beyond that of basic survival and limited arts and crafts. Since they were seasonally nomadic, it was not practical to amass personal possessions and unnecessary items. Consequently, they did not develop their craftsmanship as extensively as did more agrarian cultures. When there was leisure, the women did magnificent quill work, and this was taught to the younger females along with their domestic responsibilities.

In the early years, the Dakota lived in small villages, sometimes as small as an extended family. These villages were extremely independent and required great responsibility and self-discipline from their members. Only the very young child had no responsibilities. There were numerous chores to be done. Among the social responsibilities were preparing for the hunt, gathering roots and berries, harvesting wild rice, making maple sugar, preparing hides, and arranging and preparing for social events. The young were gradually brought into these work roles.

Although education may have been simplified, it was not insignificant or trivial. The Dakota were sustained by a highly efficient ecosystem that had a cyclical chain of events that not only provided subsistence but also brought meaning and identity. They regulated their hunting and trapping to maintain a balance of nature. The young men were thus taught to respect living animals and not to allow them to depopulate.

Education, or the passing on of knowledge, was accomplished in a variety of forms. One of these was ritual. Rituals were performed in order to recall events and certain natural laws. If the ritual was performed exactly as instructed, and the meaning was clearly explained, then whenever the ritual was performed, learning was reinforced. Another form of learning was storytelling.

Many stories and legends were passed down as soon as a young child could understand the spoken word. Stories contained moral lessons, humor, and stimulating anecdotes.

There was also much to be learned through experience. The younger males would accompany the older men on hunts and be allowed to witness warfare from a distance. Young females would start their training even earlier, accompanying the older women when they picked berries and gathered roots.

One of the most important learning experiences for the Dakota youth was the vision quest. When a vision was received, it was a monumental event. One could not easily claim a vision, because the vision had to be confirmed through a careful evaluation by the council of elders. Once confirmed, the vision gave a young man (the vision quest was typically a male experience) direction and purpose. The young person might not clearly understand the vision, but during his lifetime, he would seek its meaning.

Probably the most important learning experiences for young Dakotas were the sessions with elders. During these sessions the elders presented their experiences through the years. They would relate how their own foolishness had caused them much grief and misery in the past. In talking about their mistakes, the elders were teaching the young people the things they should avoid doing. This left the avenue clear for the youths to pursue their own visions and goals armed with wisdom about what not to do. When asked for advice or direction, elders used stories and examples that would help youths make their own decisions. This allowed young people to accomplish on their own the things they felt they should pursue. In this sense, the Dakota did not limit creativity or initiative in educating their young.

Donna Hess and Elden Lawrence

Sources for Further Study

Deloria, Ella C. Speaking of Indians. Vermillion, S.Dak.: Dakota Press, 1979.

Driver, Harold E. *Indians of North America*. Chicago: University of Chicago Press, 1961.

Eastman, Charles A. *Indian Boyhood*. New York: McClure, Phillips, 1902. Reprint. New York: Dover, 1971.

Hodge, William. *The First Americans: Then and Now*. New York: Holt, Rinehart & Winston, 1981.

Hungry Wolf, Beverly. *The Ways of My Grandmothers*. New York: Quill, 1982.

Kupferer, Harriet J. *Ancient Drums, Other Moccasins: Native American Cultural Adaptations*. Englewood Cliffs, N.J.: Prentice Hall, 1988.

Pond, Samuel W. *The Dakota or Sioux in Minnesota as They Were in 1834*. St. Paul: Minnesota Historical Society Press, 1986.

Powers, Marla N. *Oglala Women*. Chicago: University of Chicago Press, 1986.

Sandoz, Mari. *These Were the Sioux*. New York: Hastings House, 1961.

Wissler, Clark. *The American Indian*. New York: Oxford University Press, 1950.

See also: Children; Elderly; Gender Relations and Roles; Menses and Menstruation; Visions and Vision Quests.

Effigy Mounds

Tribe affected: Oneota

Significance: *Low, earthen mounds in the shape of animals, geometric forms, and other forms are among the most distinguishing features of the Woodland culture of the midwestern United States.*

Effigy mounds were constructed by mounding earth into large, low shapes. They occur mainly in groups with conical and linear mounds. The majority of mounds reported have eroded and indistinct shapes; however, others clearly represent life forms. Among the animals represented are bears, deer, felines, wolves, foxes, buffalos, and turtles, as well as eagles, swallows, and geese. Only two or three have been reported in human form. Effigy mounds are known primarily from southern Wisconsin, southeastern Minnesota, northeastern Iowa, and northern Illinois. Many have been preserved in state parks. Unfortunately, the majority have been destroyed by plowing, looting, and construction activities.

The effigies can be quite large. At Mendota, Wisconsin, one bird effigy was 6 feet tall and had a wingspan of 624 feet. In general, the mounds are no more than 2 to 5 feet high. The majority of these mounds appear to have been burial grounds. Examples have been found to contain primary or secondary bundle burials, the latter containing as many as thirty individuals, as well as cremations. These burials are usually situated in key parts of the effigies, such as the head, the position of the heart, or (in bird effigies) between the head and tail. Offerings included with the dead include pottery vessels, copper, stone axes, and tobacco pipes of various materials.

The dates for effigy mound construction are not precisely known. Artifacts found associated with burials in effigy mounds include late Middle Woodland pottery in the form of conical or round-bottomed containers decorated with techniques such as cord-marking, fingernail impressions, dentate stamping, and punctuations. These suggest that the features are roughly contemporaneous with the late Hopewell culture of southern Ohio around 200-700 c.e. There is also evidence, however, for a spread of Mississippian populations from the American Bottom in central Illinois to areas of northwestern Illinois and southern Wisconsin around 800-1000, or the early Late Woodland period, and many of the mounds may have been built around that time.

Effigy Mounds National Monument, in McGregor, Iowa, is one location where these mounds have been preserved and restored. Among the examples at this site are bird and bear effigies. The largest concentrations of effigy mounds are in southern Wisconsin, near Madison and in Sauk and Waukesha counties, where many have been preserved in parks or other public areas.

The largest and most famous effigy is the Great Serpent Mound in southern Ohio. Winding along the top of a prominent ridge, it represents an undulating snake with a tightly coiled tail; the snake appears to be holding an oval object in its mouth. The mound, including coils, is 1,330 feet long. Great Serpent Mound, unlike most effigy mounds, did not contain burials. Its age is Early to Middle Woodland (circa 200 to 400), making it several hundred years earlier than the Wisconsin mounds.

John Hoopes

See also: Mounds and Moundbuilders; Ohio Mound Builders; Serpent Mounds.

Elderly

Tribes affected: Pantribal
Significance: *Native definitions of old age are predicated on tribal custom rather than chronological age; in general, the elderly are treated with respect, although attitudes vary by tribe.*

American Indians and Alaska Natives constitute less than 1 percent of all Americans sixty-five years of age and older. The exact number of older people among Native American populations has been difficult to determine, but the 2000 census data placed the number at that time at 138,439. About 30 percent of the aged Indian population live on reservations, and perhaps another 25 percent live in rural areas.

Traditional Views. The concept of aging is quite different in many native cultures from that of European American society. Birthdays were only introduced on reservations one hundred years ago, and while birthdays are celebrated, one's chronological age is not an operative factor in defining who that person is. Among native people, grandparenting or physical disability would qualify a person as elderly, whereas reaching the age of sixty would be meaningless. In most traditional Indian tribal cultures, there was no concept equivalent to the modern idea of retirement. Older people remained active as long as they were able.

Each tribal culture and society had different attitudes toward the elderly. In some societies, when they became physically unable to care for themselves, the elderly "gave themselves back to the spirit world" by starvation or exposure to extremes of weather. At times they were assisted in this by family members. In other societies, they were "rulers of the house" and simply died of old age.

Despite the trend in many native cultures toward a quick death once productivity was impossible, elderly native people generally enjoyed high esteem because of their age and experience, very often serving in tribal positions of leadership. If capable of performing minimal, even symbolic labors, old people were treated with respect. Only at the extreme, where they became too incapacitated to function, were they either abandoned or likely to dispose of themselves.

Contemporary Issues. American Indian elders are not well-served by a definition of aging set by a chronological measure. Because native people often measure age by productive capability and social role rather than by chronology, under Title VI of the Older Americans Act, Indian tribes are permitted to define, based on their own criteria, who will be considered an older Indian and therefore will be eligible to receive Title VI services. Studies by the National Council on American Indians indicate that American Indians living on reservations at age forty-five show the same age characteristics that other Americans do at sixty-five—a reminder that many racial and ethnic groups experience premature aging under the stress of harsh living conditions.

Disruptive changes have altered much about Indian life. Many Native American senior citizens were sent away to Indian boarding schools as children, separated forcibly from their families. At many of these institutions the children were made to feel inferior and were ridiculed when they spoke their language or showed respect for their Indian heritage.

Today, the prestige associated with old age has persisted among Native Americans, and Native American elders are still, on the whole, treated with respect and honor. Retirement has also become more accepted, and because of high rates of unemployment among native people generally, it is not uncommon for elderly people to help support younger family members with their old-age benefits.

Many elderly Indian people living in urban areas were part of a large American Indian federal relocation project following World War II. This population has now reached retirement age and many have no intention of moving back to the reservation. Many American Indian elders living in cities are deprived of social contact with each other and with younger members of their tribes. Unlike other ethnic groups, city-living American Indians have not congregated in neighborhoods. Some studies also indicate that the popular image of older American Indians living in multigenerational, extended family households is greatly exaggerated in the context of an urban setting. Many native cultures, however, do maintain a tradition of communal sharing among family members and a sense of family responsibility for the care of the elderly. The fact that the elderly represent the repositories of traditional knowledge is widely recognized and is a major factor associated with their good treatment and high status.

Lucy Ganje

Sources for Further Study

John, Randy A. *Social Integration of an Elderly Native American Population*. New York: Garland, 1995.

Olson, Laura Katz. *Age Through Ethnic Lenses*. Lanham, Md.: Rowman & Littlefield, 2001.

See also: Education: Pre-contact; Kinship and Social Organization.

Employment and Unemployment

Tribes affected: Pantribal

Significance: *Before contact with Europeans, the labor of American Indians served group or tribal purposes; employment and unemployment patterns in the twentieth century reflected the profound disruption of Indian life that occurred following contact.*

In the pre-contact period, Indians had extensive trading networks throughout Canada, the United States, and Central and South America. Agricultural goods, manufactured items such as jewelry, pottery, and tanned hides, and natural resources such as seashells were bartered or sold.

Traditional Labor. Labor was required to sustain this extensive trade network, but little is known about how the labor systems were organized. Tribal groups in the Mississippi River area, the southwestern United States, and Central and South America had highly specialized labor forces in which both men and women participated. Division of labor was determined in part by gender, talent, and social position. These societies were organized hierarchically and sometimes incorporated slaves (captives from other tribes), who performed undesirable labor.

Much of North America and Canada was inhabited by nomadic hunting and gathering societies and semisedentary agriculturalists. In these societies, division of labor was based primarily on gender and was less complex, with most tribal members working toward the common goal of providing food, shelter, and clothing for survival. In these subsistence economies, there was little opportunity for members to specialize in any one area, such as art or medicine. Such cultures stressed sharing and egalitarianism as a way to ensure the well-being of the people. Everyone worked for the common good.

Arrival of Europeans. European migration to North America was primarily motivated by economic interests. The first phase of

European-Indian relations revolved around the fur trade, which required the incorporation of Indian labor. The early period of the fur trade is marked by relative equality among Europeans and native people. Indian men and women labored to supply processed hides and pelts for the fur trade. In return for their labor, Indians were paid with European trade goods—metal pots, needles, knives, guns, and a variety of domestic goods. During this period, those Indian people who obtained European trade goods would redistribute them among tribal members, thus maintaining the tribal ideal of generosity and sharing. The trade goods changed the work patterns of both Indian men and women. Guns and traps permitted more men to hunt and kill more game, and, in turn, women were required to tan more hides for trade. Indian labor during this period was still directed toward the good of the tribe, but increasingly tribal welfare depended on sources outside the tribe.

The fur trade was an important source of labor for American Indians, but the fur trade period ended as animal populations decreased and as European fashion changed. The decline in the fur trade coincides with the emergence of the United States and marks a period of change in the economic position of Indians. Indians were no longer needed as laborers in the new economy. The European American population was rapidly increasing and there was an increased desire for land. Indians became a hindrance in this emerging economic system. The relative lack of demand for Indian labor, coupled with the high demand for Indian land, caused the U.S. government to remove Indians from areas coveted by European Americans and resettle them on poor lands.

The reservation system was firmly in place by the late nineteenth century, and it caused considerable change in the work patterns of tribal groups. For the most part, hunting and fishing were no longer possible on the restricted land base, and traditional agricultural practices were not viable or were discouraged. The reservation system afforded little opportunity for Indian people to provide adequately for their families and it is directly linked to contemporary reservation poverty.

During the early reservation period, some Indian men worked for federal agents as freight haulers, policemen, and laborers. Indian women sometimes sold pottery, beadwork, baskets, or other small items. Income from these sources was small. Government policy largely confined Indian people to their reservations, so they were unable to sell their labor for wages off the reservations. Federal Indian policy, most notably the General Allotment Act (1887), reduced the Indian land base and subdivided the land among many heirs so that productive use of reservation lands became nearly impossible. High Indian unemployment rates caused gradual loosening of federal policies of confinement to reservations, and by the early twentieth century Indians commonly worked in off-reservation jobs such as laborers on farms and ranches, and in mines. The 1930 census indicates that 80 percent of Indian men were working for wages, mostly in agricultural jobs. Most of this work was unskilled, seasonal, and off-reservation.

The 1930's. In the 1930's, federal Indian policy sought to address the problem of high unemployment and poor economic opportunity on the reservations. A 1928 study, *The Problem of Indian Administration*, commonly known as the Meriam Report, criticized federal Indian policy that intentionally removed Indian control over lands and resources and contributed to the widespread poverty and unemployment that characterized reservations. Partly in response to this study, the Indian Reorganization Act was passed in 1934. This intended to enable tribes to consolidate severely checkerboarded reservation lands, take out low-interest loans to establish economic ventures on reservations, and encourage farming and ranching opportunities on reservations. The Great Depression prevented any significant business development on reservations; however, a fair number of Indian people benefited through various New Deal programs, particularly the Indian Division of the Civilian Conservation Corps, which employed and trained more than eighty-five thousand Indians in nine years. During the same period, the Bureau of Indian Affairs organized a division to place Indians in off-reservation jobs.

Changes in the Mid-twentieth Century. Thousands of Indians joined the wage labor force during World War II (1939-1945). Many Indian men and women joined the armed services or moved to urban areas to work in war industries. After the war, many Indian people remained in urban centers, while those who returned to reservations began to focus on reservation economic development and employment. Reservations remained poor and unemployment high, however. Few jobs came to the reservations, tribes had difficulty securing loans, reservation laws made business investments difficult, and many reservations were distant from markets. Additionally, off-reservation seasonal farming jobs became scarce with increasing technology. As a result, large-scale Indian urban migration continued after World War II and was encouraged by the federal policy of the 1950's known as relocation. Through the relocation program, Indians were removed to urban areas where jobs could be found. They received job training and housing assis-

An Ojibwa language professor at Bay Mills Community College. *(Raymond P. Malace)*

tance. The lack of any meaningful jobs on reservations, coupled with federal Indian policy, contributed to unprecedented Indian migration to urban areas from 1950 to 1980. By the 1980 census, more than half the Indian population resided in urban areas. Indians continue to move to cities because of poor economic opportunities on reservations. Urban Indians experience higher employment rates and per capita incomes than reservation Indians. They remain poor, however, with per capita income slightly ahead of urban African Americans and well behind urban whites, and unemployment rates more than double those of the urban white population.

The federal government abandoned relocation programs in the late 1960's and turned its attention to revitalizing reservation economies. Concurrently, tribal governments were strengthened and tribes began pursuing economic development initiatives independent of the federal government. Success has been mixed, and reservations still have high unemployment and poverty rates.

Modern Labor Force Participation. On the majority of reservations, the largest single source of jobs is government, either tribal or federal. Despite many sincere efforts, there has been little economic investment or growth on reservations, primarily due to lack of resources, capital, location, and a skilled labor force. Few businesses locate on reservations, and unemployment rates are in the 80 to 90 percent range on some reservations. Census figures on labor force calculate only those who are employed or are actively seeking employment. According to the 2000 census, 60 percent of Indians sixteen years and older were in the labor force. Many of the jobs held, however, were seasonal or part-time. A larger number of American Indians than the total population were employed in service jobs: farming, fishing, forestry, construction, or manufacturing. Fewer Indians, as compared to the total population, were employed in managerial or professional specialty occupations. In 2000, the median income of Indian workers was considerably less than that of the total population, and 26 percent of American Indians were living below the poverty level.

American Indian labor force participation on reservations continues to be low because of a lack of economic opportunities. The Indian population is young and lacks jobs experience. More significant, however, is the education deficit among Indians. Only 56 percent of American Indians graduate from high school, compared to 69 percent of the white population. Urban areas offer more job opportunities, but male Indian labor is largely confined to manual occupations, which are subject to fluctuation because of economic downturns, weather, and other factors. Female Indians are employed primarily in low-skilled, nonmanual service jobs both on and off the reservation.

During the 1980's, some tribal governments managed to attract businesses and increase employment opportunities, but overall, success was limited. Indian gaming, sometimes referred to as "the new buffalo," is being explored by many tribes as both a source of income for the tribe and as a way to provide jobs. The gaming operations have brought jobs to many reservations, but these tend to be low-wage service positions such as cashiers and waitresses. Tribal governments look to gaming as a way to strengthen reservation infrastructures and improve the lives of the people while they search for other means to address the dual need for Indian employment and real economic development on the reservations.

Indian participation in the labor force has increased as Indians have moved off reservations; however, even in urban settings, Indian unemployment remains high. Job opportunities on the reservations are scarce. Tribal governments are increasingly asserting their sovereign status and distancing themselves from the federal government in hopes of creating viable economic institutions that will bring job opportunities to the reservations. Federal law continues to frustrate these efforts.

Carole A. Barrett

Sources for Further Study
Ambler, Marjane. *Breaking the Iron Bonds: Indian Control of Energy Development.* Lawrence: University Press of Kansas, 1990. Ambler provides a historic analysis of problems, paternalistic gov-

ernment policy, and exploitation which have prevented economic development on Indian lands. She focuses on the
potential for energy development on reservations as a source of
economic revitalization for tribes.

Biolsi, Thomas. *Organizing the Lakota: The Political Economy of the
New Deal on the Pine Ridge and Rosebud Reservations*. Tucson: University of Arizona Press, 1992. Examines what happened to the
political and economic life of the Lakota people when the Indian Reorganization Act was implemented on two western reservations. The reform agenda of the IRA was not really designed to transfer power to tribal governments; as a result,
tribes continue to be hamstrung in attempts to develop economically or politically apart from the federal government.

Cornell, Stephen. *The Return of the Native: American Indian Political
Resurgence*. New York: Oxford University Press, 1988. Cornell's
book does not focus directly on Indian economic issues; rather it
takes a broad look at the complexity of Indian-white relations in
the United States. Economics is a strand woven into this tapes-
try. This broader view permits one to see clearly some of the reasons reservation economic development has been so bleak to
this point and why it is so vital for the continuation of tribal
governments.

Kasari, Patricia. *The Impact of Occupational Dislocation: The American
Indian Labor Force at the Close of the Twentieth Century*. New York:
Garland, 1999. A study comparing how urban Indians and res-
ervation Indians fare in the work force.

Lawson, Michael. *Dammed Indians*. Norman: University of Oklahoma Press, 1982. Explores the devastating economic impact of
dams along the Missouri River to Sioux reservations. In the
1950's a series of dams upset reservation economies and caused
long-lasting economic and cultural hardships.

Littlefield, Alice, and Martha C. Knack, eds. *Native Americans and
Wage Labor: Ethnohistorical Perspectives*. Norman: University of
Oklahoma Press, 1996. A collection of ten essays examines how
wage labor was critical not only to Native American individuals, but to community survival.

Meriam, Lewis, et al. *The Problem of Indian Administration*. Baltimore: The Johns Hopkins University Press, 1928. This seminal work appraises the failings of the federal government to give Indian people a true voice in their governance and destiny. It explores in depth the poor economic conditions on reservations in the 1920's and the reasons for them. Much of the analysis is still meaningful.

See also: Agriculture; Ranching; Relocation; Urban Indians.

Ethnophilosophy and Worldview

Tribes affected: Pantribal
Significance: *Despite the diversity among indigenous American cultures—their environments, beliefs, and adaptations—the underlying philosophy of these cultures is a respect for the natural world and their place within it.*

Around the world and throughout history, indigenous peoples have developed belief systems that shape their lifestyles to their natural environment in order to enhance their survival within it. Such has been the case among the indigenous peoples of North America.

Definitions. The ethnophilosophy, or worldview, of any culture is a description of how that culture explains the structure and workings of the world in which it lives. It is based on experience, observation, and intellectual inquiry. In many cultures, this worldview is relatively distinct from other aspects of its ideology. One of these other aspects that is especially important is religion, which might be defined as the description of a group or individual's relationship with that world, a behavioral guide that relies to some extent on emotional appeal. Myths are a link between philosophy and religion.

The distinction between worldview and religious influence,

however, is much less clear-cut in North American native cultures. This blending has been both a strength and a weakness for the indigenous American peoples since Europeans came to their lands. The extent to which these closely tied phenomena shape the daily lives and activities of indigenous peoples has been unrecognized or disregarded by the dominant, immigrant culture.

Recurrent Themes. As cultures and individuals, most North American natives consider their lives to be constant expressions of their abiding respect for the natural world and their place in it. Although there are many different belief systems and rituals among the groups, there are several recurrent themes that appear across the spectrum of differences. These are the acceptance of visions and dreams as legitimate realities, brotherhood with particular plants or animals, the necessity for maintaining balance in all aspects of life, and the sanctity of the circle. These motifs appear repeatedly in art and decoration, music, dance, and many rituals. Reverent, constant attention to these themes is an integral experience of daily life.

In many Native American cultures, dreams and visions are welcomed, even sought, as sources of wisdom. There are rituals to prepare seekers for a vision experience. Spending a period of time in a sweatlodge is often part of the preparation. Fasting and solitude are also common practices. In some cultures, the use of hallucinogens facilitates the vision experience. Sometimes, though, these experiences are spontaneous. Whatever information is gained is considered reality, though perhaps reality in metaphor. It is wisdom.

Wisdom is always a gift. There are always sacred and unknowable "great mysteries." Their existence is recognized and appreciated as part of the bond that ties people to life. It is not only foolish but also disrespectful to ask too much about the great mysteries. Although shamans and members of secret religious societies might have more insight than the average tribe member into the ultimate and unknowable, even they are barred, by reverence for its infinite sanctity, from too much direct inquiry: All that they are to know will be revealed to them.

Usually during one of these dream or vision experiences some animal or mythical being communicates with the participant. Its message is shared with the tribe and may become part of the myth system for that tribe. Imagery from the dream or vision may be used later by their artists who make masks or who paint pottery. It may be woven into the pattern of a blanket or basket or may become part of a costume worn during a ceremonial dance.

Native Americans accept their place in the natural world as being a part of creation rather than being separate from it. They share equal status with other parts of creation, both living and nonliving.

Plants, Animals, and Mother Earth. Because of Native Americans' traditional reliance on the abundance of the land, certain plants and animals have always been accorded special status. Corn, squash, beans, rice, and tobacco were traditional crops. Buffalo, caribou, deer, fish, and whales were common sources of game food. Wolves, eagles, bears, and snakes are important symbols of wisdom and strength. Cedar trees, which provided Northwest Coast Indians with material for their homes, boats, clothing, and containers for storage and cooking, are revered in that region. In many indigenous cultures, when a person needs to kill something to use it, he apologizes to it first or explains to it the necessity for its death. Although North American natives' lives were particularly dependent on these living things, they recognized the worth of all forms of life and took care not to harm them if possible. Nonliving parts of the natural world were also valued.

The earth as mother is a major theme both in myth and in daily life. All life comes from and is dependent upon Mother Earth. Several groups believe that they emerged as a people from the earth. Some believe that future generations are developing within the mother now and will emerge from the mother as long as humankind exists. Many believe that after death their spirits will return to their source within Mother Earth. Crops emerge from the earth and are nourished by her. Animals are sustained by the plants that the earth supports. Therefore, the only way to regard Mother Earth is with gratitude and reverence.

Certain mountains or rock formations, caves, or rivers, as well as the ocean, are considered sacred to those who live near them. These sites may be revered because the natives believe that their ancestors originated there or because their ancestors are buried there. It may be that the tribe believes that its future lies there—that the coming generations will need those places for their lives. Therefore, it is the responsibility of those currently living to take care of the site both physically, by not scarring or polluting it and spiritually, by regarding it with respect.

On a somewhat smaller scale, certain gems and minerals have particular symbolic importance. Solid forms may be fashioned into amulets or may be used in rituals; clay and various pigments, for example, are used for ceremonial body paint. Even a plain-looking small stone can carry a prayer if it is handled reverently.

Life in Balance. Balance in the natural world and in individual lives is seen as crucial for survival. In their relationship with the environment, Native Americans see it as their responsibility not to disturb natural balances. They must not take more resources than they need for their survival or take more than the environment can bear to give. They must treat with respect all that is taken from their surroundings.

Balance must also be maintained in relationships within their communities. Political systems have varied widely among groups. In pre-contact days, some North American tribal leaders were monarchs, and their subjects lived within strict caste systems. Other groups enjoyed relative democracy, their governments involving representatives in voting councils. The model for the United States' government was influenced by the Iroquois' Confederacy of Six Nations, which is one of the oldest continuously functioning systems of governance in the world.

Personal lives must be kept in balance by respectful attitudes, ethical behavior, and avoidance of excess in order to maintain physical and mental health. When a person is suffering because he or she is out of balance, a healer or shaman may be able to help find the cause. The sufferer may not even remember a seemingly minor transgression committed several years before, or a child may be suffering because one of his or her parents unknowingly did something before the child was even conceived. Whatever the cause, once the source of the problem is recognized, the healer or shaman performs ceremonies and offers advice to help the sufferer regain the balance necessary for good health.

All creation is bound by a sacred circle, and since the indigenous people live within it, they must take care not to break it by either carelessness or intentionally destructive behavior. The circle expresses itself repeatedly throughout the natural world—in the rounded vault of the sky, in the cycle of the seasons, in the shape of the sun and moon, and in the nests of birds and the webs of spiders. The circular pattern is reiterated in the shape of many tribes' houses, in the hoops of games, in the choreography of dances, and in the form of religious structures.

While these motifs are prominent in nearly all indigenous cultures of North America, many of the ways in which they are honored might not seem obvious. Factors as basic as the name by which a tribe knows itself and its environment, as major as the education of its children, and as seemingly insignificant as the proper way to move about in the home are all matters related to the philosophy of respect for the worlds among which the various American indigenous cultures live.

Tribal Names and Traditions. Most tribes credit mythical figures or their ancestors with having provided tribal names. Because of the sacred source for these names, tribal membership offers spiritual as well as social identity. Frequently a tribe is named for its location or for some trait of its community. For example, the Pimas' indigenous name is Akimel O'odham, which means "River People," and their Papago neighbors, the Tohono O'odham, are the "Desert People." Many tribes are known in their native tongues simply as "the People." Among them are the Dine (Navajo) of the American Southwest, the Nimipu (Nez Perce) of eastern Washington state, the Kaigini (Haida) of the Pacific coast, and the Maklaks (Klamath) of the mountainous California-Oregon border region. A few variations on this are Ani-yun-wiya (Cherokee), or "Real People"; Kaigwu (Kiowa), or "Main People"; Anishinabe (Chippewa), "First Men"; and Tsististas (Cheyenne), "Beautiful People."

In every tribe, Indian children are given instruction in the proper way to behave and are introduced to their origins through stories and myths told by parents and relatives or by tribal storytellers. Children are discouraged from asking too many questions. Instead, they are advised over the years to listen to stories several times. As the children grow up in this oral tradition, they come to understand the metaphors and realities that are the bridges connecting their people's history, philosophy, religion, and traditions. Everything the children learn must be relevant to their lives; it is vital for the physical, spiritual, and social survival of the children individually and for the tribe as a whole. The oral tradition continues to be a sacred responsibility for both the teller and the listener.

Among some tribes, even the way people move about within the group or inside their homes or religious structures is an expression of respect. Children are taught not to cross between the fire and their elders so that they are not deprived of any heat or light. In some tribes, the pattern of movement in the homes is always in a clockwise direction, the way that the sun moves across the sky. Participants in nearly all religious and political meetings gather in a circle.

Sentimentalization Versus Reality. It is important to realize that one should not become carried away with oversentimentalizing the worldviews and practices of Native Americans. (This type of sentimentalizing was prominent in the eighteenth century, with the European concept of the "noble savage.") Certain tribal hunting techniques, as well as some tribes' capturing and selling of slaves and cruelty in warfare, attest the side of Indian life that sentimentalists do not consider.

Before they had horses to use in their hunting expeditions, the method that several tribes used to slay buffalo was to herd and stampede them into running off cliffs. Although it was customary for the hunters to apologize to the dying and dead, the number of animals lost was in excess of what their tribes could use, and many carcasses remained at the foot of the cliffs to become carrion.

Taking slaves was a common practice for tribes in many parts of the continent. Often these slaves were captured from other tribes during raids for that purpose. Sometimes non-natives were enslaved, including African Americans taken by the Cherokee. Comanches took Spaniards as slaves. In the Pacific Northwest, a large portion of the Chinook economy was the slave trading that they did up and down the coast. The Ute captured people for other tribes to use for slaves, trading them for horses. Several tribes in the Southeast captured other natives for the English and Spanish to use on their ships and in the Caribbean colonies.

Human sacrifice and cannibalism were not unknown. Most tribes that practiced human sacrifice used prisoners who had been captured in conflicts. Those who were not suitable for slaves or sacrificial purposes, or who would not make good wives, were often tortured before they were killed. The Pawnee sacrificed captured females—or one of their own, if necessary—as part of a ritual to ensure an ample harvest. Most cases of cannibalism involved using the victims' hearts to gain the enemies' valor and strength.

The potlatch, the celebration among British Columbian and Pacific Northwest natives that has been seen as a symbol of generosity and a ceremony of sharing the host's wealth among the guests, was not always an altruistic event. The Kwakiutl, for example, also used it as a political tool to humiliate their enemies and to gain power over them.

Immigrant Philosophy Conflict. Throughout their history with European immigrants, Native Americans have suffered near annihilation—physical, cultural, and spiritual—because of the ethnophilosophical differences between the two groups.

When Europeans began arriving on the shores of North America, they brought with them a philosophy that was radically different from that of the natives they encountered. The newcomers did not see themselves as being an integral part of their natural environment, participants in it who had to obey its laws. They saw themselves as separated from it by their level of civilization—by how far they believed they had risen above the brutality and unpredictability of the natural world and by how well they had managed to exploit its resources. The essential difference in worldview was, and continues to be, a source of conflict that has been disastrous to Native American communities across the continent.

Marcella T. Joy

Sources for Further Study

Beck, Peggy V., and Anna L. Walters. The Sacred: Ways of Knowledge, Sources of Life. Tsaile, Ariz.: Navajo Community College Press, 1977. Discusses several North American cultures while concentrating on southwestern peoples. Many photographs and maps. Extensive bibliography and film lists.

French, Lawrence. *Psychological Change and the American Indian: An Ethnohistorical Analysis.* New York: Garland, 1987. Academic, theoretical approach. Well organized and well documented. Focuses on educational policies with discussion of pre- and post-contact attitudes among Cherokee, Athapaskan/Apache, and Plains Sioux.

Highwater, Jamake. *The Primal Mind.* New York: Harper & Row, 1981. Philosophy in elegant, simple language. The author's views are based on academic studies and on life experience in both Blackfeet (Blood) and non-native cultures. Extensive bibliography.

Inter Press Service, comp. *Story Earth: Native Voices on the Environment.* San Francisco: Mercury House, 1993. Essays by the world's indigenous peoples, including American Indians, compiled by a global newswire. Introduction by the prime minister of Norway. Interesting non-American editorial perspectives.

McLuhan, T. C., comp. *Touch the Earth: A Self-Portrait of Indian Existence.* New York: Simon & Schuster, 1971. Native Americans' quotations from the last three hundred years. Many photographs. Insightful and visually beautiful. Well documented; includes suggested readings.

Nerburn, Kent, and Louise Mengelkoch, eds. *Native American Wisdom*. San Rafael, Calif.: New World Library, 1991. Short quotes from numerous Native Americans, past and present, discussing ways that philosophical concepts are expressed in daily life.

Ridington, Robin. *Trail to Heaven: Knowledge and Narrative in a Northern Native Community*. Iowa City: University of Iowa Press, 1988. Anthropological study of the philosophy, social life, and customs of the Beaver Indians in British Columbia. Some photographs and a long reference list.

Suzuki, David, and Peter Knudtson. *Wisdom of the Elders: Honoring Sacred Native Visions of Nature*. New York: Bantam Books, 1992. Views of indigenous peoples from around the world, including North America. Scholarly but readable. Several epigraphs by scientists from many disciplines, theologians, and social scientists. Romanticized non-native assumptions are examined. Well documented.

Vecsey, Christopher. *Imagine Ourselves Richly: Mythic Narratives of North American Indians*. New York: Crossroad, 1988. A broad-ranging anthology. The introduction includes academic discussion of sources and functions of myths in general and of their value to Native Americans specifically.

Wall, Steve, and Harvey Arden. *Wisdomkeepers: Meetings with Native American Spiritual Elders*. Hillsboro, Oreg.: Beyond Words, 1990. Long quotations from interviews with several American Indians. Not an academic work but informative and insightful. Moving text and photographs.

See also: Children; Mother Earth; Oral Literatures; Religion; Religious Specialists; Sacred Narratives; Sweatlodges and Sweatbaths; Visions and Vision Quests.

False Face Ceremony

Tribes affected: Iroquois tribes

Significance: *During the False Face Ceremony, certain tribal members don special masks which they believe give them the power to cure disease.*

The False Face Ceremony refers both to the rite performed by members of the False Face Society during the Midwinter Ceremony and to individual healing practices during which members of the society control sickness with the power of the spirit in the mask and the blowing or rubbing of ashes on the patient's body. At midwinter, the society comes to the longhouse to enable people to fulfill particular dreams or to renew dreams during a ritual called the Doorkeeper's Dance.

The False Face Society uses wooden masks with deepset eyes; large, bent noses; arched eyebrows; and wrinkles. The mouths vary, but they are most often "O"-shaped or spoon-shaped (a horizontal figure-eight shape). Often spiny protrusions are carved on the mask. The original "Great False Face" comes from an origin story and is depicted as a hunchback with a bent nose. His name links him to the legend of the test of moving a mountain, in which he engaged with Hawenio, or Creator. The Great False Face is the great trickster figure, although tricksters occur in Iroquois legends with many names and manifestations.

Hawenio, recognizing that Shagodyoweh-gowah (one of the names for the Great False Face) has tremendous power, tells the Great False Face that his job is to rid the earth of disease. Shagodyoweh-gowah agrees that if humans will make portrait masks of him, call him "grandfather" or "great one" (gowa), make tobacco offerings, and feed him cornmeal mush, he will give the humans the power to cure disease by blowing hot ashes. Shagodyoweh-gowah travels the world using a great white pine as a cane, without which he would lose his balance. His movement is mimicked during the Doorkeeper's Dance.

Glenn J. Schiffman

See also: Masks; Midwinter Ceremony; Tricksters.

Feast of the Dead

Tribes affected: Algonquian, Huron, Iroquois
Significance: *The Feast of the Dead provided an outlet for mourning the dead and promoted tribal unity.*

The Feast of the Dead was a Native American religious ceremony that provided several villages a chance to gather together, reestablish friendships, and collectively mourn their dead. Though the Feast of the Dead is frequently referred to as an Algonquin ceremony, it was also practiced by Huron and Iroquois nations.

Every few years, tribal councils gathered and announced the date and location for a Feast of the Dead. The bodies of the dead were disinterred from their temporary burial sites to be reburied in a common grave. Family members exhumed the bodies and prepared them for the ceremony. They removed the flesh, which was burned, and wrapped the remains in beaver robes. Each village then traveled to the placed selected by the councils. At the site, a large pit was dug. The inside was lined with beaver robes. The bones of the dead and the goods that had been buried with them were suspended from a platform. In turn, each family threw their deceased and grave goods into the pit, which was covered with mats, bark, and logs.

When the Northeastern Indian nations broke up and moved west or north, it became increasingly difficult to gather tribes for a Feast of the Dead. The Mohawk and Seneca tribes continued to practice a variation of the ceremony into the twentieth century.

Leslie Stricker

See also: Death and Mortuary Customs; Feasts; Religion.

Feasts

Tribes affected: Pantribal

Significance: *American Indians traditionally celebrated special occasions with special meals; feasts as part of sacred ceremonies usually included specified dishes and practices, while secular feasts usually had greater flexibility.*

Native Americans, in common with most peoples around the world, celebrated special occasions with communal meals, generally rendered as "feasts" in English. Some feasts formed part of seasonal sacred ceremonies, others accompanied meetings of secular voluntary societies, and still others commemorated family events, such as the visit of a dignitary, a success in diplomacy or war, the naming of a child, or the completion of a house. In general, feasts that were part of a sacred ceremony were more formalized in their structure and might include fixed prayers or practices, while the more secular feasts followed less rigid guidelines of expected behavior and courtesy.

Common Features. Regardless of the type of feast, there were certain common features. Unlike European and Asian feasts, American Indian feasts tended not to be elaborate affairs, and they were presented with the same implements that would be used in everyday eating. While the meals often included ingredients and dishes that might appear at any meal, feasts usually featured choice ingredients and a wider diversity of foods than other meals.

The sponsor was expected to provide food for a feast, and kin often would be called upon to assist; their assistance would be repaid later when they were sponsoring feasts and needed assistance. Family feasts were sponsored by the family as a communal unit, although a head of the household usually was conceived as the sponsor. In many tribes, this would be a man, but some of the matrilineal tribes considered a woman to head the family, and she would serve as sponsor. Feasts accompanying the meetings of secular societies usually were sponsored by a person or persons who were seeking membership in the society or by the person at whose house the meeting was to be held. Feasts accompanying sacred ceremonies would be sponsored by the tribe as a whole or by its chief as its representative. The sponsor had to take special care that no foods were included that would be taboo for any of the diners.

Typically, food was prepared by female members of the sponsoring group and was then ladled out by them from a communal pot onto each diner's bowl or plate. Small family feasts usually would be served by the female head of household. Under certain conditions, particularly if a feast was to honor a prominent person, the sponsor and his immediate kin might abstain from eating during the feast, appointing another guest to do the serving. Details of manners varied from tribe to tribe, but the male head of household, chief, or religious leader usually would signal the beginning of the feast by lifting up a bit of the food, sometimes presenting it to the four cardinal points, then dropping it to the ground or into the fire. This thanksgiving offering to the gods was performed in silence.

Many feasts were part of the ceremonies surrounding the beginning of the season when an important food became available. Among the Nootka of the Northwest Coast, for example, salmon captured during their fall spawning runs were dried for use throughout the year, and this staple was recognized as critical to survival. The first catch of salmon, regardless of who caught them, would be presented to the chief, who would sprinkle them with goose down while greeting the fish with a formalized welcome. Women, except those menstruating, would be designated to prepare the salmon, and everyone (except menstruating women) would partake of the food. Bones and innards from this feast would be returned to the water, ensuring that future generations of salmon would be plentiful and well-formed.

Agriculturalists also held feasts within harvest festivals. Many Eastern tribes, such as the Cherokee, held a four- or eight-day ceremony, often called the Green Corn Dance, at the time of the earliest corn harvest. This ceremony included social dances, the rekindling of fire, the forgiving of transgressions, and a feast centered on the new corn. Ceremonies serving similar purposes were conducted by Pueblo agriculturalists at harvest time.

Memorial Feasts. Other sacred ceremonies focused on the dead. Many tribes maintained that a feast should be held in honor of a recently deceased person at a fixed number of days after that person's death. For most of the Plains tribes, the feast was held after four days, while the Iroquois waited ten days; some groups waited several months. These feasts typically were family-sponsored.

Other tribes held special memorial feasts for all the dead of the tribe at a certain date or season. The Huron, for example, held the Feast of the Dead in autumn, at which time they disinterred their dead from the previous year, reverently stripped the remaining flesh from the bones, dressed them in the best of clothes, and laid them to their final rest in a communal burial pit. This was accompanied by a feast in the evening, sponsored by the entire community and dedicated to the well-being and memory of the dead. The Inuit and most Northwest Coast tribes also held communal feasts for their dead in the winter, when the dead were conceived to return for the feast, enjoying the food that was given them by placing it on the ground or passing it through the fire.

Calendric Festivals, Societies, and Guests. Other feasts were part of calendric festivals, such as the myriad religious ceremonies held by the Hopi. Major ceremonies lasted eight days, while minor ceremonies lasted only four days; given the number of ceremonies per year, fully one-quarter of the year could be taken up with ceremonies. To share the burden of sponsorship, different villages would sponsor different ceremonies each year, and participants would travel to that village. The feasts that were part of these ceremonies served the practical purpose of feeding visitors and others whose ritual obligations kept them from regular eating arrangements. These feasts were viewed as a secular part of the overall ceremonies, and women and others not permitted to participate in the sacred kiva rituals were welcomed at the feasts.

The meetings of volunteer societies, especially in the Plains, were characterized by a feast following the other activities. These feasts followed different protocols, depending on the tribe and the society. Sometimes food was brought ready-cooked to the meeting, kept warm, and ladled out to members; in other cases it was prepared during or after the meeting. Two common threads, however, united these feasts. First, there was no public invitation, since only members were expected to attend and a herald notified them individually. Second, each person brought his or her own bowl, and they were served from a communal pot or pots.

Feasts held by families to commemorate special events were the most variable. Unlike feasts held with ceremonies or institutional activities, they seldom had a rigorous, prescribed structure. Instead, they were flexible, permitting the sponsoring family to adjust according to circumstances.

Among the best-known early Indian feasts are those honoring guests, since these were the ones that early European writers were most likely to have witnessed and recorded. Europeans, even those inclined to disparage Indian culture, universally were impressed by Indian hospitality. Time and again, accounts noted that even in times of famine or personal tragedy, the arrival of a significant visitor was celebrated with a feast of the best foods available. Alvár Nuñez Cabeza de Vaca, the early sixteenth century Spanish traveler who entered North America through Florida and left it through the Southwest and West Mexico, described dozens of feasts at which nearly starving Indians marshaled their scant resources to honor him. Other writers echoed this experience, one that had been shared by thousands of Indian visitors before the coming of the Europeans.

The Royal Feast. Feasts north of Mexico were communal affairs, to be shared by members of the tribe, a voluntary society, or family. Farther south, in Mexico, an additional type of feast also existed: the royal feast. This meal was sumptuous, often involving extravagant numbers of dishes unavailable to commoners and served only to the Aztec emperor. As described in native and European books, the emperor would have up to three hundred different dishes prepared for his dinner. The emperor ate alone, separated even from his retainers (servants) by a gilded door, so that he would not be seen in the act of eating. He would sample the various dishes, passing one or another on to a retainer on the other side of the screen, as a special favor. Leftovers were eaten by guards. This type of feast, aggrandizing a single individual and setting that person apart from others, was entirely alien to Indian practices north of Mexico, where feasts were an act of community.

Functions. Feasts served many functions in traditional Native America. They filled the bellies of those involved, which was significant in terms of ceremonies at which large numbers of visitors were present. In a broader sense, these feasts permitted those experiencing bad years to share in the good fortune of those with abundant food; over a lifetime, every community would experience good years and bad years, and the generosity of one year would be repaid subsequently. In addition, feasts gave people an opportunity to demonstrate their common bond, since food sharing is a universal human symbol of oneness. For many ceremonies, the entire community or tribe feasts together and demonstrates its commonality; in other ceremonies, it is only a voluntary society of perhaps only a single family, but the principle is the same. Ceremonies for the dead, at which the living eat the food and the dead share symbolically, bond the dead with the living members of the tribe. Other ceremonies unite the spirits and the people in the sharing of food.

Russell J. Barber

Sources for Further Study

Beck, Mary Giraudo. *Potlatch: Native Ceremony and Myth on the Northwest Coast.* Anchorage: Alaska Northwest Books, 1993. A very readable book treating major ceremonies, including feasts, of the Northwest Coast tribes. Emphasizes the cultural context of feasting.

Benitez, Ana M. de *Pre-Hispanic Cooking—Cocina Prehispánica.* Mexico City: Ediciones Euroamericanas, 1974. An excellent distillation of information on Aztec foodways, drawing on the Florentine Codex and other primary sources. Bilingual in Spanish and English.

Dietler, Michael, and Brian Hayden, eds. *Feasts: Archaeological and Ethnographic Perspectives on Food, Politics, and Power*. Washington, D.C.: Smithsonian Institution Press, 2001. A compilation of fifteen essays examines the cultural, economic, and political significance of feasts from such places as the Americas, Africa, and Asia.

Highwater, Jamake. *Ritual of the Wind: North American Indian Ceremonies, Music, and Dance*. New York: Viking Press, 1977. A widely available compilation of several ceremonies from different tribes. Little detail on feasts as such, but information of the ceremony of which they are part.

Kimball, Yeffe, and Jean Anderson. *The Art of American Indian Cooking*. Garden City, N.Y.: Doubleday, 1965. The most widely available of American Indian cookbooks. The introduction provides a historic (though somewhat romantic) context for the recipes, which are divided by culture area.

Root, Waverly, and Richard de Rochemont. *Eating in America: A History*. New York: William Morrow, 1976. A general history of food and cooking in North America, devoting four chapters to Native American foods and cooking.

Swanton, John R. *The Indians of the Southeastern United States*. Bulletin of the Smithsonian Institution, Bureau of American Ethnology 137. Grosse Point, Mich.: Scholarly Press, 1969. This classic and massive work contains detailed descriptions of the tribes of the Southeast, including considerable information on feasts and food. Includes some extended quotations from early accounts describing feasts.

Waugh, Frederick W. *Iroquois Foods and Food Preparation*. Memoir of the Canada Department of Mines, Geological Survey 86 (Anthropological Series 12). 1916. Reprint. Ottawa: National Museums of Canada, National Museum of Man, 1973. Perhaps the best work of its kind, this monograph summarizes food, food preparation, feasts, and related subjects for the Iroquois tribes in great detail.

See also: Feast of the Dead; Food Preparation and Cooking; Green Corn Dance; Potlatch.

Feathers and Featherwork

Tribes affected: Pantribal
Significance: *Indian tribes used feathers for decorative and symbolic purposes.*

Feathers obtained from native birds were an important natural material used by North American Indians for both decorative and symbolic purposes. Although not believed to possess inherent power, feathers could be used to represent spiritual powers and actual achievements of the wearers.

Among the items of spiritual significance that were decorated with feathers were the calumet, or peace pipe, the prayer stick, and the wand. The calumet shaft was often heavily decorated with feathers and even the skins and heads of birds. The feathers on the shaft might be painted red when war was planned.

By far the most valued and significant feathers used were those of the eagle. Indians preferred the feathers of the less common golden eagle found in the western mountains, and birds were sometimes raised from eaglets and then plucked at maturity. Another way to acquire eagle feathers required a hunter to conceal himself in a covered pit near a baited noose and overpower the snared eagle attracted to the food. This was a courageous act, as the eagle was taken alive. Feathers would also be obtained through trade. Eagle feathers were especially important in constructing war bonnets and as "exploit feathers." A white feather with a black tip was preferred. Among the Dakota Sioux, each of these exploit feathers had a particular meaning depending on how it was shaped or painted. A red spot painted on top represented the killing of an enemy; if the feather was cut off at the top it meant that the enemy's throat had been cut. The number of notches in a feather indicated if a warrior had been second, third, or fourth in counting coup on an enemy. If the edges were cut, he may have been fifth. A split feather served as a medal of honor, indicating the warrior had been wounded in battle. Eagle feathers were also considered best for feathering arrows.

Feathers served a symbolic as well as decorative function in the ceremonial dress of Native Americans. *(Unicorn Stock Photos)*

Other bird species used for various purposes included the wild turkey, hawk, woodpecker, meadowlark, quail, chaparral cock (or roadrunner), duck, bluejay, and blackbird. Some California tribes were reputed to have used the scalps of certain small birds as a form of currency. Feathers of the roadrunner, called "Medicine Bird" by the Plains tribes, were believed to bring good luck if hung within the lodge. Roadrunner feathers were also fashioned into whistles for use in the Medicine Dance.

Woodland Indians of the eastern United States used turkey, crane, and heron feathers to fashion their headdresses. Other tribes made caps of overlapping circles of small feathers, sometimes topped by a single eagle feather. Sometimes feathers of small birds were prepared and used for decoration in the same manner as porcupine quills.

Elaborate feather robes were constructed by eastern tribes, and also by some tribes in the west. Both feathers and skins of birds were used, the skins sometimes being cut into strips and interwoven to form the garment. Elaborate figures or patterns were often created in these feather robes.

Heavy depredations by American and European fashion designers in the late nineteenth century threatened many native bird species, and by the early twentieth century, laws such as the Lacey Act of 1900 were passed to protect native birds. In 1916, the Migratory Bird Treaty, also aimed at protecting birds from extensive predation, was signed between the United States and Great Britain (for Canada), and other treaties with nations such as Mexico followed. Although allowances were made for American Indians, this has sometimes caused difficulty for those who wished to continue to use certain feathers for decorative and symbolic purposes.

Patricia Masserman

See also: Beads and Beadwork; Dress and Adornment; Headdresses; Quillwork; War Bonnets.

Fire and Firemaking

Tribes affected: Pantribal
Significance: *Fire was the Indian's most versatile tool; it cooked food, provided the focal point for religious ceremonies, and altered the environment.*

The origins of human use of fire go so far back in prehistoric time that no one can say exactly when it began. It seems probable that when the ancestors of the North American Indians crossed the land bridge between Siberia and Alaska they brought fire with them.

The Indians are known to have used several methods of making fire. The Indians of Alaska used stones to generate sparks, in the fashion of the flint stone. Much more widespread, however, was firemaking by wood friction. A hearth of wood, with pits in it, was placed on the ground and held firmly in place by the knees of the fire maker; he or she had already prepared some very dry vegetable material, shaved or rubbed to act as tinder. A "drill"—a stick that is rotated rapidly with the hands with one end set in one of the pits of the hearth—was used. The drill-stick shed fine material onto the hearth, and the friction generated by rapid movement produced enough heat to make the material on the hearth smolder; it could then be blown into life and the tinder touched to it. Rapid rotation of the drill could also be produced by looping a string around it and tying both ends to a bow; the bow was moved back and forth.

The possession of fire made many Indian practices possible. It made it possible to bake the pottery that was so widely used for containers; it made it possible to brew a variety of drinks; it made it possible to bake foods and to boil water. Fire made it possible to keep warm in the colder months that all Indians experienced. Fire made it possible to cook the meat that Indians obtained by hunting wild animals. Fire was essential for cooking the beans, squash, and corn that were central to the Indian diet.

Fire was also central to the religion of many tribes. Religious ceremonies nearly always took place around a fire. Fire was a cleansing and purifying agent. Keeping a fire going was a religious duty; when the Indians wanted to mark the end of a cycle, they put out the old fires and started a new one. Tribal deliberations took place around the council fire.

Most important of all, fire was the tool that Indians used to shape the natural environment to meet their needs. When they cleared a plot of land of trees to create a field in which to plant crops, they burned the vegetation. In so doing they not only disposed of unwanted plant material but also added lime and potash to the soil to make it more fruitful.

It was common practice, widely noted by the first Europeans to come to America, for the Indians to burn the woods each year. This was done to eliminate underbrush and make it easier to move about in the woods. It served another purpose: It drove game animals into groups so they could more easily be hunted. Many of the trees that are associated with Indians of the forest grow only in areas that have been burned over; the birch is the most widely known of these, but pitch pines also grow best in burned-over areas. Without fire, many of the cultural practices commonly associated with American Indian societies would have been impossible.

Nancy M. Gordon

Source for Further Study
Boyd, Robert, ed. *Indians, Fire, and the Land in the Pacific Northwest.* Corvallis: Oregon State University Press, 1999.

See also: Food Preparation and Cooking; Religion.

Fish and Fishing

Tribes affected: Pantribal
Significance: *Fish were a dietary mainstay in northern and northwestern North America and a significant part of the diet in most other regions of the continent.*

With the exception of a few tribes, such as the Hopi, for whom fish are taboo, all Indians utilized fish for food. Fish were captured by an impressive array of technology, including hooks and lines, gorges (double-pointed spikes on lines, swallowed by fish), harpoons, bows and arrows, leisters (spears with grabbing hooks alongside their points), fish traps, and nets. Hooks, gorges, and traps sometimes were baited. Nets were set, thrown, or dipped; weirs (fencelike fish traps) sometimes incorporated set nets. In some places, vegetable poisons were thrown into pools to bring stunned or killed fish to the surface. When spawning fish were dense, they might be clubbed out of the water or simply grabbed with the hands. All these techniques were widespread in North America. Men most frequently did the fishing, though women often collected fish after they had been poisoned.

Shellfish were collected by different methods. Most mollusks were collected by hand or by digging, work that usually was considered to be like plant gathering and was done by women. Lob-

This Yurok fisherman was photographed in 1923 by Edward S. Curtis. *(Library of Congress)*

sters, crabs, and other crustaceans usually were captured in nets or traps by men. Although shell heaps left from such gathering sometimes are extensive, few tribes relied on shellfish heavily.

The degree of reliance on finfish varied around North America. The greatest reliance was in the Pacific Northwest, where salmon runs provided vast quantities of food that was preserved for use through the year. In this culture area, the salmon run was a critical annual event surrounded by religious and social ritual to ensure success. Less intensive river and ocean fishing secured a variety of other fish, including the olachen, a fatty fish used for candles. The Inuit of the Arctic also used a considerable amount of fish, though sea mammals provided the greater part of their diet. Tribes of the northern forests of Canada used large quantities of lake fish seasonally, when mammals were less available. Fish were important to tribes of the Atlantic coast, the interior woodlands, and California, but they did not assume the importance they did in the aforementioned areas. Fish were relatively unimportant in the Plains and the arid Southwest and West.

Most fish come together in great numbers during seasonal spawning, and maximum advantage of their abundance can be taken only if their flesh can be preserved. In the far north, this can be accomplished by freezing, but elsewhere the technology must be more complicated. Placing fish on racks over low fires dries the meat and impregnates it with chemicals from the smoke. These chemicals flavor the meat and inhibit the growth of microorganisms, and fish can be preserved for several months by this method. Such drying-smoking racks are known archaeologically from as early as 6000 B.C.E. in New York's Hudson Valley. There is no evidence that any Indian tribe used salt to preserve fish or other meat.

Russell J. Barber

See also: Hunting and Gathering; Salmon; Weirs and Traps; Whales and Whaling.

Flutes

Tribes affected: Pantribal

Significance: *Flutes were played in many American Indian cultures, usually by shamans and participants in ceremonies.*

Flutes, rattles, and hand drums are the oldest and most widespread musical instruments in the New World, and they were probably derived from Old World paleolithic prototypes. The flute and similar wind instruments such as pan-pipes and ocarinas were commonly revered by shamans and curers as sacred instruments for contacting the spirit world, in many cases literally manifesting the "voice" of the spirits.

Though flutes were widespread throughout the Americas, the majority of archaeological specimens have been recovered from preserved deposits in the western and southwestern United States, Mexico, and South America. Flutes could be constructed of any appropriate material, including wood, reed, bone, and ceramic. Most versions were simple hollow tubes with four or five finger holes to control pitch.

Major cults centered on the playing of flutes arose in several locales throughout the Americas and flute players are commonly depicted in paintings, ceramics, and jewelry from South America, western Mexico, and the American Southwest. Flute players figure prominently in several Native American myths and legends. In South America, reed flutes up to 6 feet in length, called *queñas*, were played during male initiation ceremonies, and several pre-Columbian deities, such as Tezcatlipoca, the Aztec god of darkness, deception, and shamanic power, were commonly depicted as flute players.

A particularly strong version of a flute cult appeared in the American Southwest around 500 C.E. The central character in this cult is a figure identified by modern Hopi as "Kokopelli," a mythological hump-backed figure, sometimes depicted as an insect or ithyphallic male and commonly recognizable by his playing of the flute. Masked representations of Kokopelli appear in modern

Hopi ceremonials, and a seasonal dance called the Flute Ceremony is specifically devoted to the playing and honoring of large wooden flutes. Flute playing was traditionally restricted to male shamans and ceremonial participants.

James D. Farmer

See also: Dances and Dancing; Music and Song.

Food Preparation and Cooking

Tribes affected: Pantribal
Significance: *Cooking techniques among indigenous North American peoples varied according to whether a tribe was mobile or sedentary and whether it used pottery.*

Most foods in traditional North American Indian cuisines were eaten cooked. While a few, such as animal livers and berries, commonly were eaten raw, the rest were transformed through techniques constrained by the available ingredients, technology, and energy sources.

The greatest constraints surrounded heat for cooking. Much of North America had plentiful wood supplies, though parts of the arid West and the Arctic were deficient. Wood typically was burned in an open fire, with food or cooking vessels suspended over it or buried in its coals. Flat rocks could be used as griddles. Sometimes, especially in the East, the fire was made in a pit and covered with dirt, forming a slow-cooking earth oven (above-ground ovens were not used anywhere). The masonry bread oven of the Pueblos was introduced by the Spanish. While ceramic pots could be exposed to fire, skin and bark vessels would burn up. Tribes who made only the latter had to heat liquids in them by adding hot stones, never obtaining more than a low simmer.

These factors meant that the more mobile tribes, most of whom made little or no pottery, were quite limited in their cooking techniques, especially if they lived in an area with limited fuel. The

A northern Plains woman preparing a meal in the nineteenth century by blending traditional techniques with European American customs. *(Library of Congress)*

Washoe, for example, prepared most of their food by simmering ground seeds and tubers, often mixed with greens, meat, berries, or whatever was available. Other foods were wrapped in leaves and roasted in the coals.

Sedentary tribes usually made pottery, and they could exploit full boiling. The Wampanoag, for example, ate primarily stews and gruels, based on cornmeal with various additions. Biscuits were made on rock griddles, and dumplings were made from leaf-wrapped dough. Meat often was roasted on racks above a fire, while vegetables usually were roasted in the coals.

Desert agriculturalists of the Southwest had a special problem: dense populations with limited fuel. There, the Pima developed sautéing as an adjunct to boiling, baking, and roasting. Sautéing is quick and conserves fuel, but it requires a fat that will not burn easily, as will most animal fats. The Pima grew cotton and extracted oil from its seeds, using it for sautéing and seasoning. The Pueblo peoples had no cotton from which to extract oil, but they developed other fuel-saving practices. Stews and soups, the most common meals, were cooked in large pots for an entire extended family, then ladled into individual serving bowls. Some dishes, like paper-thin piki bread, cooked almost immediately.

Without refrigeration, storing food became a major challenge, and drying was most commonly used. Some foodstuffs, such as beans and corn, dry easily and well, while others pose greater difficulties. Fish and meat require a smoky fire to produce a nonperishable product, and the resultant taste became a flavoring for other dishes. Indeed, eating large chunks of meat was unusual, and most tribes used meats to complement the plant seasonings collected and cultivated. Pemmican, a tasty mixture of dried meat, berries, and fat, was widely used in the East.

Every tribe had distinctive rules surrounding cooking and eating. Some foods were taboo, while others were relished. Certain foods might be eaten politely only with the hands, while others required the use of spoons or leaf scoops. Many tribes offered a prayer before eating. These and other social conventions made eating an event with cultural, as well as nutritional, significance.

Russell J. Barber

See also: Agriculture; Buffalo; Corn; Feasts; Fire and Firemaking; Hunting and Gathering; Pemmican; Salt; Subsistence.

Gambling

Tribes affected: Pantribal

Significance: *Gambling facilities have brought needed income to some native peoples, but some tribe members protest its presence on reservations.*

During the late twentieth century, commercial gambling became a major source of income on Indian reservations across the United States. While many Native American cultures practiced forms of gambling as a form of sport (such as the Iroquois peachstone game), there was no prior large-scale experience with gambling as a commercial enterprise. The arrival of gaming has brought dividends to some native peoples, but it has brought controversy culminating in firefights and death to others.

Four Paiute Indians playing a gambling game in southwestern Nevada during the late nineteenth century. *(National Archives)*

Development of Gambling. The history of reservation gambling begins in 1979, when the Seminoles became the first Indian tribe to enter the bingo industry. As state-run lotteries became legal and proliferated throughout the United States, Indian tribal governments, not subject to state regulations, saw a means of increasing their revenues by offering bingo games with prize money greater than that allowed by the U.S. state's law. When challenged, the tribes sued in federal court and won (*Seminole Tribe v. Butterworth*, 1979; *California v. Cabazon Band*, 1987).

By early 1985, between seventy-five and eighty of the federally recognized Indian tribes in the United States were conducting some sort of organized game of chance. By the fall of 1988, the Congressional Research Service estimated that more than one hundred Indian tribes participated in some form of gambling, which grossed about $255 million a year. In October of 1988, Congress passed the Indian Gaming Regulatory Act, which officially legalized gambling on reservations. The act also established the National Indian Gaming Commission to oversee gaming activities. The provisions of the law were two-edged: They required tribes to negotiate with states on types and rules of gaming, but they also guaranteed that ownership of gaming facilities and their revenues would belong to the tribes. For the first time, gaming was sanctioned as a legitimate method of tribal economic development, and gaming revenues began to subsidize reservation infrastructure, schools, hospitals, roads—and, most important, jobs.

By 1991, 150 native reservations recognized by non-Indian governmental bodies had some form of gambling. According to the U.S. Department of the Interior, gross revenue from such operations passed $1 billion that year. Individual prizes in some reservation bingo games were reported to be as high as $100,000, while bingo stakes in surrounding areas under state jurisdiction were sometimes limited to one hundred dollars. Marion Blank Horn, principal deputy solicitor of the Department of the Interior, described the fertile ground gambling enterprises had found in Indian country:

Casino Morongo in Cabazon, California.

The reasons for growth in gambling on Indian land are readily apparent. The Indian tribal governments see an opportunity for income that can make a substantial improvement in the tribe's [economic] conditions. The lack of any state regulation results in a competitive advantage over gambling regulated by the states. These advantages include no state-imposed limits on the size of pots or prizes, no restrictions by the states on days or hours of operations, no costs for licenses or compliance with state requirements, and no state taxes on gambling operations.

Death at Akwesasne. While gambling brought benefits to some Native American communities, it brought violence to the Akwesasne Mohawks of St. Regis in upstate New York. As many as seven casinos had opened illegally along the reservation's main highway; the area became a crossroads for the illicit smuggling of drugs, including cocaine, and tax-free liquor and cigarettes.

Tension escalated after early protests against gambling in the late 1980's (including the vandalizing of one casino and the burning of another) were met by brutal attempts by gambling supporters to repress this resistance. Residents blockaded the reservation to keep the casinos' customers out, prompting the violent destruction of the same blockades by gambling supporters in late April,

1990. By that time, violence had spiraled into brutal beatings of antigambling activists, drive-by shootings, and night-long fire-fights that culminated in two Mohawk deaths during the early morning of May 1, 1990. Intervention of several police agencies from the United States and Canada followed the two deaths, and outside police presence continued for years afterward.

Benefits. By the early 1990's, gambling was providing a small galaxy of material benefits for some formerly impoverished native peoples. A half-hour's drive from Minnesota's Twin Cities, black-jack players crowded forty-one tables, while 450 other players stared into video slot machines inside the tipi-shaped Little Six Casino, operated by the 103 members of the Shakopee Mdewakanton Sioux. By 1991, each member of the tribe was getting monthly dividend checks averaging two thousand dollars as shareholders in the casino. In addition to monthly dividends, members became eligible for homes (if they lacked them), guaranteed jobs (if they were unemployed), and full college scholarships. The tribe had taken out health insurance policies for everyone on the reservation and established day care for children of working parents. The largest casino to open by mid-1991 was the three-million-dollar Sycuan Gaming Center on the Sycuan Indian Reservation near El Cajon, a suburb of San Diego, California. Since that time, despite continued state challenges, Indian tribal casinos and other gaming centers have proliferated, and voters—such as California's electorate, which approved Proposition 105 in 1998—have shown support for Indian gaming. According to the National Indian Gaming Association, in 2002 two-thirds of the American public supported Indian gaming.

Regulation and Ongoing Controversy. Because of the provisions of the Indian Gaming Regulatory Act (IGRA), Indian gaming is highly regulated and not solely under the jurisdiction of tribal governments. The IGRA divides gaming into three classes: social or cultural forms (Class I); bingo and other nonbanking card games lawful within the states as a whole (Class II); and all other gaming, including casino games (Class III). The latter two classes are subject to regulation by the tribal gaming commissions (TGCs), of which there are nearly two hundred. Class III gaming is subject to compacts between TGCs and state regulatory agencies. In addition, national agencies, including the Internal Revenue Service, the Federal Bureau of Investigation, the Bureau of Indian Affairs, and the Justice Department, all have roles in the regulation of Indian gaming. Starting in 1996, Indian casinos became subject to Title 31 of the Bank Secrecy Act.

Today Indian gaming is big business, with state-of-the-art casinos across the nation that attract patrons from surrounding areas and beyond. The National Indian Gaming Association (NIGA) is the primary advocate and defender of Indian gaming, which continues to provoke controversy, opposition, and litigation by large non-Indian gaming interests as well as states. Nevertheless, Indian gaming continues to thrive, and at least for those tribes with large interests the industry has spawned some improvement in the socioeconomic status of tribal members and reservation infrastructure. According to the NIGA's Web site, "gaming has replaced the buffalo as the mechanism used by American Indian people for survival."

Bruce E. Johansen, updated by Christina J. Moose

Sources for Further Study

Cozic, Charles P., ed. *Gambling*. San Diego, Calif.: Greenhaven Press, 1995. A collection of articles covering all perspectives, from investigative reports to a letter to *60 Minutes*. Bibliography, list of gambling organizations.

Eadington, William, ed. *Indian Gaming and the Law*. Reno: University of Nevada, 1998. A collection of essays by participants in the North American Conference on the Status of Indian Gaming with different perspectives. Appendices include the Indian Gaming Regulatory Act and transcripts from the Cabazon case.

Gabriel, Kathryn. *Gambler Way: Indian Gaming in Mythology, History, and Archaeology in North America*. Boulder, Colo.: Johnson Books, 1996. Covers traditional Indian gaming in myth, history, and modern times, including politics and current issues. Bibliography, notes.

Lane, Ambrose I., Sr. *Return of the Buffalo*. Westport, Conn.: Begin and Garvey, 1995. Covers the historical development of California's Cabazon band of Mission Indians and the landmark case that established the beginning of Indian gaming. Bibliography, index.

Levine, Jerome L, and Wendy Parnell, eds. *Indian Gaming Handbook*. Los Angeles: Levine and Associations, 1999. An overview and compendium of the law surrounding Indian gaming: the Indian Gaming Regulatory Act, National Indian Gaming Commission regulations, related federal statutes and regulations, taxes on wagering, the Bank Secrecy Act, the Department of the Interior's gaming guidelines, Internal Revenue Service publications, and more.

U.S. Congress. Senate Select Committee on Indian Affairs. *Gambling on Indian Reservations and Lands*. Washington, D.C.: U.S. Government Printing Office, 1985. Established federal standards and regulations for the conduct of gaming activities.

See also: Games and Contests; Tourism.

Games and Contests

Tribes affected: Pantribal
Significance: *Games reflected the importance of athleticism to most Indian tribes, provided entertainment, and helped develop skills for work, hunting, and war.*

American Indians traditionally participated in a variety of games and contests. Children tended to mimic adult activities to ready themselves for work and war, while men tested themselves in preparation for hunting and warfare, developing their skills and endurance. Both men and women found entertainment in playing games, including games of chance.

Athletic games involved wrestling, throwing spears, shooting arrows, kicking sticks or balls, running, and many other activities. These games tested the strength, stamina, and courage required for survival in the Americas. Pre-Columbian Native Americans played forms of field hockey, ice hockey, soccer, and football, and they developed canoes, sleds, snowshoes, kayaks, toboggans, stilts, swings, and rubber balls. Many Native American games involved teams playing against each other, in contrast to the more individualistic sports of pre-contact Europeans. Unlike the spectator sports of today, there was more total participation, and participation was more important than winning, even though betting on outcomes was universally common.

Games also had a religious aspect, and their history and rules were often bound up in the traditional beliefs of the tribes. According to Stewart Culin, who did an extensive study of Indian games, they were played to drive away sickness, produce rain, and fertilize crops

Races and Ball Games. Different tribes had various forms of foot races. In pre-Columbian America, hunters literally ran down deer and other game, while communication within and among tribes took place using swift couriers. Inca runners ran thousands of miles, uniting their empire. Pueblo Indians would get up at dawn and run to their cornfields located miles away. Various forms of races were held to develop the endurance of runners, including shuttle relay races, kick-stick, and kickball races. In 1980, the Pueblo Indians celebrated the tercentennial of the Pueblo Revolt of 1680 by reenacting the part played by the runners who spread the word of the rebellion.

Plains tribes played a form of dodge ball in which the batter tossed and batted a rawhide ball. Fielders would try to catch the ball and then throw it at the batter, who would try to dodge out of the way. Football games were played across the continent, even by Inuits (Eskimos). Inuits also did a blanket toss, spreading a blanket like a trampoline and throwing participants as high as fifteen or twenty feet in the air. Various forms of kickball were played, including what was known in the 1980's as hackeysack. In the Southeast, ball games were used to earn hunting privileges, to settle disputes, or to determine who were the best warriors.

The Choctaw played a game called *kabocca* with a wooden ball about the size of a golf ball. As many as seven hundred players on one team would try to move the ball toward one or another of the goalposts, which were as much as a mile apart, using sticks with cup-shaped ends to catch and throw the ball. Games could be very rough and could last several days—scores could run into the hundreds. The Iroquois called kabocca the "little brother of war." This game, now known as lacrosse, was uniquely American.

Shinny is a form of hockey that was played throughout North America. The ice version was played by both sexes, but the field version was played mainly by women. Doubleball was a variation of shinny that used two baseball-sized balls that were tied together with a half-foot leather strap. A player carried the double ball or threw it with a hooked stick.

Some tribes played games involving throwing or shooting arrows, either at circular targets drawn on the ground or through rolling hoops. Crow Indians still practice an arrow-throwing game involving throwing arrows at a circular target drawn on the ground.

Various forms of bowling were practiced. The Cherokee pitched stones at clay pins. Another Cherokee game involved rolling or sliding a disk-shaped stone while contestants simultaneously threw poles to land where they guessed the stone would stop. In the Southwest, corncob targets were knocked down with wooden balls.

Gambling Games. Gambling games were popular. Stick games that involved guessing which hand held a hidden marker were widespread. Crow Indians played the stick game with teams, and each team had supporters that dressed similarly and sang as the game was played to give their players power and to confound the opposing team. The Menominee would shake dice-like objects in a bowl and then throw them out. Other tribes would place an object in one of several moccasins, with the object of correctly guessing the moccasin hiding the object.

Jim Thorpe, in a football uniform, at the Carlisle Indian School circa 1919. (National Archives)

Children's Games. Children participated in a variety of games. Girls would put up miniature dwellings and play "house," while boys hunted small game to feed their "families." Northwest Coast children played games such as fish trap, a form of tag in which the "fishers" simulated a net while the "fish" tried to avoid getting caught.

Famous Athletes. While usually any recognition given outstanding Indian athletes was fleeting at best, in the twentieth century Indians have participated in non-Indian athletic events, and there have been a number of Olympic-class Indian athletes. Billy Mills (Sioux) won the gold medal for the ten-thousand-meter race at the 1964 Olympics, and in the process he beat the United States Olympic record of Louis Tewanima (Hopi), who had won the silver medal in the same event in 1912. The greatest Indian athlete was Jim Thorpe (Sauk and Fox). According to an Associated Press poll in 1950, he was considered the greatest athlete of the half-century. He won the gold medal for the pentathlon and decathlon in the 1912 Olympics and went on to play professional football and baseball. An American Indian Athletic Hall of Fame was established in 1972 at Haskell Indian Junior College to honor Indian athletes.

Jon Reyhner

Sources for Further Study

Anderson, Madelyn Klein. *North American Indian Games*. New York: Franklin Watts, 2000. An examination of the orgins and significance of games such as lacrosse, shinny, dice games, and guessing games to Native Americans.

Culin, Stewart. *Games of the North American Indians*. New York: Dover, 1975. First published in the twenty-fourth *Annual Report of the Bureau of American Ethnology* (1902-1903), this is the most extensive study of Indian games available. It includes detailed drawings of the various implements used in the games.

Grueninger, Robert W. "Physical Education." In *Teaching American Indian Students*, edited by Jon Reyhner. Norman: University of Oklahoma Press, 1992. Describes a variety of Indian games appropriate for schools.

Macfarlan, Allan, and Paulette Macfarlan. *Handbook of American Indian Games*. Illustrated by Paulette Macfarlan. New York: Dover, 1958. Describes various Indian games; intended to teach children how to play the games.

Nabokov, Peter. *Indian Running: Native American History and Tradition*. Santa Fe, N.Mex.: Ancient City Press, 1987. Describes the races held as part of the tercentennial commemoration of the Pueblo Revolt of 1680. In addition, discusses the history and accomplishments of Indian runners.

Oxendine, Joseph B. *American Indian Sports Heritage*. Champaign, Ill.: Human Kinetics Books, 1988. Comprehensive history and description of Indian games along with short biographies of Indian sports figures.

Schoor, Gene, with Henry Gilfond. *The Jim Thorpe Story: America's Greatest Athlete*. New York: Julian Messner, 1951. A biography of one of the most famous athletes of the twentieth century.

See also: Ball Game and Courts; Children; Gambling; Hand Games; Lacrosse.

Gender Relations and Roles

Tribes affected: Pantribal
Significance: *Gender roles are culturally defined entities that serve to structure social organization; Indian societies were marked by variation in the types of gender categories present and in their manifestation over time.*

Gender is typically regarded as a cultural or social construction, in contrast to the biologically defined sexual division between male and female. The creation of gender is an active process that may involve more than simply two-gender categories and that may vary through time among different cultures.

Engendering Native Americans. Much of our understanding of North American Indians and their history and prehistory is "degendered"; that is, it is a tale of interactions among sexless cultures rather than among gendered individuals. Even those accounts of Native Americans which incorporate gender commonly only include male roles, for as Alice Kehoe ("The Muted Class," in Cheryl Claassen's *Exploring Gender Through Archaeology*, 1992) explains: "Dominant groups dominate discourse. Subordinated groups whose discourse differs from the dominant mode may not be heard." Typical of androcentric (male-oriented) writing is Claude Lévi-Strauss's statement: "The entire village left the next day in about 30 canoes, leaving us alone with the women and children in the abandoned houses" (remarked upon in Alison Wylie's "Gender Theory and the Archaeological Record," in Joan M. Gero and Margaret W. Conkey's *Engendering Archaeology*, 1991). The implication is that women and children are unimportant and do not contribute to village society. Such male-centered research creates obvious problems for an adequate understanding of human interactions and behavior, which involve both men and women.

Accounts of American Indian prehistory manifest similar problems. Generally, prehistories demonstrate cultural differences through archaeological studies of material culture, typically pottery or stone tools. Elizabeth Graham ("Women and Gender in Maya Prehistory," in Dale Walde and Noreen D. Willows' *The Archaeology of Gender,* 1991) succinctly explains: "Pots and lithics [stone tools] seem to move of their own accord across ancient landscapes, and tools are dropped here and there by faceless, sexless beings defined mainly in terms of the space in which they move, or the energy they expend." Such reconstructions of the past may demonstrate differences in manufacturing styles among groups but generally do not advance understanding of the interactions among the men and women who composed these groups.

Typical androcentric studies concerning Native Americans generally include such erroneous assumptions as the following: Gender roles and relationships are irrelevant for the understanding of other cultures, only two gender roles are found in other cultures, gender relationships among Native American societies correspond directly to those found among European groups, gender arrangements are unchanging through time, women's activities are defined in accordance to their reproductive capabilities, and women are passive and their work is of little value (whereas men are active and their work is socially important). For some American Indian groups, a few of these assumptions may be correct, while for others they may be completely inaccurate. The point is, these broad generalizations are often applied to Native Americans with little attempt to verify their truth.

Since the 1970's, but more intensely during the 1980's and 1990's, feminist studies have had an impact on the fields of anthropology, archaeology, history, Native American studies, and other fields which typically ignored gender among Indians. Some of this feminist-inspired research has a political component and is explicitly directed toward the empowerment of certain groups, such as women, American Indians, and gay populations. Not all is politically motivated, however, and not all is even concerned with women. The unifying theme underlying gender research is a theoretical outlook which views gender relationships as the fundamental structural component to social organization, much as the "manland" relationship was typically seen as fundamental to cultural

ecology. Gender studies also may stress social diversity by emphasizing the presence of multiple "voices" or "narratives" within a
group.

Generally, gender research concerning American Indians includes three types of study: the investigation of women's behavior
and history, the identification of more than two gender categories
and their activities and history, and the development of theories to
explain the identified gender relationships.

Early twentieth century Cahuilla woman carrying berries or nuts she has gathered. (Library of Congress)

Investigation of Women's Behavior and History. This aspect of gender research includes many types of research, among them studies of famous women, women as gatherers and horticulturalists, women as tool-makers, and women in the colonial period. Studies of famous women represent attempts to balance a male-dominated history by showing the contributions of important women. Toward this goal, researchers have written biographies of well-known Indian women and of women anthropologists, archaeologists, and other scholars who have worked with Native Americans or Native American concerns.

Increased attention directed toward women's roles has focused research on their gathering activities. Studies have demonstrated that this anthropologically undervalued occupation can generate a large proportion of the household's daily diet. Previously, it had sometimes been assumed that male hunting contributed the major portion of the diet, based primarily on data from male-focused ethnographics. Other assumptions concerning women's collecting behavior have been similarly corrected. Previously, it had been assumed that women's biological functions (the bearing and rearing of children) limited their ability to roam far from home to obtain plants or raw materials. Among some cultures, however, gathering women, whether working as a cooperative group or on their own, do not remain consistently close to their home or camp, nor do these women always take their children with them on excursions. In fact, once women have given birth, varying strategies of child care are possible, and children may be looked after by other mothers (who can nurse the infant), other women, siblings, fathers, mother's brother and family, or other members of the group.

Based on the ethnographic data concerning women as gatherers and horticulturalists (practicing nonmechanized farming), there is an obvious linkage between women, plants, and crop domestication. Generally, studies of prehistoric North American Indians assume that the women gathered plants and that the men hunted animals. Hunting by males was regarded in the literature as an innovative and active event, whereas gathering was depicted as routine, passive behavior. An undervaluing of female roles appears to explain why descriptions of the development of horticulture commonly involve a process whereby "plants virtually domesticate themselves," rendering human (likely women's) actions or abilities unnecessary (according to Patty Jo Watson and Mary C. Kennedy in "The Development of Horticulture," in Gero and Conkey's *Engendering Archaeology*).

In addition to studies concerning women's contributions to household subsistence, some researchers have examined women's tool-manufacturing abilities. In the past, archaeologists and ethnographers typically emphasized "*man* the toolmaker." The role of women in tool manufacturing was commonly ignored, downplayed, or denied. Archaeologists and members of the public are commonly interested in aesthetically appealing, elaborate stone pieces which display complex flaking patterns; these items are typically identified as male hunting tools (such as arrowheads or spear points, termed "projectile points" by archaeologists). Of less interest are skinning, scraping, and food-preparing tools (such as knives), usually associated with women. In most cases, however, researchers have not conducted edge-wear analyses (microscopic examinations of stone tool edges), which demonstrate whether the items were used for piercing (point) or slicing (knife) functions, or on what material these actions were performed. Typically, the projectile-point identification is applied in excavated contexts ranging from open woodlands to domestic campsites, despite the fact that open areas might be more likely locations for points, while campsites are the more likely locations for knives and scraping implements. Joan M. Gero ("Genderlithics: Women's Roles in Stone Tool Production," in *Engendering Archaeology*) suggests that based on two assumptions—that "females comprised approximately half of all prehistoric populations" and that "these women carried out production activities at prehistoric sites"—then surely "women can be expected to be most visible and active in precisely the contexts that archaeologists are most likely to excavate: on house floors, at base camps, and in village sites, where women would congregate to carry out their work."

In addition to the fact that women's roles as stone-tool users or manufacturers typically vanish in archaeological reconstructions, their roles in ceramic production may also be over- or understated. Anthropologists often indicate whether women or men are the "potters" among the society studied, but in many cases, this category is meaningless for traditional kinship-oriented groups. If the entire household participates in ceramic manufacturing, through the gathering of clay, water, fuel, fire-tending, decorating, and so on, then the actual shaping of the clay may not be the most important part of the process, although this role may be the only one which is recorded by the investigator.

Generally, discussions of North American prehistory assume that Indian women were the prehistoric potters if the historically documented communities had women potters. It has been ironically remarked by anthropologists with an interest in gender that women suddenly "appear" in the archaeologies of regions with the advent of ceramic manufacturing, much as men earlier "appeared" with the use of stone tools.

Despite dissatisfaction with such simplistically applied assumptions, it must be admitted that the identification of prehistoric gender-correlated activities is not an easy process. Even in cases for which historic documents exist, observers may provide only a partial account of events. For example, sixteenth century writings describing the involvement of Aztec women in weaving and cooking may not mention other roles, such as healing or marketing, shown in accompanying illustrations.

Scholars and Native Americans have worked to demonstrate women's participation in areas in which their influence is commonly denied. These include prestigious wealth-generating occupations (among Hopi, Iroquois, Ojibwa, and Tlingit), religion (among Blackfoot, Cree, and Kiowa-Apache), trade (Hidatsa and Mandan), and warfare (Cheyenne, Crow, and Pawnee).

A high proportion of the research concerning women's roles in American Indian societies has been directed toward the demonstration of changes which occurred with the encroachment of the European social and mercantile system. For example, many studies have concentrated on how changing trading priorities may have affected gender relationships. Research on Plains (such as Lakota Sioux), and Northeast (such as Ojibwa and Cree) cultures suggests that the European fur trade added value to the traditional production of prepared skins. Theoretically, a hunter (typically a man during the contact period for these groups) could obtain an infinite number of skins, but each skin had to be prepared (typically, the women's occupation at that time and place) before it could be exchanged with Europeans. As pelts increased in value, there was increased pressure for a man to create relationships with more women who could treat the animal skins. This could be achieved through polygynous unions (marriage to more than one wife). In this manner, women became producers within a system controlled by men, rather than being the producers and organizers of their own economic enterprises. It has been suggested that this situation probably resulted in decreased power for the women of these groups. Other effects of Indian-European contact have also been investigated. Several studies, for example, have examined the influence of missionization on traditional gender roles.

Identification of More than Two Gender Categories. Descriptions of American Indians have often ignored common culturally accepted changes in gender typical of many Native American groups. Relatively recent emphasis on the understanding of diversity has led to a greater study and recognition of gender transformations among American Indians. Patricia C. Albers' research, as described in "From Illusion to Illumination: Anthropological Studies of American Indian Women," in Sandra Morgen's *Gender and Anthropology* (1989), indicates that as many as 113 American Indian groups recognized transformative gender statuses and that among these, male transvestism (biologically male individuals who took on the cultural roles typical of women) predominated. There is abundant literature discussing the *berdaches* (typically defined as males who dress and behave as women) in the historic period. Within many Native American cultures, berdaches constituted a culturally accepted component of society. They were found across North America and have been identified during the historic period in the Arctic (Aleut, Pacific Inuit, Baffinland Inuit, and Quebec Inuit), the Subarctic (Hare and Ingalik), the Great Basin (Eastern Shoshone, Kawaiisu, and Paiute), California (Chumash, Salinan, Tolowa, Wiyot, and Yokuts), the Southwest (Karankawa and Navajo), the Great Plains (Lakota Sioux), the Northeast (Delaware, Illinois, Miami, possibly Tuscarora and Winnebago), and the Southeast (Timucua and Natchez).

Traditionally, anthropologists discussed the berdache phenomenon in the context of cultural relativism (the concept that cultures must be evaluated based on their own values, and not on those of outside groups), specifically as an example of how notions of normal and abnormal behavior are culturally defined within individual societies. Studies of berdaches from the 1970's onward have instead tended to discuss transformative behavior within its specific social context and to include women gender transformers (women behaving as men) in addition to identifying other gender categories.

Research has confirmed the expectation that gender varies culturally and that many Indian groups had roles for female gender transformers. Among them were the Atsina (or Gros Ventres), Canadian Blackfoot, Cherokee, Cheyenne, Kutenai, Lakota Sioux, Navajo, Ottawa, Piegan, and Tlingit. There are, or were, various gender categories within different cultural groups, and each of these has (or had) varying roles and social status. In some cases, individuals determined their own genders, while among other groups, parents or other adults could change the gender of a child. For example, among the historic period Inuit, girls were often dressed as boys if the parents had desired a son or if they wished the child to take on the name and characteristics of a deceased male.

Theories to Explain Gender. American Indian studies have concentrated more on the identification and description of different gender categories than on the explanation of these categories' creation or function. Theoretical works generally focus on the discussion of two gender categories—heterosexual men and heterosexual women—and often examine their relative status and power through time (typically precolonial versus colonial), using the variables of occupation or marital relationship. Activities do provide a strong indication of the demarcated gender role within the society (traditionally discussed under "divisions of labor"), although there are always exceptions. Among some groups, individuals could adopt the behavior of the opposite sex without changing their gender, whereas among other groups, such behavior was interpreted as a change in gender.

It has been suggested that in cases where women contributed noticeably to the household's subsistence (as among the Hopi and Iroquois), women had greater status than in societies where women contributed less to the daily diet. Many of the societies with socially valued women also granted women claims to the resources they generated, to the land, or to their homes.

Marital rights are also examined as an indicator of the relative freedom of women and men. Among some societies (as among Blackfoot, Hopi, Iroquois, and Ojibwa), women played an active role in the selection of a spouse and were able to divorce their husbands. Broadly, it seems that women have more freedom in marital matters when descent is traced through the women's line (matrilineal descent).

Improvement in women's social status generally is correlated with a number of factors. It is related to their economic contribution (such as their ability to contribute to the daily diet); it is also related to their control over basic resources (such as homes or land) and to the yields from these resources (such as crops). Additionally, it is related to their influence on the heredity of their offspring through matrilineal descent patterns. Societies having all these attributes (Hopi society, for example) tend to be marked by the presence of powerful, independent women.

Colonization resulted in many changes in the relationships between Indian women and men. In some cases, such as with the nomadic buffalo-hunting groups of the Plains, the European mercantile system seemed to decrease the status of women. In other cases, such as among the horticultural Iroquois, the European trading system may have advanced the status of women. During the later prehistoric and early historic period, Iroquois women controlled horticultural production (most importantly, corn) in the fields surrounding their villages. With the arrival of Europeans, Iroquois men became fur traders, and as prey became scarcer in the vicinity of their settlements, they ventured farther afield in search of fur-bearing animals. These extended absences from villages, both in fur trading and in raiding, meant that women assumed greater control of village organization and resources. For nomadic Plains groups, this male involvement in buffalo hunting (for hides and meat) did not translate into increased female status, since women were eliminated from the cooperative buffalo hunts and, as Albers notes, "became workers in a highly specialized production process over which men had ultimate control. As a result, the means of wealth accumulation and prestige were increasingly in the hands of men."

The most important result of gender research is that it has increased awareness of the variation among Native American populations. It is now recognized that anthropological descriptions which fail to take gender into account are incomplete at best, often misleading, and sometimes completely inaccurate. New perspectives on gender have had a profound impact on the understanding of society and culture in general and of Native Americans in particular.

Susan J. Wurtzburg

Sources for Further Study

Ackerman, Lillian A. *A Necessary Balance: Gender and Power Among Indians of the Columbia Plateau*. Norman: University of Oklahoma Press, 2003. An examination of gender equality in four areas: domestic, economic, political, and religious.

Allen, Paula Gunn. *The Sacred Hoop: Recovering the Feminine in American Indian Traditions*. Reprint, with a new preface. Boston: Beacon Press, 1992. Gunn's Laguna Pueblo and Sioux heritage influences her essays concerning Native American women, including gay women. Comprehensive index, no illustrations.

_____, ed. *Spider Woman's Granddaughters: Traditional Tales and Contemporary Writing by Native American Women.* New York: Fawcett Columbine, 1989. Anthology of fictional and traditional prose. Brief authors' biographies and suggestions for further reading.

Bataille, Gretchen M., and Kathleen Mullen Sands. *American Indian Women: Telling Their Lives.* Lincoln: University of Nebraska Press, 1984. Essays concerning Native American autobiography. Comprehensive index and useful bibliography.

Bowker, Ardy. *Sisters in the Blood: The Education of Women in Native America.* Newton, Mass.: WEEA, 1993. Informative analyses based on interviews with 991 northern Plains women. Index, no illustrations.

Claassen, Cheryl, ed. *Exploring Gender Through Archaeology: Selected Papers from the 1991 Boone Conference.* Madison, Wis.: Prehistory Press, 1992. Anthology of papers by archaeologists providing research on gender issues. No index.

Gacs, Ute, et al., eds. *Women Anthropologists: Selected Biographies.* Urbana: University of Illinois Press, 1989. Biographical data concerning women anthropologists, many of whom wrote about Native Americans.

Gero, Joan M., and Margaret W. Conkey, eds. *Engendering Archaeology: Women and Prehistory.* Oxford: Basil Blackwell, 1991. Anthology of articles by specialists, most dealing with North America. Good theoretical introduction. Comprehensive index, charts, drawings, maps, and photographs.

Morgen, Sandra, ed. *Gender and Anthropology: Critical Reviews for Research and Teaching.* Washington, D.C.: American Anthropological Association, 1989. An anthology of articles focusing on the synthesis of research and teaching methods, including lesson plans and film suggestions. Contains useful review of research concerning American Indian women by Patricia C. Albers. No comprehensive index.

Spector, Janet D. *What This Awl Means: Feminist Archaeology at a Wahpeton Dakota Village.* St. Paul: Minnesota Historical Society Press, 1993. An innovative archaeologist's search for evidence and understanding of Dakota women. Index, charts, maps, illustrations and photographs.

Walde, Dale, and Noreen D. Willows, eds. *The Archaeology of Gender: Proceedings of the Twenty-second Annual Chacmool Conference.* Calgary, Canada: University of Calgary Archaeological Association, 1991. Selection of papers, most of which concern prehistory or history of Native Americans. No index.

See also: Berdache; Children; Education: Pre-contact; Marriage and Divorce; Menses and Menstruation; Puberty and Initiation Rites; Women.

Ghost Dance

Tribes affected: Pantribal
Significance: *The Ghost Dance was one of many religious rituals and movements that arose in the wake of European contact in response to permanent changes in traditional lifeways for native peoples.*

The Ghost Dance began in 1890 as a result of the visions of a Paiute Indian from Nevada called Wovoka. As a result of his visions, Wovoka began delivering a series of prophetic messages that described a future which would restore Native Americans to their life as it had been before contact with the European American settlers and would drive away or destroy the settlers on Native American traditional lands.

Crisis Movements. The Ghost Dance movement is usually described by scholars as an "apocalyptic" or "prophetic"-type movement (borrowing descriptive terms from the study of biblical history). Such movements usually involve someone describing bizarre or frightening visions of a catastrophic change in world events, and these movements are often found among populations who are experiencing severe crisis. These crises can be natural (earthquakes, massive fires, volcanoes) but are more typically associated with political/military conquest by a foreign people who seem strange and overwhelmingly powerful. Such a description clearly fits the experience of Native American tribes who found their lifestyle severely disrupted by the newly arrived settlers. The old way of life, with its familiar routines, was disrupted forever, and the old ways were seen as a "golden age" to which many people wished to return.

Ghost Dance as a Crisis Movement. In the case of the Ghost Dance of 1890, the movement and its widespread popularity are usually attributed to the disastrous disruption of the traditional life of the indigenous populations of North America that came in the wake of European settlement beginning in the sixteenth century. White encroachment had disastrous effects on the native peoples in the West in the nineteenth century. Although the Ghost Dance movement became widespread in 1889-1890, Wovoka had begun having his revelatory visions and experiences in 1887. Also known as John (Jack) Wilson, Wovoka's most influential and serious supernatural experience was, as he himself described it, a visit to the spirit world on the occasion of the total eclipse of the sun on January 1, 1889.

The precise content of the visions of Wovoka and the teachings and implications which he derived from these visions are difficult to describe with confidence, since virtually all existing reports are second- and third-person contacts. The classic source is James Mooney's government-supported study, "The Ghost Dance Religion and the Sioux Outbreak of 1890," published in 1896. This study was conducted within memory of the events described. Mooney, as a white government official, had to interview sources and interpret his reports as best he could. The major difficulty with this procedure is that the Ghost Dance movement was typically hostile toward white settlers' presence, and one must suspect that reports collected by Mooney would have been delivered in a more conciliatory tone than discussions among Native Americans themselves.

The United States government's interest in the Ghost Dance movement was a direct result of the fact that the message of

A depiction of the Arapaho Ghost Dance circa 1900. *(National Archives)*

Wovoka had a very rapid impact that quickly crossed tribal lines. The movement was deeply implicated in the historic massacre of Chief Big Foot's band at Wounded Knee in Pine Ridge, South Dakota. The Ghost Dance was interpreted in different ways in different tribal contexts; it took a relatively militant turn among the Lakota (Sioux) who were active in the movement.

Representatives from many other tribes were sent to hear of Wovoka's revelations, and through these messengers the movement spread widely among the Sioux, the Northern Cheyenne, and the Northern Arapaho. It was also influential on related movements, such as that based on the visionary experiences of John Slocum, a member of the Coast Salish tribe whose own prophetic experiences led to the founding of the Indian Shaker Church.

Wovoka's Visions. Included among the visions of Wovoka, and related by him to his followers and representatives of other tribes, were such basic ideas as the resurrection of tribal members who had died, the restoration of game animals, a flood which would destroy only the white settlers, the necessity and importance of the performance of a dance ritual (the Ghost Dance itself), and a time that is coming which would be free of suffering and disease. Of these major ideas, the primary focus seemed to be on the ideas of resurrection and the restoration of important elements of the old ways, as well as the performance of the dance itself. Related developments of the Ghost Dance movement were certain ethical precepts and, at least among the Sioux, the creation and wearing of distinctive "ghost shirts," which identified adherents to the movement and were used in the performance of the ritual dancing itself.

In Indian descriptions of the Ghost Dance precepts to white researchers such as Mooney, the motif of the destruction of whites was muted, and many interviewees stressed that the visions of Wovoka actually taught a peaceful coexistence with the white settlers. It is certainly possible that ideas varied, depending on the views and experiences of the tribes appropriating the basic message of Wovoka.

Roots of the Ghost Dance. An interesting summary of the Ghost Dance movement that emphasizes the important role of Wovoka himself is provided by Thomas Overholt, who compares Wovoka with certain prophets of the Bible such as Jeremiah. Overholt also suggests that the Ghost Dance of 1890 was preceded by, and possibly influenced by, similar visionary/apocalyptic movements, such as the Ghost Dance of 1870 (which also occurred among the Paiutes, initiated by a visionary named Wodziwob) and the Southern Okanagan Prophet Dance around 1800.

Attempts to trace a prehistory of the Ghost Dance of 1890, however, must also reckon with the very high probability of some influence from the Old Testament biblical prophets through early contact with European missionary teachers. Wovoka himself, for example, did have some contact with missionaries, as reported by Mooney. Yet it is also true that such visionary movements were not uncommon among western American tribes from the beginning of the nineteenth century.

As predicted dates for the cosmic events described by Wovoka came and passed, the initial fervor of the Ghost Dance and Wovoka's teachings in general began to dissipate. Among some tribes, however, the focus shifted from apocalyptic expectations of events to a longer-term stress on daily ethics. In short, the movement became partially institutionalized, which is not uncommon for religious groups whose roots lie in visionary experiences.

Daniel L. Smith-Christopher

Sources for Further Study

Bailey, Paul. *Wovoka: The Indian Messiah*. Los Angeles: Westernlore Press, 1957.

Hittman, Michael. *Wovoka and the Ghost Dance*. Edited by Don Lynch. Expanded ed. Lincoln: University of Nebraska Press, 1997.

Mooney, James. "The Ghost Dance Religion and the Sioux Outbreak of 1890." In *Annual Report of the Bureau of American Ethnology*. Vol 14. Washington, D.C.: Government Printing Office, 1896. Reprint. Chicago: University of Chicago Press, 1965.

Overholt, Thomas. *Channels of Prophecy: The Social Dynamics of Prophetic Activity*. Minneapolis: Fortress Press, 1989.

Wilson, Bryan R. *Magic and the Millennium*. New York: Harper & Row, 1973.

See also: Dances and Dancing; Visions and Vision Quests.

Gifts and Gift Giving

Tribes affected: Pantribal
Significance: *Gift exchange was an essential mode of strategic interaction with other tribes and with the colonial powers.*

Gift giving was a central feature of exchange customs common to North American Indians. Treaties, trade, and other interactions demanded the distribution of various gifts among the parties. These presents symbolized the social bonds between the participants. Indians presented gifts to make and sustain alliances and to demonstrate continued control to the colonial powers. They used this gift giving to symbolize, sustain, and equalize human relationships. Presents were also given to create and alter social relationships. Other functions of gift giving were to establish an identity, to maintain peaceful interactions, to provide a basis for genuine friendships, to foster an egalitarian social order, and to create an economic order based on the redistribution of wealth.

The European powers were forced to comply with a gift-giving political economy in order to obtain commercial advantages. They presented gifts to guarantee loyalty from tribes and chiefs, to buy service from Indian leaders, to counter influence from rival colonial governments, and to foster trade. In addition, European gift giving served to create kinship ties to important chiefs and to signify respect for Indians.

There were many varieties of items in the gift-exchange economy. Among these items were artifacts such as looms, baskets, textiles, leather goods, and clothing. Plants, animals, shells, skins, food, and medicines were also offered as gifts. In addition, rituals could produce presents of songs, stories, or healing ceremonies. After European contact, commodities such as manufactured goods, rum, brandy, and other products were introduced into the gift-exchange economy.

Gift giving was supplanted by European-style commerce. Gift giving had always been in conflict with commercial economic activity. The Europeans first participated reluctantly in gift exchange to receive commercial advantage. Over time, however, Native Americans were drawn away from gift exchanges and toward commercial exchanges. This resulted in much destruction of their culture. For example, subsistence hunting was replaced with the near extinction of species because of the commercial desire for certain pelts in the fur trade. This commercial activity also countered the community-forming function of gift exchange by bringing Indians into conflict through commercial competition.

William H. Green

See also: Money; Potlatch; Trade.

Gold and Goldworking

Tribe affected: Aztec
Significance: *Using a variety of techniques, Aztec goldworkers produced jewelry, ornaments, and implements of great beauty.*

Before the Spanish conquest of Mexico in the sixteenth century, Aztec goldsmiths produced gold jewelry and implements of extraordinary beauty. Archaeological evidence suggests that goldworking was introduced from South America into Central America and Mexico relatively late; the Toltec culture was working gold around 900 C.E. Goldworking was not widespread in the pre-Columbian cultures of Mexico; the occasional gold pieces found in Mayan sites, for example, appear to have been the result of trade rather than local manufacture. Aztec goldworkers used gold nuggets or dust, or so-called virgin gold, for their artistry; there is no evidence for the smelting of gold ore in pre-Columbian cultures.

Goldworking was a highly valued skill among the Aztecs. It was a specialized task at the time of the Spanish conquest, with goldsmiths being divided into those who hammered or beat gold and those who cast it in molds; within these divisions, there were many categories of artisans, depending on the kind of work they produced. Gold was used by the Aztecs as a means of tallying tribute obligations; gold also had religious connotations. In the Aztec language, Nahuatl, the word for gold was *teocuitlatl*, or "excrement of the gods." Aztec goldworkers had their own patron god, Xipe Totec; anyone guilty of stealing gold was flayed alive to propitiate this deity.

The first pre-Columbian Mexican goldwork involved shaping nuggets by grinding and hammering them. Later it was discovered that gold dust and grains could be formed into ingots of workable size by fusing them, using a blowpipe to quicken the flame; Aztec drawings show goldworkers using blowpipes. Cold-hammering of gold nuggets or ingots into sheets eventually makes the gold springy and unworkable, but pre-Columbian smiths learned that heating the beaten gold returns its malleability. The process of alternately hammering and heating gold is called annealing, and it was widely used in Mesoamerica to produce not only gold but also various alloys of copper.

Aztec goldworkers also used the "lost-wax" method of working with gold. In this technique, a goldworker first makes a wax model of the desired piece, which is then covered with clay; the wax form is covered with powdered charcoal so that it will release smoothly from the clay mold. Vents are left in the clay to allow the wax to drain from the mold when it is heated. Molten gold is then poured into a vent, and after cooling the mold is broken apart. The lost-wax technique allows for the production of intricate and finely wrought gold jewelry or ornamentation. In addition, Aztec goldworkers learned to solder intricate pieces together using gold alloyed with copper or silver.

No archaeological evidence has yet been able to date precisely the emergence of the various skills in pre-Columbian goldworking. Similarly, no goldworking shop has been discovered or excavated. Detailed descriptions of Aztec goldworking are contained in Spanish historical records, however, along with extensive inventories of golden objects seized by the conquerors. The Spanish were astonished by the volume and value of Aztec gold, much of which they melted down into ingots or reformed into Spanish coins. Yet enough goldwork remains intact from the pre-Columbian and early contact period to testify to the great skill of Aztec goldworkers.

David J. Minderhout

Source for Further Study

Baxter, Paula A. with Allison Bird-Romero. *Encyclopedia of Native American Jewelry: A Guide to History, People, and Terms*. Phoenix, Ariz.: Oryx Press, 2000.

See also: Aztec Empire; Dress and Adornment; Metalwork; Ornaments; Silverworking; Turquoise.

Gourd Dance

Tribe affected: Kiowa
Significance: *Part of a four-day ceremony honoring a Kiowa victory in a major battle.*

In 1838, the Kiowa defeated the Arapaho and other enemies in a major battle along the Missouri River in Montana. Skunkberry bushes full of red berries covered the battleground. A warrior who became lost after the victory wandered around for days, seeking his people's encampment. Then he heard music coming from a red wolf, who taught him to dance to a beautiful tune accompanied by a gourd rattle. The wolf told him to take the song back to his people and teach them the dance.

The warrior returned, and in celebration of the victory and the return of the lost comrade, a Gourd Dance Society formed and shook red-painted gourds covered with representations of skunk-berry bushes while dancing the dance of the red wolf. Only males performed the dance, which featured the dancers, a drummer, a whip man to keep the dancers moving, and a director who set the pace. Skunkberries were a symbol of endurance and bravery, and the Gourd Dance became part of a four-day festival until it was banned by reservation authorities in 1890. In 1955, the Kiowa brought back the dance as part of a newly established Gourd Day celebration taking place on the Fourth of July.

Leslie V. Tischauser

See also: Dances and Dancing; Drums; Music and Song.

Grass Dance

Tribes affected: Arapaho, Arikara, Assiniboine, Blackfeet, Crow, Gros Ventre, Hidatsa, Iowa, Kansa, Lakota, Menominee, Ojibwa, Omaha, Pawnee, Ponca

Significance: *The Grass Dance is a men's competitive dance believed to give the participants the power to heal burns.*

The Grass Dance is a men's competitive dance. It may have originated with the Pawnee dance known as the *iruska*. Iruska means "the fire inside of all things." The Pawnee man Crow Feather was given this ceremony of fire-handling and dancing, which confers on participants the power to heal burns. In modern times, the Grass Dance is a part of the dance competition at pow-wows along the summer circuit in the United States. Grass dancers wear grass tied to their costumes. During the dance there is a considerable amount of athletic jumping, bending, and stomping. Dancers perform either individually or in pairs.

Grass Dance societies typically have a number of officers: a leader, a pipe keeper, whip bearers, food servers, drummers, and singers. The Grass Dance has developed a large repertory of drumming and singing sequences. There are music groups among some tribes that specialize in Grass Dance songs. The Grass Dance is regarded not only as a competitive event but also as a celebratory occasion.

T. J. Arant

See also: Dances and Dancing; Drums; Music and Song; Pow-wows and Celebrations.

Grass House

Tribes affected: Primarily California, Great Basin, and Southwest
  tribes
Significance: *The grass house was constructed by covering a pole framework with layers of grass that formed both the walls and roof.*

There were basically two types of grass house: the conical beehive
and the larger, elongated house, which could accommodate several extended families. In wet areas, grass houses were essentially
dwellings set on exposed bearing poles several meters off the
ground, with a ladder entrance. The beehive structure was formed
by running straight or bowed poles to a vertical support center

A nineteenth century Bannock family pictured outside their grass tent. *(National
Archives)*

pole or simply by tying the slanted poles together at the apex. The longhouse was also constructed with vertical and horizontal poles.

The grass covering was applied in one of several ways. Most commonly, long grass was bunched, with the top third folded over a horizontal cane or thin wood pole, and tied with grass to the longer outside length; grass was added until the course was completed. The next course would overlap or shingle the lower row, providing, when finished, effective water-shedding. This layering continued to the long, longitudinal ridge pole, where the opposing topmost rows were tied together. Some grass house coverings were better secured by stitching external horizontal willow or cane rods to the internal frame. Because of accumulated smoke residue and general deterioration, grass houses would be rethatched every three to five years, using the original frame.

John Alan Ross

See also: Architecture: California; Architecture: Great Basin; Architecture: Southwest; Wickiup.

Green Corn Dance

Tribes affected: Cherokee, Creek (Muskogee), Seminole, others in the Southeast
Significance: *This was the principal dance performed in the most important harvest ceremony of the southeastern tribes.*

Dance is a central component of Native American ceremonial life. Nowhere is this more evident than in the Eastern Woodland Green Corn Rite. Ritual dance is an important feature of this ceremony, which takes place in July or August at the final corn harvest. The Green Corn Dance is a necessary part of the planting of the corn. Great spiritual benefit is believed to derive from the performance, which occurs in the newly cleaned and sanctified town square. The square contains the sacred fire, which binds the community to their deceased and to their deity. Into the newly kindled fire, such items as new corn, tea leaves, meat, and medicine are offered.

As it is presently performed in the Southeast, the dance has four stages, each of which is divided into various movements. Music includes the sounds of stone-filled gourd rattles as well as singing. Men and women, in their finest attire, dance separately but simultaneously around a high pole adorned with green boughs that provide shade for the musicians seated on benches below.

First the men begin to dance. A leader followed by a column of ten to twenty men carrying guns circles counterclockwise in an area a few hundred yards from the town square. The leader sings and plays a rattle while the other men shoot their guns at various times. The first man in the column shoots first, then the second, and so on until the last man, who shoots twice. By shaking his rattle, the leader thus directs the shots. The rifle shots are supposedly symbolic of the sound of thunder. This men's part of the dance takes place in the morning. At about noon participants break to eat food that the women have provided.

The women dance in a single line and side by side in the main square. They are directed by a woman leader who uses leg rattles to keep time. This second stage of the dance performance symbolizes the fertilization of corn. Men come to the central square and combine with the women's column, led by the men's dance leader. All the men and women then commence to circle counterclockwise. After this portion of the dance, the whole community takes part in a feast.

In the evening, the third stage of the dance begins. The men and the women are again separate, as in the beginning. The men carry guns and circle counterclockwise around the women. This movement continues until the sun sets. The fourth stage is done the next night, accompanied by animal sacrifices.

At the conclusion of the Green Corn Ceremony, the individual, the family, the clan, and the nation are all renewed for another year.

William H. Green

See also: Corn; Corn Woman; Dances and Dancing; Mississippian Culture; Music and Song.

Grooming

Tribes affected: Pantribal

Significance: *Though grooming and personal adornment were univer-sally valued by American Indian peoples, the specific ways these were practiced varied from tribe to tribe.*

Bodily grooming and adornment performed a number of signifi-cant functions for individuals and groups throughout Native North America. Gender-specific norms related to personal appear-ance for both everyday life and special occasions existed in all In-dian communities. Such norms prescribed methods by which men and women could make themselves attractive or could call atten-tion to their special ranks and achievements.

Tattoos and Body Painting. Among the most widespread of such grooming techniques were body painting and tattooing. The colors and designs associated with each of these practices were quite often used to symbolize an individual's attainment of a spe-cific status or accomplishment that was valued by his or her fellow community members. Thus, for example, among the Lakotas or Teton Sioux, the right side of the face of the lead *akicitapi*, or camp marshal, was marked with four stripes of black paint. In many tribes, face and body painting was an important element in rites of passage, including girls' and boys' puberty rituals and funeral cer-emonies. Aside from marking social status, numerous Indian com-munities also used facial and body painting as a means of warding off evil spirits believed to cause illnesses during their curing cere-monies. Thus, for example, Siberian Inuits would paint the faces of sick persons with stripes of red ochre during their healing prac-tices.

Perhaps the most extensive use of body painting was practiced by the now extinct Boethuk tribe of the Northeast coast who col-ored their entire bodies, hair, clothing and equipment with a mix-ture of red ochre and grease. It is thought that the term "Red In-dian" was first applied to the members of this tribe for that reason.

The men and women of the Plateau's Thompson tribe also painted and tattooed themselves on a daily basis with a similar combination of fat and pigment. Tattoos were used extensively by Indians of the Northwest Coast, including decorating their arms, legs, and chests with family crests. It was common for the women of Indian tribes from northern California to the northern Northwest Coast decorated their chins with tattoos.

Body Piercing. Body piercing served similar functions among many tribes as those already mentioned in connection with painting and tattooing. The Seminoles, like many other tribes, bored their earlobes in order to wear rings and bobs. Numerous Inuit peoples practiced the custom of perforating parts of their faces in order to insert labrets and pins. In many cases, these practices were

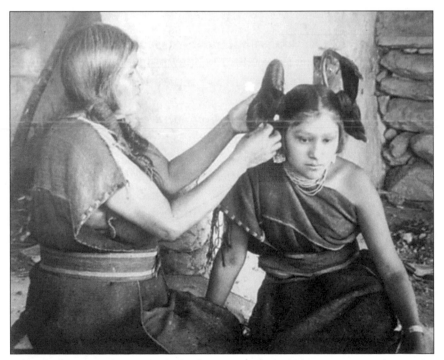

A Hopi woman arranges the hair of an unmarried girl into an appropriate style. *(National Archives)*

A woman attends to the hair of this Hopi man. *(National Archives)*

performed in association with a rite of passage. For example, two puberty ceremonies among the Mackenzie Delta Inuits involved piercing the cheeks and earlobes as preparation for labrets.

Hair Styling. Manners of dressing and wearing hair were also important among most tribes. Such customs differed markedly from one group to another. For instance, whereas St. Lawrence Inuit males generally shaved their scalps, leaving only an encircling circumference of hair, men belonging to southern Tiwa groups reversed this pattern so that the unshaven scalp hair resembled a skullcap. Women's hair displayed similar variations in style, sometimes braided, sometimes tied in a top knot, or worn in whorls over the ears, as was typical of many southwestern Indian groups. Occasionally younger and older women of the same tribe would wear their hair differently. Thus, for example, Hopi girls sported the distinctive whorl style, but after marriage they generally wore their hair in braids.

Modes of tending and wearing one's hair many times held religious and social significance. The Western Apaches and the Kiowas, for instance, held ceremonies to mark the first cutting of a child's hair. Among many Plains Indians, individuals cut their hair as part of ritual cycles connected with mourning.

Hair styling and care involved the use of tonics, most commonly made of grease or marrow. The Lenni Lanape, or Delawares, also employed sap for this purpose. Many tribes utilized combs made of various materials, including wood and porcupine tail, as part of their styling and grooming regime. The use of tweezers to remove unwanted facial hair was also found among many Indian groups.

Impact of Assimilation. From the late eighteenth through early twentieth centuries, Native American modes of bodily grooming, hair styling, and hair care underwent drastic changes due to the influence of federal assimilation policy and missionary work. As part of the so-called civilization and Christianization regime followed in both government and religious boarding schools, schoolmasters and matrons routinely cut and styled the hair of their young charges according to white fashion. Students were also expected to adopt western standards of personal grooming and adornment as signs of their cultural progress. With the revitalization of tribal values during the last few decades, however, some individuals have attempted to return to the traditional grooming and hair care practices of their tribes, especially during ritual or social celebrations. The influence of Hollywood and the media has also led to a stereotyped, "Pan-Indian" version of these practices, patterned after that of Plains Indians.

Harvey Markowitz

Source for Further Study
Dubin, Lois Sherr. *North American Indian Jewelry and Adornment: From Prehistory to the Present*. New York: Henry N. Abrams, 1999.

See also: Dress and Adornment; Gender Relations and Roles; Rites of Passage; Tattoos and Tattooing.

Guardian Spirits

Tribes affected: Pantribal

Significance: *According to a belief held by many American Indian cultures, an individual may obtain contact with the supernatural world by seeking a guardian spirit to serve as a personal guide and protector.*

For many American Indians, the concept of a guardian spirit was most commonly associated with the natural world through the visible representation of animals or birds, such as the bear, wolf, or eagle. The particular association of a guardian spirit with a certain animal was the result of either ancestral ties (most typical of the Northwest Indians), the personal vision quest (common among Plains Indian tribes), inheritance (more typical of the Indians of the Southwest and Mexico), or, least often, transference or purchase.

In the Northwest the guardian spirit of the clan is represented in the totem. The clan members obtain protection from the clan totem at the puberty ceremony. The totem can also become a guardian spirit offering personal as well as communal protection. Totem poles depict the guardian spirit of the ancestral father and other figures from the natural and supernatural world.

Guardian spirits may also be obtained through a vision quest ritual in which the individual seeks a vision of the guardian spirit in a secluded place. At its appearance, the guardian spirit gives the individual some kind of special capacity and a medicine bundle to be used in hunting rituals. The vision quest is usually preceded by fasting, a sweatlodge experience and bathing, and a preparatory ascetic style of living. The spirit generally appears as an animal, but not in form and shape identical to a natural animal. An individual may cause the guardian spirit to depart if any taboos are violated, and not everyone who seeks a guardian spirit through the vision quest receives one. The vision quest is still practiced today, although not for hunting purposes in the way it was practiced prior to European contact.

Guardian spirits had the most significance among the hunting tribes because they helped in providing game during the hunt. It was taboo to eat the animal represented by the guardian spirit. Agricultural tribes of the Southwest and Mexico relied more on a variety of spirits for assistance in regard to fertility cycles and typically did not seek a personal guardian spirit, believing that one had already been received at birth. Boys more often than girls sought a guardian spirit, and obtaining a guardian spirit was often done as a puberty rite directly relating to future hunting success.

An American Indian's relationship to his or her guardian spirit is personal and intimate, expressed physically by wearing the fur, claws, or feathers of the spirit and symbolically by incorporating the animal's name into his or her own. The shaman or medicine man was often believed to be able to change into his guardian spirit.

Diane C. Van Noord

See also: Bundles, Sacred; Puberty and Initiation Rites; Religion; Religious Specialists; Shields; Totems; Visions and Vision Quests.

Guns

Tribes affected: Pantribal
Significance: *Guns obtained from Europeans altered patterns of intertribal warfare and Indian-white warfare as well as traditional native economies.*

The introduction of guns by European traders and settlers powerfully reshaped American Indian patterns of warfare, intertribal politics, and economic life. Early seventeenth century muskets had a much greater effective range than traditional bows, and they inflicted more lethal wounds. Warriors armed with bows were easily defeated by smaller numbers of Europeans armed with guns. As Indians along the Atlantic coast learned of the effectiveness of the unfamiliar weapons in war and in hunting, they eagerly traded furs, the native commodity Europeans chiefly sought, to obtain them.

After their introduction by Europeans, guns were widely used by Native Americans as illustrated by this Paiute Indian in the late nineteenth century. *(National Archives)*

Tribes situated along the coast became middlemen in the exchange of European goods for furs from tribes in the interior. As tribes trapped out the beaver or other animals in their own territories, they made war on less well-armed neighbors to take possession of their hunting grounds, so that guns and the accompanying fur trade created an entirely new and more deadly source of intertribal warfare. The mid-seventeenth century destruction of the Huron Confederacy by the better-armed Iroquois is the best-known example. The trade in furs and skins for guns and other European goods disrupted the traditional subsistence economies of Indian peoples, making them dependent on the Europeans, but no one could risk ignoring the new weapons. Guns spread steadily into the interior, reaching the Great Plains in the early nineteenth century. Armed with guns, Indians became a far greater military threat to Europeans.

Bert M. Mutersbaugh

Source for Further Study

Taylor, Colin F. *Native American Weapons*. Norman: University of Oklahoma Press, 2001.

See also: Bows, Arrows, and Quivers; Warfare and Conflict; Weapons.

Hako

Tribes affected: Plains tribes, especially Pawnee
Significance: *The hako ceremony symbolizes the transferral of life forces from generation to generation.*

The word *hako*, which means "pipe" in the Wichita language, has been applied to a number of Indian ceremonies that center on the use of feather-ornamented hollow shafts of wood. In some general but not fully accurate descriptions, hako is deemed to be synonymous with the easily recognized calumet, or pipe ceremony, popularly associated with the "peace pipe." In the early twentieth century writings of American ethnologist Alice C. Fletcher, however, who is still recognized as the first authority on hako, the much broader cultural symbolism suggested by the Pawnee term *hakkwpirus*, or "beating [in association with] a breathing mouth of wood," is apparent.

Early Observations. Feather-decorated pipe ceremonies that could be considered prototypes of what Fletcher and her associates studied under the general label of hako were first observed, but not fully understood, in the last quarter of the seventeenth century by the French Jesuit Jacques Marquette among the Illinois tribes. Similar traditions appeared in ceremonies practiced by Algonquian and Siouan peoples. Very little was known about the specialized symbolic content of hako, however, until Fletcher carried out and published, in 1906, what remains the most extensive fieldwork on the subject. The ceremonies she described reflected the traditions of Plains Indians in particular.

Fletcher must have encountered a high degree of secrecy among the Omahas, where she first observed hako ceremonies during the 1880's. After failing over a number of years in her efforts to learn the meaning behind the Omaha ceremonies, she turned to the Pawnees, where a Chawi tribal holy man, Tahirussawichi, gave her essential explanations and some ceremonial texts. The latter were eventually translated with the assistance of her main Pawnee assistant, James Murie.

Meanings of the Ceremony. Before considering the hako ceremony itself, a description of the central "breathing mouth of wood" and accompanying ritual objects is essential. Usually the wood used (two pieces) consisted of stems three or four feet in length with burned-out piths to allow the passage of breath. One stem was painted blue to represent the sky. A long red groove symbolizing life stood for the path that would be symbolized in several phases of the ceremony. Ceremonial wood was always decorated with feathers on the forward tip to "carry" communications associated with hako. As in more general Indian belief systems, the brown eagle in particular is believed to have the power to soar to the domain of higher powers in the sky. Other forces were represented in the attachment of the breast, neck, and mandibles of a duck to the downward (earthward-pointing) end of the hollowed stem. The duck symbolized daily familiarity with all elements affecting life: land, water, and sky. A second white eagle-feathered stem, called *Rahaktakaru* (to contrast it with *Rahakatittu*, the "breathing mouth of wood with dark moving feathers"), was painted green for the earth. Its position in the hako ceremony was always different from its brown-feathered counterpart. The unconsecrated nature of the white eagle, and thus Rahaktakaru's association with the male father, warrior, and defender, kept it separate from two other symbolic elements of hako, namely the mother and the children. The former, the giver of fruit and abundance, was represented by an ear of white corn (*atira*, or mother breathing forth life), with a blue-painted tip (the sky, dwelling place of the powers) from which four blue-painted strips, or "paths," allowed powers to descend to join the red (life) grooves of the Rahakatittu.

Unlike many Indian ceremonies, hako was not associated with a particular seasonal activity, such as planting, harvesting or hunting. As a ceremony celebrating life, it could occur at any time when signs of life were stirring, either in mating (spring), nesting (summer), or flocking (fall), but not during winter dormancy. In a hako ceremony there is always a symbolic position reserved for participants representing the "parents" and a second reserved for the "children." The latter are traditionally from a group that is distinct from the host, or parent group. This element underlines the universality of the union of otherwise distinct groups in that all benefit from the cycle of life.

Journey of Mother Corn. Hako ceremonies symbolize a journey taken by Mother Corn leading from the place of origin in the group or tribe of the fathers to a destination in the group or tribe of the children. The importance of the "breathing mouth of wood" bearing the power of the brown eagle feathers is that it allows Mother Corn to attain the blue-domed abode of the powers before redescending to the ceremonial lodge. When the journey is concluded, Mother Corn will seek out the son, who is considered the paramount representative of the children. Successful conclusion of Mother Corn's passage symbolizes assurance of safe passage of life's bounty from one generation to another.

The songs accompanying the ceremony describe various stages in the arrival and reception of Mother Corn in the village and then in the lodge of the son. After a song proclaiming her arrival, the tribe's chief stands at the doorway to the ceremonial lodge holding Mother Corn. He is flanked by the Ku'rahus (spiritual "headman") and his assistant, holding the brown eagle-feathered stem and the white eagle-feathered stem, respectively. As the son receives the bounty represented by Mother Corn, the central power image is the stem bearing the brown eagle feathers. Fletcher's 1906 description of the meaning of the stem's power is poignant: "*Kawas* [the brown eagle] has the right to make the nest and seek help from *Tira'wa* [the heavens] for the children." A following stanza describes kawas's flight inside the receiving lodge itself, the flapping of its sacred feathers driving out evil influences before a nest is made.

Overall the ceremony is intended to ask for the gift of children and sustenance for the next generation, as well as for a firm bond between the parent and child. It also can symbolize the wish for peace and prosperity between those bearing the sacred objects and those who receive them. Hence, hako is associated with a ceremony of peace between tribes, one representing the fathers, the other the children.

It is important to note that, although there is always a point in the hako ceremony for the offering of smoke to Tira'wa, and therefore the use of a ceremonial calumet, this aspect is not as important as the "true" symbol of the pipe in the ceremony, which is tied to the two "breathing mouths of wood" bearing the eagle feathers.

Byron D. Cannon

Sources for Further Study

Driver, Harold E. *Indians of North America*. 2d ed., rev. Chicago: University of Chicago Press, 1969. A general guide that can be used to compare forms of symbolism that place Hako in a broader cultural context.

Fletcher, Alice C. *The Hako: A Pawnee Ceremony*. Twenty-second Annual Report to the Secretary of the Smithsonian Institution. Washington, D.C.: Bureau of American Ethnology, 1904. This original work remains the most extensive description of Hako.

_____. "A Pawnee Ritual Used When Changing a Man's Name."

American Anthropologist, n.s. 1 (1899): 82-97. Shows ways in which Hako symbolism extends to other realms.

Murie, James. *The Ceremonies of the Pawnee.* Smithsonian Institution Contributions to Anthropology 27. Washington, D.C.: Smithsonian Institution Press, 1979. General coverage, by Fletcher's primary assistant, of rituals that occur among the same tribes that practiced the "model" hako ceremony.

See also: Calumets and Pipe Bags; Corn Woman; Feathers and Featherwork.

Hamatsa

Tribes affected: Kwakiutl
Significance: *The Hamatsa, or Cannibal Dance, is intended to inspire fear and awe in the audience.*

The Hamatsa, a dance performed by the Kwakiutl of British Columbia, Canada, is used primarily to induct novice shamans into the Hamatsa Society. Their membership in this society assures them of higher status as community healers. The Hamatsa dance is also occasionally performed at ceremonial potlatches.

The Hamatsa or "cannibal," is the central figure of the dance. Before each performance, a fire is lit in a large ceremonial plank house. After the fire has burned down to coals and the proper mood has been established, the dance begins. Through repetitive arm gestures, shuffling of the feet from side to side, exaggerated and contorted facial expressions, and manipulations of the eyes, the Hamatsa dancer attempts to instill a sense of fear and awe in the audience. The skill of a Hamatsa dancer is measured by the reactions of people in the audience. If they seem uneasy and spellbound, the dance is considered successful.

The dance roughly follows the story of a "wild" or "unkept" cannibal who lives in the forest and occasionally comes near villages to devour unsuspecting children. It is interesting to note that although most Kwakiutl dances require the use of masks, they are not typically employed by Hamatsa dancers because so much of the effect of the dance relies on the improvisational use of facial contortions. To embellish the role of a wildman, the dancer's face must be visible.

Researchers who have worked with the Kwakiutl have speculated about the underlying functions of the dance. Some have suggested that it reaffirms a basic symbolic separation between things that are well-ordered, such as village life, and things that represent disorder, such as the forest. Thus, the Hamatsa theme might reinforce cultural values for village and societal togetherness, and at the same time point to what can happen if those values are neglected.

Michael Findlay

See also: Dances and Dancing; Potlatch.

Hand Games

Tribes affected: Pantribal
Significance: *Hand games were an important source of entertainment; they were used by shamans to dramatize their magic and by storytellers to illustrate important events.*

Native Americans played a wide variety of hand games, primarily for entertainment and for developing and displaying skill and dexterity. Hand games were frequently the basis of different games of chance and even gambling, and both genders and all ages participated. Children were encouraged in hand games at an early age, to help them develop hand-eye coordination. The more common hand games were jackstraws, stick games, basket dice, tops, ball juggling, four stick, tip cat, hidden ball/object, pebble games, ring and pin, shell game, whirling game with hemp, dice games, and cat's cradle.

Shamans used special hand games that involved legerdemain (sleight of hand), to demonstrate the user's religious power during

Hand games served as the basis for gambling games such as kose-kaw-nuch. *(Library of Congress)*

curing rituals or prophesying. Skilled shamans could make game objects "speak" using ventriloquism, implying that the game had its own power or spirit. These special hand game objects were "fed" and sung to by their owners. Elders and skilled storytellers employed certain hand games to illustrate or dramatize events in creation stories or mythological accounts. Gifted hand game players frequently acquired status, and during winter confinement they would be called upon for entertainment.

John Alan Ross

See also: Children; Games and Contests.

Hand Tremblers

Tribes affected: Navajo
Significance: *Hand trembling is a distinctive cultural practice among the Navajo, an expression of the Navajo view of the world as ruled by harmonious balance.*

Hand trembling is one of the most common techniques for divination, or obtaining knowledge by ceremony, used among the Navajo, also known as the Diné. The two other widely used techniques are stargazing and listening. In stargazing, the diviner uses quartz crystals to interpret flashes of light or images outdoors in order to obtain information about an illness or some other problem. A listener finds the cause of a problem by hearing and interpreting some meaningful sound, such as that of thunder, after a ritual. Stargazers and listeners tend to be men, while hand trembling is reported to be more common among women. Researchers of Navajo culture and religion have suggested that both stargazing and listening have declined over the years, while the use of hand trembling has increased.

Hand trembling is thought to have been borrowed by the Navajo from the Apache after 1860. Its usual uses are to diagnose illnesses, to identify witches, and to find lost objects or lost children. While the knowledge obtained from stargazing and listening is said to come from the dangerous Coyote spirit, hand tremblers get their information from the spirit of the Gila Monster. Traditional Navajo believe that the Gila Monster sees everything that happens and watches the actions of every person, so that it is able to tell where a child has strayed, what taboo a person has violated to bring on an illness, or what witch has cursed a sufferer.

Hand trembling is usually signaled by the uncontrollable shaking or trembling of the right arm. After someone shows signs of hand trembling, a ceremony must be performed to enable the individual to bring on the state at will. Without the ceremony, there is a danger that the trembling will become a disease.

When an object is missing, the one who has lost it will sit or kneel in front of the hand trembler, who will shake the hand before the seeker. For an illness, the ceremony involves sprinkling pollen over the sufferer, singing four special songs, and presenting gifts to the Gila Monster, who takes possession of the hand trembler. The answer to the question about the location of the lost object or about the nature of the sickness comes either from interpreting the motions of the shaking hand or from a direct revelation to the trembler by the Gila Monster.

The hand trembler does not cure illnesses, but prescribes the ceremony and the song needed for a cure. This generally involves sitting or lying on a sand painting while a singer performs the needed ritual. The diagnosis by hand trembling and the healing ritual are based on the Navajo idea that the world is ruled by harmony. If something goes wrong, it is a result of a disruption of harmony by someone's unintentional actions or by the intentional selfishness of a witch. Ceremonies help to re-establish a harmonious balance.

Carl L. Bankston III

Sources for Further Study

Goodman, James. *The Navajo Atlas: Environments, Resources, People and History of the Diné Bikeyah.* Norman: University of Oklahoma Press, 1982.

Hill, W. W. "The Handtrembling Ceremony of the Navaho." *El Palacio* 38 (1935): 56-68.

Levy, Jerrold E., Raymond Neutra, and Dennis Parker. *Hand Trembling, Frenzy Witchcraft, and Moth Madness: A Study of Navajo Seizure Disorders.* Tucson: University of Arizona Press, 1987.

See also: Chantways; Medicine and Modes of Curing: Postcontact; Medicine and Modes of Curing: Pre-contact; Music and Song; Religion; Sand Painting.

Headdresses

Tribes affected: Pantribal
Significance: *A symbol of tribal or clan affiliation and of connection to specific spiritual powers, the headdress indicated the status and wealth of the wearer and suggested the response appropriate from others.*

Headdresses were worn as the spirits guided or as honors were bestowed. Everyday head coverings were artfully made, but practical. For ceremonial headdresses, however, there were no limits. All available materials were used: fur, fabric, leather, wood, metal, and bone. Decorations and adornments included feathers, beads, quills, stones, shells, and various metals. The simplest headdress was a single eagle feather, a symbol of status among the Plains people. The brave became a warrior after his first killing of an enemy and was permitted to wear the feather. The familiar fillet headband of fabric, fur, or leather was often beaded or quilled. It also took the form of braids of sweetgrass or crowns of cottonwood leaves or sage.

Eastern Woodlands. A bear claw on a headband held power for dancers; others might dance in a whole bearskin, head and all. The ceremonial crowns of Algonquian men had dozens of turkey feathers fastened only at the quill-tips so that they were kept in motion as the wearer moved. The Seneca used a deerskin cap lined with woven willow twigs for protection in battle. For ceremonies a silver headband was worn with a large bunch of feathers on top. In the Ojibwa Midewiwin (Grand Medicine Society), a headband with upright eagle feathers was used in healing rites.

Southeast. Fur or deerskin headdresses trimmed with heron feathers were favored in the Southeast. At the Green Corn Ceremony the Creek chief wore a duckskin headdress. Warriors and chiefs had wampum or quill-decorated fillets with crane or heron feathers fastened at center front. The Hopewell shaman performed a burial ceremony in a hood made of a human skull trimmed with deer hide fringe and human hair tassels. Shamans-in-training often had a stuffed owl perched on their heads.

Plains. The ceremonial war bonnet of the Plains chiefs had a beaded headband, ermine tails, many eagle feathers slanted back, and more eagle feathers forming a trailer. At times one or two eagle feathers designated warriors or chiefs, such as Sitting Bull and Red Cloud, who had also earned the right to wear the full war bonnet.

The majestic buffalo horn headdress had a cap of buffalo fur, beaded headband, ermine tails, buffalo horns, and a trailer of eagle feathers. Four Bears, a Mandan chief, had a buffalo-horn and eagle-feather bonnet. A red wooden knife fastened through the cap indicated that he had killed with such a weapon.

Men of the Hidatsa Dog Society wore a headdress with a huge spray of magpie feathers, a fan of large upright turkey feathers at the back of the head, and one eagle plume at the crown. Cheyenne and Oto men wore wide headbands of fur decorated with feathers, beaded medallions, or small mirrors. Some Crow warriors perched a full stuffed crow at the back of their heads.

The Pawnee warrior made a striking image with his partly shaved head painted red and topped with a red roach of deer tail hairs and an upright eagle feather. Sometimes on the Plains a full grizzly bearskin was used with the bear's head as a helmet or with the snout upright.

Southwest. Apache men wore braids of yucca fibers or a folded bandanna. The mountain spirits (Gans) danced in black hoods with turquoise or shell ornaments. Red scarves covered their faces. They wore long horns of yucca or a two-foot-high wooden slat frame, decorated with powerful symbols. Women in the Corn Dance wore the spectacular "tablita," a large, brightly painted wooden headdress, while men danced with a bunch of small red-dyed feathers on top of their heads.

The Pueblo Deer Dance headdress was made of spruce boughs and deer antlers trimmed with feathers. Hopi men tied their headbands of red cloth, leaving the ends hanging down. For ceremonies, the Snake priest wore a large spray of feathers. In the Southwest Yaqui Deer Dance, the headdress was an actual deer head with red scarves wrapped around its antlers. It was tied upright on the dancer's head over a white scarf.

California. The woodpecker's bright red feathers were prized by the Hupa. Their men's Jumping Dance headdress had more than fifty red woodpecker scalps on a white fur band. The Pomo

An important part of Native American dress was the headdress—often very elaborate in style. *(Library of Congress)*

used orange and black flicker feathers to decorate similar headbands. An elder in the Hupa Jumping Dance had a crown of sea lion teeth. The finely woven basket hat of Hupa women was decorated with painted images. The California Kuksu cult dancers wore enormous headdresses of feathers and long willow sticks. A trailer of yellow woodpecker feathers swayed as they danced.

Northwest. The young Northwest Coast bride proclaimed her family's wealth with a headdress of thousands of slender dentalium shells, glass beads, and Chinese coins, so long it touched the ground. Kwakiutl people wove basket hats with wide brims and conical tops, trimmed with copper and disk-shaped shells. The Nootka conical hat was waterproof, woven of spruce roots, and painted with stylized animal images. A headdress of long upright feathers was the symbol of power for the Nootka female shaman. Impressive Haida dance headdresses featured the clan animal crest of carved wood trimmed with ermine tails, feathers, and sea lion whiskers. The Kwakiutl dance crest was surrounded by swansdown and feathers and topped with long splints of whalebone.

Tlingit people carved a full-head battle helmet of wood. Their shaman's spirit mask worn on the forehead held a small carved wood face trimmed with feathers and white down. The Tlingit chief's woven hat had a tall cone with rings declaring the number of potlatches he had sponsored.

Arctic. The Aleut men of northwestern Alaska used long whiskers of the sea lion, beads, and paint to decorate their extended-visor caps made of steamed and shaped wood. Aleut women's headbands were beaded with a stylized floral pattern.

Post-contact Influence on Headdresses. Styles and new fabrics from Europe and England led to changes in clothing and headdresses. To replace his deerskin cap, Cherokee chief Sequoyah adopted the silk turban. Seminole leader Osceola topped his turban with three ostrich plumes. When Shawnee warrior Tecumseh joined the British as a general during the War of 1812, his uniform included a red cap with an eagle feather. The famous Apache Geronimo wore the rolled scarf headband. After his surrender to General Miles in 1886, he was photographed wearing a wide-brimmed European hat.

When a delegation of Osage leaders visited Washington, D.C., President Thomas Jefferson presented them with dark blue U.S. military tunics and top hats trimmed with red and white ostrich feathers. These became traditional wedding outfits for the Osage bride and groom.

Never overshadowed by European styles, the distinctive Plains headdress has been, rather stereotypically, the one considered American Indian. In 1990, the United States Postal Service issued a set of commemorative stamps featuring several eagle-feather war bonnets.

Gale M. Thompson

Sources for Further Study

Billard, Jules B., et al. *The World of the American Indian*. Washington, D.C.: National Geographic Society, 1974.

Brown, Joseph Epes. *The North American Indians: A Selection of Photographs by Edward S. Curtis*. New York: Aperture, 1972.

Dubin, Lois Sherr. *North American Indian Jewelry and Adornment: From Prehistory to the Present*. New York: Henry N. Abrams, 1999.

Gattuso, John, et al. *Insight Guide: Native America*. Reprint. Boston: Houghton Mifflin, 1993.

Mails, Thomas E. *Mystic Warriors of the Plains*. Garden City, N.Y.: Doubleday, 1972.

Sturtevant, William, gen. ed. *Handbook of North American Indians*. Washington, D.C.: Smithsonian Institution Press, 1978-2001.

See also: Beads and Beadwork; Dress and Adornment; Feathers and Featherwork; Masks; Pow-wows and Celebrations; Quillwork; War Bonnets.